Encounter

Encounter
Williams College Museum of Art

Edited by Vivian Patterson
with Elizabeth Athens, Dana Pilson,
and Kathryn Price

Williams College Museum of Art
Williamstown, Massachusetts

This book is dedicated to the Williams family—students, faculty, staff, alumni, and community members—all of whom have embraced the appreciation of art, the encouragement of creativity, and the promotion of cross-cultural understanding.

This publication has been made possible with the generous support of the Edith and Herbert Lehman Foundation and the Williams College Museum of Art Fellows.

First Edition
© 2006 The President and Trustees of Williams College

All rights reserved under International and Pan-American Copyright Conventions

Printed and bound by
The Studley Press
151 East Housatonic Street
Dalton, Massachusetts 01227

Editor: Vivian Patterson
Copy Editor: Fronia W. Simpson
Design and Production: Diane Gottardi
Indexer: Kathleen Friello

Cover: Detail of *Eyes*, 2001, Louise Bourgeois, American, b. 1911, Granite, bronze, and electric light. Commissioned on the occasion of the 75th anniversary of the museum with funds from the Museum Fellows, friends, and museum endowments. Wachenheim Family Courtyard given by Edgar Wachenheim III, Class of 1959, and Chris Wachenheim, Class of 1994 (M.2001.14.1–10). Photograph by Arthur Evans

Page iv: Class of 1935 Gallery, 1986, designed by Charles Moore and Robert Harper of Centerbrook Architects & Planners. Photograph by Blake Gardner

Pages 2–3: Lawrence Hall, East Wing, 1903

Pages 12–13: Detail of *Festa del Redentore,* ca. 1899, by Maurice Prendergast, watercolor and pencil on paper, Gift of Mrs. Charles Prendergast (91.18.5)

ISBN 0-913697-28-1
Library of Congress Control Number: 2006901723

Contents

ix   Directors' Foreword
      Lisa G. Corrin, Marion Goethals, Linda Shearer

xi   Notes
      Vivian Patterson

2   Timeline and History

12   The Collection: Selections
      (in chronological order)

40   Collections Survey: Prints

56   Collections Survey: Animalier

72   Collections Survey: Prendergast

94   Collections Survey: African Art

112   Collections Survey: Drawings

133   Collections Survey: Mellon

142   Collections Survey: Modern and Contemporary

152   Collections Survey: Labeltalk

166   Collections Survey: Photography

191   Authors

192   Index

195   Credits

196   List of Publications Cited

Directors' Foreword

DIRECTORS

Karl E. Weston
1926–48

S. Lane Faison, Jr.
1948–76

Whitney S. Stoddard
Acting Director
1960–61, 1968

Franklin W. Robinson
1976–79

Milo C. Beach
Acting Director
1979

John W. Coffey II
Acting Director
1979–80

Thomas Krens
1980–88

Charles Parkhurst, Jr.
Co-Director
1983–84

W. Rod Faulds
Interim Director
1988–89

Linda B. Shearer
1989–2004

Marion Goethals
Interim Director
2004–5

Lisa G. Corrin
2005–

The Weston Gallery, given in honor of Karl E. Weston (Williams 1896), founder and Director from 1926 to 1948, by Andrew S. Keck (Williams 1924)

A MUSEUM ENCOUNTER may be between a person and an artwork, between people, or between a student, a teacher, and a museum full of art. Each encounter has its own personality—profound, challenging, and even transformative. After such an encounter, we never forget the work of art, often visiting it again and again, to relive the intensity of that first extraordinary experience. Within this book, we hope to reflect the kinds of exchanges that happen daily at the Williams College Museum of Art (WCMA), which leave lasting impressions on our students and general public alike. This experience is what has, since its founding in 1926, made WCMA so beloved by alumni and visitors as a sanctuary for contemplation and, equally, as an arena for dialogue about issues that connect us to one another, eliding boundaries of historic time and culture. As you look through these pages, much as you might go through the museum itself, you will experience the ways in which firsthand exposure to works of art have affected artists, faculty, students, staff, and friends of WCMA.

We are deeply grateful to the artists—ancient to contemporary—whose work at WCMA deepen our perceptions of the world. Thanks are also due to those who have helped build the collections; their generosity rewards us again and again as the ever-changing student body confronts artistic creativity anew. Past directors, each in his or her own way, guided acquisitions of more than twelve thousand objects, especially Karl Weston, S. Lane Faison, Jr., Thomas Krens, Linda Shearer, and Marion Goethals. Many alumni of Williams College such as Lawrence Bloedel, faculty members such as Milo Beach, and enlightened patrons such as Eugénie Prendergast have profoundly contributed to ensuring the collections could evolve. Within these pages, then, please enjoy the efforts of all these individuals who have made this a great teaching museum.

This handbook was first shaped during the tenure of Linda Shearer, Director from 1989 to 2004, and came to fruition under Marion Goethals, Interim Director. Vivian Patterson, WCMA's long-standing Curator of Collections, conceived its unique personality, bringing together multiple interpretative voices rather than the usual single and oftentimes authoritative voice of the institution. Her encyclopedic knowledge of the museum collections and generous spirit have resulted in a book that reaffirms and values the varied ways we encounter art as scholars and as individuals. We are grateful to Vivian, to the many authors, to the Edith and Herbert Lehman Foundation, and the Museum Fellows for support of this project, and to Williams College for support of the whole. We now invite you to participate in a dialogue on the page that we hope is as memorable as your encounters with the artworks themselves.

Lisa G. Corrin   Marion Goethals   Linda Shearer

Notes

Indian
Chauri Bearer
ca. 2nd century
Red sandstone
28 3/4 x 7 3/4 x 4 in.
Museum purchase, Anonymous fund, Karl E. Weston Memorial Fund (91.14)

THIS VOLUME IS NEITHER a conventional museum guide nor a handbook. It can only stand as an outline for a visitor's encounter with the museum. What unfolds are sketches—arranged chronologically according to date of an object's creation—that we hope will prompt a personal adventure through WCMA or spark and reward the fond memory of an excursion through the galleries. In keeping with the museum's long-standing relationships with departments across campus, the effort has been to explore and understand works in the collection from the perspective of myriad disciplines and through the eyes of faculty, students, community members, and museum staff. While some of the interpretations and descriptions of the works included will guide you, they do not presume to provide all the answers, nor do they eliminate the possibilities of alternatives. WCMA will ultimately be seen and experienced through your eyes.

Celebrating close to eight decades of dedication to teaching and learning about art, this book alludes as well to astonishing and sometimes spellbinding stories of acquisition and bears witness to the visions of individual directors, faculty, and curators; changing philosophies of taste; the generosity and unfaltering support of alumni and friends of Williams College; and just plain chance. The paintings, sculptures, and works on paper seen here, selected from more than twelve thousand objects, offer fresh insight and perspective to the multiplicity of forms, historic periods, individual expressions, and diverse world cultures present within the collection.

A generous grant from the Edith and Herbert Lehman Foundation along with funds from the Museum Fellows have enabled the Williams College Museum of Art to produce this long-overdue publication featuring some of the finest and most distinguished art in the museum's permanent collection. Twenty-seven years have passed since Director Emeritus S. Lane Faison, Jr. published the first handbook of the collection, and it would be an understatement to say that both the institution and its collection have dramatically evolved. Since 1979 the museum has reinvented itself, expanding architecturally, increasing its holdings tenfold, and establishing itself as a major museum both in this country and abroad.

This volume can only suggest the remarkable democratic scope and depth of one of the premiere college art collections in America. It demonstrates the extent to which WCMA's collecting activities have developed to sustain the museum's mission as a teaching institution, nurturing its vital connection to the college's curriculum while contributing to ongoing art scholarship and research.

WCMA does not take lightly its responsibility to advance learning through lively and innovative approaches to art or its intent to provide its audiences with immediate exposure to objects that are both concretely present and documents of a past. And through its acquisitions, exhibitions,

Charles Willard Moore
American, 1925–1993
Untitled Sketch
ca. 1985
Ink on napkin
5 x 5 in.
Gift of Charles W. Moore
(85.38.2)

and programs, the museum continues to encourage the encounter, appreciation, and analysis of images, objects, built environments, and installations, which can provide a basis for critical thought and visual literacy.

Many people have shared generously of their time, knowledge, and enthusiasm in the production of this handbook. At the heart of the effort is the staff of the Williams College Museum of Art, who undertook and sustained the innumerable tasks related to the organization and production of *Encounter*. But for their teamwork, the project would never have come to fruition—their investment, dedication, and loyalty to WCMA know no bounds. Deserving of special note are former Director Linda Shearer, under whose tenure this project was initiated and Interim Director Marion Goethals who helped guide this project to completion; their commitment to promoting WCMA's mission of art and learning has been a driving force in the development of this publication.

We also would like to extend our sincere thanks to all the authors—past and present Williams faculty and students, museum staff, and community members—for their enlightening entries on objects in the collection; to the photographers whose pictures beautifully illustrate this volume; to the Williams College Archives and Special Collections; to both Fronia W. Simpson, copy editor, and Diane Gottardi, designer, who energetically supported this publication; The Studley Press and Suzanne Salinetti for their expert attention to WCMA's project; and to the Edith and Herbert Lehman Foundation Publication Assistants—Elizabeth Athens, Dana Pilson, and Kathryn Price—whose zeal and initiative have sustained the preparation of this manuscript.

Vivian Patterson
Curator of Collections

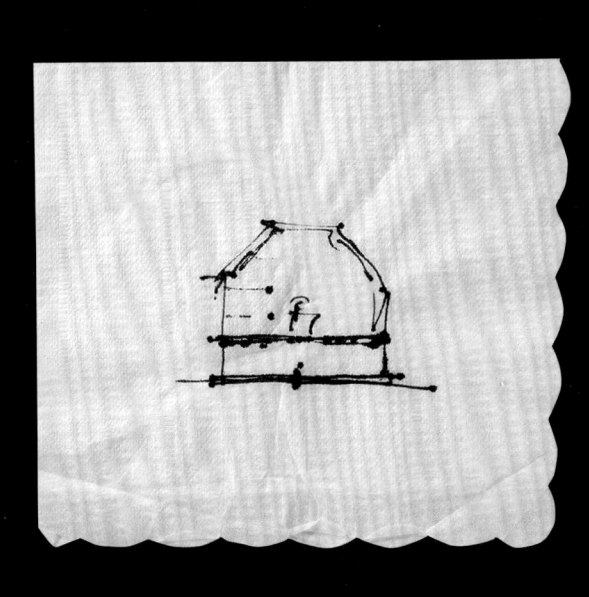

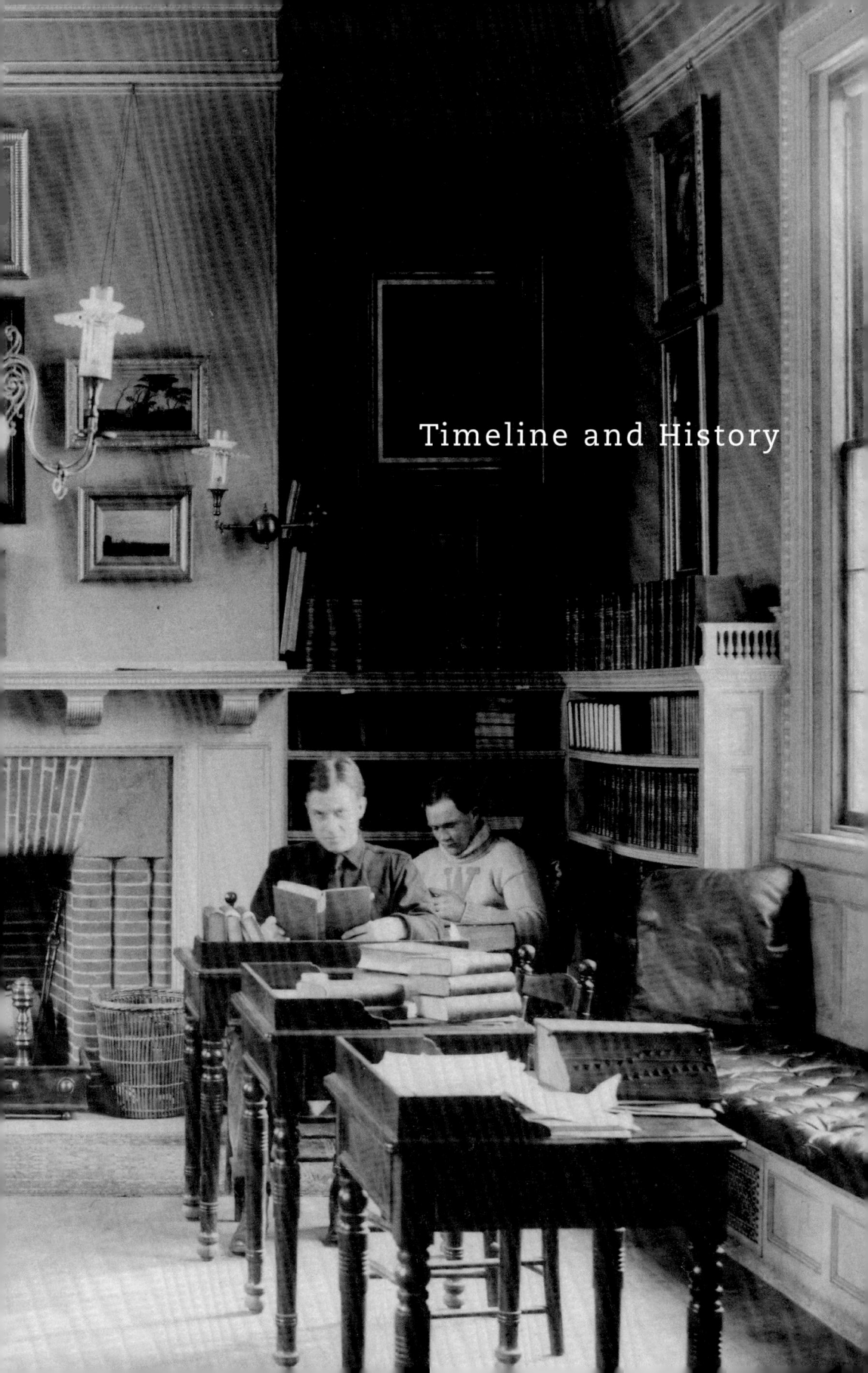

Timeline and History

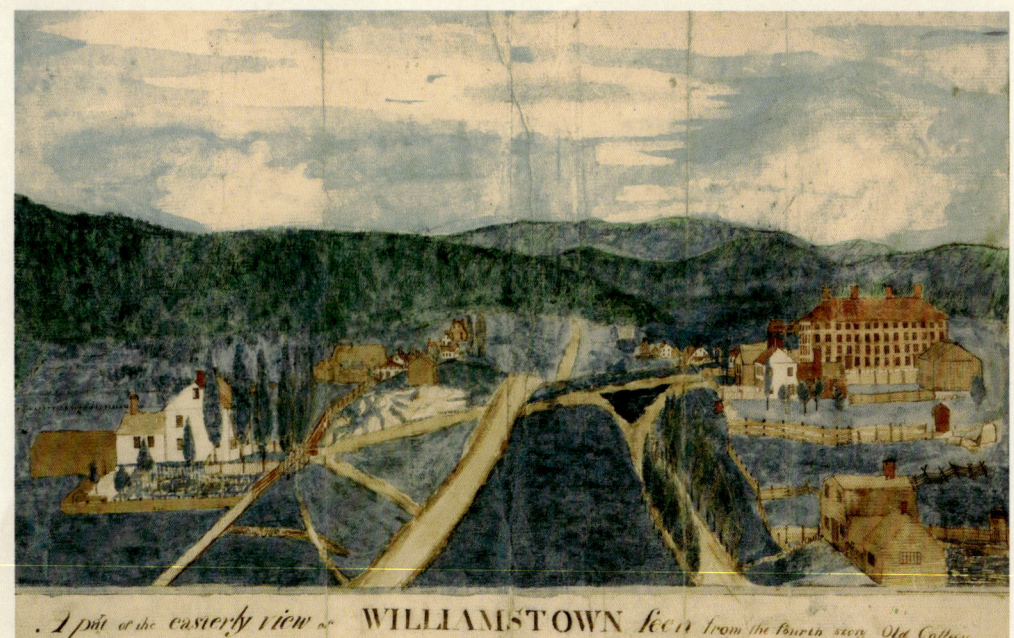

1793
Williams College is granted an official charter by the Commonwealth of Massachusetts [1].

1835
Students establish what is to be a fourth Greek fraternity on campus, Phi Beta Theta, but decide to forgo secret rituals in favor of pursuing scientific interests and organizing expeditions. Under the name the Lyceum of Natural History, students amass a collection of scientific specimens that range from the botanical and geological to the archaeological and later raise money for an independent building, Jackson Hall [2a, b].

1846–47
The core building in the complex of structures that currently houses the Williams College Museum of Art and Department of Art is designed by Thomas A. Tefft of Providence, Rhode Island, as the first college library [3a, b]. The two-story octagonal brick structure is named for the merchant-manufacturer and self-made millionaire Amos Lawrence [4], who contributes the funds for its construction [6].

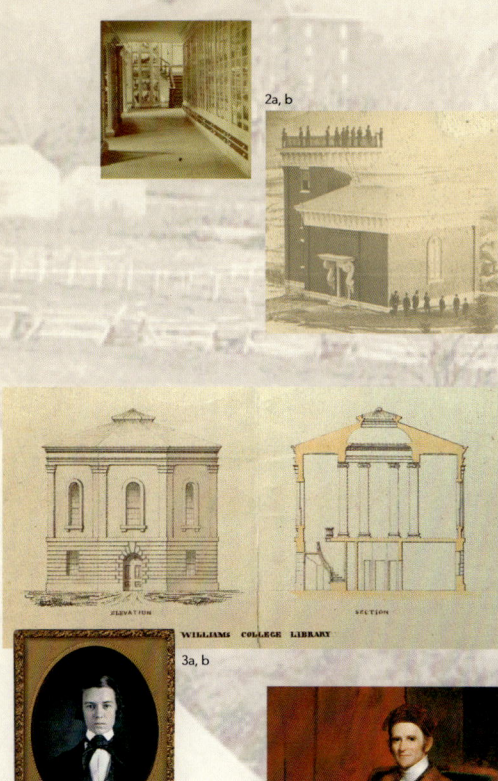

1851

Williams receives its first major works of art, acquired not as art but as artifacts of an ancient culture: three ninth-century B.C. Assyrian stone reliefs from the Palace of Ashurnasirpal II at Ninevah [5a, b].

1858

The Williams Art Association is founded to promote the study of art on campus. The association demands classes in art and aesthetics and asks for donations of "oil paintings, water-color, crayon and fine pencil drawings, photographs, prints, sculpture and casts." The group collects fine reproductive engravings of paintings by the old masters and offers a number of exhibitions in various rooms on campus. They elect a curator and hanging committee, whose duties include assessing acquisitions and, as stated in Article VII of the association's constitution, to "arrange the pictures and sculpture for exhibition." The association tries to hold exhibitions in Lawrence Hall but without success. Instead, they settle for an "Art Room" in South College, and later in Hopkins Hall [7].

1860–61

The Williams Art Association renews its call for donations in the *Williams Quarterly*: "A large number of the pictures at present are engravings, some of them inferior ones, . . . Paintings and crayon sketches will be sought as specimens of higher art and therefore better, as subjects for study." In the beginning, the objects the college collected were an amalgam of fine art and study aids, with reproductions far outnumbering original works of art.

1869

The Williams Art Association disbands, discouraged by difficulties in accumulating an impressive art collection and trouble in finding a correspondingly impressive gallery.

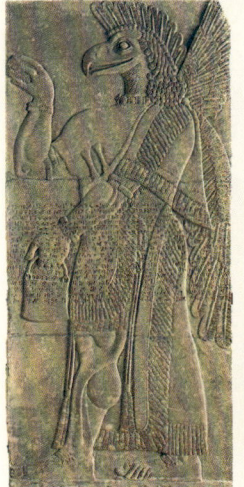

5a, b

6

7

8 (background) Williamstown looking northeast, late 1800s

1886
The Williams Art Association revives when the college's priorities for teaching with art change, thanks in part to the Aesthetic Movement. Style, sensual pleasure, and originality become a focus for learning, as does a more archaeological approach to the history of art.

1887–90
Eliza Peters Field memorializes her husband, John W. Field, by donating their large art collection to Williams: 85 objects, including 74 oil paintings—the first substantial art collection to be accepted by the college. She also donates funds to build wings east and west of the octagon to house the collection [11, 17]. The completed rooms display John La Farge's *Magnolia Grandiflora* [9] and John Frederick Kensett's *Lake George* [10], as well as Greek, Etruscan, Roman, and pre-Columbian artifacts and nineteenth-century French bronzes in glass and wall cases.

1897–98
The Williams College catalogue lists courses in "History of Art—A study of the forms and history of the arts of design, especially as expressed in architecture and ornament."

1903
The college establishes a chair in art and the history of civilization.

1926–27

Karl E. Weston (Williams 1896) [12], the college's Amos Lawrence Professor of Art, establishes the Lawrence Art Museum. The museum is intended to provide Williams College students with the opportunity for firsthand observation of fine works of art, a practice Weston maintains is essential to the study of art. The museum opens in Lawrence Hall on April 19, 1927, and a wing is added in the rear for instruction in art and the classics. This addition brings art and classrooms together, leading to a new approach in the educational use of the art object. Professors use the collection in weekly conferences with students.

12

1938

Another addition, composed of one gallery on the ground floor and two galleries on the second, is added to the Lawrence Art Museum. Funds for construction were donated by Edwin Howland Blashfield's widow and his sister. The gift also included original work by the painter [13], memorabilia, photographs he owned, and a number of works of European art [14].

13

14

1944

Twenty-one paintings from the Museum of Fine Arts, Boston are exhibited at the museum [15]. The MFA stores a significant portion of its collection at Williams during World War II.

1947

The *North Adams Transcript* runs an article with the headline "Cole Porter Gives Museum 7 Paintings." Among the gifts the composer and lyricist gives to the museum are Grant Wood's *Death on the Ridge Road* [16] and Paul Cadmus's *Point O'View*. Porter maintained a house in Williamstown until his death in 1964.

15

16

17 (background) Lawrence Hall, ca. 1895–1900

1948

S. Lane Faison, Jr. (Williams 1929) [18] is appointed to the directorship of the Lawrence Art Museum. During his 28-year tenure, both the college's art history curriculum and the museum's art collections significantly expand. The museum's collections policy emphasizes American art, modern and contemporary art, and the art of Asia and other non-Western civilizations.

1953

George Alfred Cluett (Williams 1896) [19] gives a significant collection of primarily Spanish and Italian Renaissance art objects to the museum. Among these is the dramatic painting entitled *The Executioner* [20], created by the Spanish painter Jusepe de Ribera in the mid–seventeenth century.

1956

Karl E. Weston, the museum's founder and first director, dies at age 81. In his will, he bequeaths funds to the museum for the acquisition of works of art, which he requests be named the Ruth Sabin Weston Art Fund, after his late wife. This fund is used for the purchase of notable artworks, including a seventeenth-century still life by the Spanish painter Juan van der Hamen y León [21].

1962

The Lawrence Art Museum changes its name to the Williams College Museum of Art (WCMA).

1972

A masters program in the history of art is jointly established by Williams College and the Sterling and Francine Clark Art Institute.

29 (background) Charles Willard Moore (American, 1925–1993) and Arthur Andersson (American, b. 1951) East Elevation with Anne & Patrick Poirier Sculpture, 1986; pencil and colored pencil on yellow trace; Gift of Charles W. Moore; 88.27.13

1976

Planning begins for an addition to WCMA to meet the needs of an expanded Department of Art and the museum's growing collections and programs. Architect Charles Moore designs a four-story addition [22, 29] in a Postmodernist style that echoes the original architecture of the building. As well as new galleries, the addition includes classrooms, faculty and staff offices, art storage, and preparation areas. State-of-the-art security, climate control, and display systems are built into all areas of the new structure.

S. Lane Faison, Jr. retires from the directorship of the museum.

1977

Lawrence H. Bloedel (Williams 1923) [23] bequeaths a large portion of his private collection to WCMA. Among the works donated is Edward Hopper's *Morning in a City* [24].

1980

Thomas Krens (Williams 1969) [25], Williams professor of studio art (undergraduate) and of art history (in the college's graduate program) becomes director of the museum.

1981

Scholars begin work on a catalogue raisonné of the works of Maurice and Charles Prendergast [26a, b], the beginning of the museum's long-standing relationship with the Prendergasts' art and Mrs. Charles (Eugénie) Prendergast [27]. Although not earlier affiliated with the college, Mrs. Prendergast's strong support for the use of art objects in education led her to Williams. She subsequently donates approximately 400 works by Maurice and Charles Prendergast to the museum [28].

26a, b

1982

The Estate of Kathryn Hurd establishes a fund at WCMA for the purchase of artwork by living American artists. Paintings in Mrs. Hurd's personal collection, such as Georgia O'Keeffe's *Skunk Cabbage (Cos Cob)* [30], are also donated to the museum.

1989

Expansion of WCMA's facilities and programs gains it a national reputation as one of the finest college art museums in the country. Linda Shearer [31], formerly the curator of contemporary art at the Museum of Modern Art, New York, becomes director. During Shearer's 15-year directorship, the museum increases the interdisciplinary and curricular use of its holdings and continues its commitment to contemporary art and the art of world cultures.

The Prendergast catalogue raisonné is completed and published in 1990.

1991

WCMA receives a generous bequest of 73 Indian and Persian art objects from the Estate of Mildred K. Frost, adding depth and diversity to the museum's collection of Asian art [32, 33].

37 (background) WCMA atrium, looking east

34

2001

To celebrate its 75th anniversary, the museum commissions *Eyes* [34], a permanent outdoor sculpture by the renowned artist Louise Bourgeois. For the museum, the work symbolizes an ongoing dedication to the best of contemporary art and living artists while providing students and visitors a unique outdoor meeting place and central artery to the museum's front entrance.

2004

The museum's facilities are once again updated with the construction of the Rose Study Gallery in the spring. Converted from a public exhibition space, the Rose Study Gallery is a museum classroom where Williams College faculty can teach with art objects not on display in the museum's galleries. The Rose Study Gallery enables WCMA to continue its mission as a teaching museum, advancing learning through lively and innovative approaches to the instruction of art [35].

35

2005

Lisa G. Corrin, formerly deputy director of art and the Jon and Mary Shirley Curator of Modern and Contemporary Art at the Seattle Art Museum, is appointed to the directorship of WCMA [36].

36

The Collection: Selections

ASSYRIAN

Winged Guardian Spirit
ca. 880 B.C.

Guardian Spirit
ca. 880 B.C.

Gypsum
83 x 39 3/4 x 3 in.
Gift of Sir Henry Layard through Dwight W. Marsh, Class of 1842
(1851.1)

Gypsum
92 x 38 1/2 x 3 in.
Gift of Sir Henry Layard through Dwight W. Marsh, Class of 1842
(1851.2)

In Kahlu, nine centuries before Christ, these carved slabs of gypsum were but two of many hundreds that lined the walls of the Northwest Palace built by order of Ashurnasirpal II (r. 883–859 B.C.). The palace, situated within the town walls of Kahlu, served as the seat of the Assyrian Empire for a little over a century. Like other rulers before him, Ashurnasirpal II aspired to create a grand city to honor him and according to his specifications. Before the king's building campaign, Kahlu had been a small, sleepy settlement located between two of the larger cities of the empire—Ninevah and Ashur. When completed, Kahlu encompassed 890 acres and included several temples as well as the Northwest Palace, which served both as Ashurnasirpal II's home and administrative headquarters.

Enormous reliefs such as these decorated the walls of the palace. Besides being beautifully and delicately carved, they were also brightly painted; traces of pigment are still visible on the feet of both carved figures. They represent variants of the *apkallu*, a deity that protects the supplicant from evil. In addition to repelling evil, the two *apkallus* participate in what many scholars believe was a purification ritual involving a stylized tree, images of which were next to these figures in the palace. Each *apkallu* holds in its right hand a fir cone, or "purifier," as described in Assyrian texts, and a bucket filled with either water or pollen in the left. The tree's symbolic meaning is still unknown, but it may represent the prosperity and strength of the empire. The figures, therefore, not only purify the tree but protect it and, by extension, the empire at large.

The text on these reliefs—as on all the reliefs—describes the palace's original appearance, as if in the king's words:

I built thereon (a palace with) halls of cedar, cypress, juniper, boxwood, teak, terebinth, and tamarisk(?) as my royal dwelling and for the enduring leisure life of my lordship. Beasts of the mountains and the seas, which I had fashioned out of white limestone and alabaster, I had set up in its gates. I made it (the palace) fittingly imposing. I bordered them all around with bronze studs. I mounted doors of cedar, cypress, juniper, and terebinth in its gates. Silver, gold, tin, bronze, iron, my own booty from the lands over which I ruled, as much as possible, I brought (to the palace); I placed it all therein.

—Elyse Gonzales (Williams M.A. 2000), Assistant Curator, The Institute of Contemporary Art, University of Pennsylvania. Adapted from *Stones of Assyria: Ancient Spirits from the Palace of Ashurnasirpal II*, 2001

My great desire and prayer is that students who look upon the relics of the past may think wisely of time and be led to take a deeper interest in the efforts made to rescue the degraded from the beastliness of their present life, and the eternal dangers impending. Would that every active imagination would hear the stones cry out. Asia has claims upon New England.

—Dwight W. Marsh to Rev. Mark Hopkins, Mosul (present-day Iraq), August 7, 1865

I was the only American in Mosul from the Spring of 1850 to that of 1851. It was the last year of [British archaeologist Sir Austen Henry] Layard's stay there, and he was very polite and kind to me as the only representative of my country occasionally inviting me to dine with him, once about sundown on the roof of his house in Mosul . . . and whenever new treasures of sculpture were found asking me to enjoy the new sights in the trenches.

Finding him to be a great admirer and friend of America, it occurred to me in mentioning how many in our land were reading his works to suggest that my Alma Mater would be very glad to get some samples of the sculptures at Nimrood where I knew there were duplicates. He at once offered to put two as good slabs as the best at my disposal the only drawback being their close likeness to a pair already in the British Museum.

I at once gratefully accepted them and thanked him in the name of the college and then I wrote asking the college authorities if they would pay the expense of transportation: to which they assented.

Then arose the question of route. All slabs sent by Layard to Europe had gone down the Tigris and by Persia and India to England. That was an entire water route but requiring too many transshipments to get to America. I concluded to take an entirely new course to reduce the thickness of the slabs by sawing from about a foot to about four inches, and then to make each slab into three, making in all, six pieces, which were boxed with thick planks and made three camel loads. These were loaded and unloaded night and morning the long journey of about four hundred miles to the Mediterranean and so eventually from Beirut in an American woolship to America.

—Dwight W. Marsh to Prof. A. L. Perry, Amherst, Mass., November 29, 1882

Archaeological sites and artifacts are not merely relics of the past; they can also be potent and conspicuous symbols of national identity. In the modern Middle East, with its volatile political climate and unusually rich archaeological heritage, the political manipulation of history and its relics has been both widespread and hotly contested.

Nowhere has the politicization of archaeology been more apparent than in Iraq. For most of the twentieth century, fashioning a distinct Iraqi national identity was a fundamental challenge in the political process. Ever since the establishment of the Hashemite kingdom of Iraq in August 1921, the political leaders of the state have been faced with the formidable task of nation-building among peoples of diverse religious and ethnic backgrounds. To overcome these vast cleavages in Iraq's social fabric, Iraqi politicians increasingly turned to archaeology in an attempt to convince Iraqis of the legitimacy of the state and of a common heritage and history.

This trend reached its apex under the presidency of Saddam Hussein (r. 1979–2003). Hussein, in his typical tyrannical and megalomanic style, sought to prove that his presidency was the climax of successive Iraqi civilizations and empires. In this presentation, Hussein was merely the latest ruler in the long line of glorious rulers and the embodiment of the "spirit" of Nebuchadnezzar or Hammurabi. During his reign, therefore, pre-Islamic artifacts, such as

objects from the Assyrian Empire, became closely identified with his oppressive despotism and symbols of Ba'ath party power. When governmental power was tenuous, such as during the uprisings after the 1991 war or in April 2003, Iraqis attacked and ransacked national and regional museums. The looters were surely seeking valuable artifacts. But they were also demolishing important vestiges and symbols of authority.

These two Assyrian reliefs are magnificent objects of immense historic and artistic significance. Their importance from an art-historical point of view is considerable. Their arrival at Williams is a fascinating story not least because of the role of Austen Henry Layard, who first popularized archaeology with his best-selling books and spectacular finds in Mesopotamia in the nineteenth century. Yet interpretation and meaning are so often predicated on context. Here, far removed from modern Iraq, their aesthetic qualities can be appreciated without any Iraqi political strings attached.

—Magnus T. Bernhardsson, Assistant Professor of History

TROILOS PAINTER
Greek, active ca. 520–480 B.C.

Red-figured Stamnos Vase
ca. 500–480 B.C. (Late Archaic Period)

Side A: Poseidon attacks the giant Polybotes;
Side B: Three drunken youths make merry
Terracotta
14 in. high, 22 5/16 in. diameter
Museum purchase, Karl E. Weston Memorial Fund (64.9)

Challenged with—"If Keats could do it, why can't you try?"—Barbara Howes wrote an ode to a Grecian urn which the Williams College Museum of Art acquired in 1964 for its permanent collection. . . . The challenge, hurled by Professor S. Lane Faison, Jr. (Williams 1929), director of the Williams College Museum of Art, refers to Keats's "Ode on a Grecian Urn." The gauntlet was picked up by Miss Howes (Mrs. Barbara Howes Smith of Pownal, Vermont). . . . Faison stated, "We are proud to have played even so small a part in the genesis of a work of art, and proud, too, that an ancient one in our collection was instrumental in the history of a creative art."

—Williams College, *Alumni Review*, February 1966

Ode to Poseidon, Lines on a Grecian Urn Recently Acquired by the Williams College Museum of Art

Well, hail, Poseidon! Old mariner who was caught
Between brothers—Zeus and Hades—but
There you are, bent
On sinking your new trident
Into the vitals of poor Polybotes.
Who rears back upon space as if a cot
Waited; only his shield,
A lion, will not yield,
But, switching its black teardrop tail,
Glares out only at us; Poseidon, hail!

On the vase's other side live three students
Dancing home, exams over, brains spent;
Life in their heels, they clown
The cobbled road on down
To celebrate. The central boy knows
What it is to want to dance, he fools and shows
Them who is actor, they
Are end men; so they play,
Lifting imagined wine in wassail
The students should: Poseidon, hail!

One wed Poseidon, from whom Pegasus
Spring; no mean feat; many of us
Know that most able horse,
Whose love ran with the muse,
Could braid by the very rhythm of his hooves
The formal circlet this vase wears and weaves . . .
As to a theatre-in-the-round,
To lives, music, and sound,
How well this wine jar brings us in!
Oh, navigator, hail! Poseidon!

—Barbara Howes, originally published in *The New Yorker* © 1965

ROMAN

Sarcophagus Fragment of
Hercules, Triumph of Dionysos
late 3rd century

Marble
33 11/16 x 25 3/16 x 8 15/16 in.
Museum purchase, John B. Turner
'24 Memorial Fund (86.19)

What do we see? A broken slab of marble. Drill holes form a lacy pattern. Step back and it falls into place. A bearded muscleman, crowned by cupids. He drives a chariot and holds out a cup to be filled. He drinks and drives? Who is this? The muscliest of them all, Hercules/Heracles. His story starts badly: he's Zeus's bastard son. Hera, his stepmother, forces him to be a weaker man's slave. Twelve labors later, twelve lifetimes later, he is pitied by the gods, snatched from the pyre, and granted immortality, the chance to sit among the gods. He ascends to Heaven/Olympus. That's the part we see. The ascent. But what is immortality without eternal youth? In Heaven he will wed Hebe, the goddess of youth. That's where the cupids come in. Our hero undergoes a makeover at the hands of flying babes. And what of immortality? The sarcophagus's owner, desiring Hercules' fate, chose an imperishable material. But his bones were dumped out by tomb robbers; his marble coffin smashed and sold piecemeal to antiquities dealers. What do we see? One man's bargain with Heaven, broken. A single fragment survives. The fractured moment of becoming a god.

—Elizabeth McGowan, Professor of Art. Adapted from *Labeltalk*, 1996

MAYAN, MEXICO, CAMPECHE

Gadrooned Bowl with
Hieroglyph Rim Text
ca. 600–900 (Late Classic)

Mold-made terracotta with orange and black polychrome
6 ½ in. high, 6 ¼ in. diameter
Gift of Herbert D. N. Jones, Class of 1914 (21.1.14)

For additional information, visit www.famsi.org, kerr number: 8713

"ca-ca-wa"

Modern scholars have noticed that the rim inscriptions around Maya pots such as this one are frequently composed of the same symbols. The hieroglyphic message usually begins by describing the pot, then notes whether it is painted or carved, then names the contents, and finally gives the names and titles of the pot owner and/or his or her scribe. This painted vase has a sixteen-glyph inscription that states, among other things, that the young noble owner of the pot was just twenty years old when he earned the honorific title of "sacred bloodletter" and that he died shortly afterward. Translated, the entire inscription reads: "This drinking cup contains fresh new cocoa and is owned by Spine-Hand the Blood-Scatterer, the twenty-year old kin [possibly son] of the forty-year-old Lord of Naman."

Two glyphs, *D* and *E*, are in the shape of the same fishlike head. The second glyph differs in its curl-like suffix. We know that the ancient Maya read the fish-head glyph as making the sound "ca"; the curl-suffix added a phonetic "wa." Hence together the two glyphs were pronounced "ca-ca-wa"—cocoa. Our modern word derives from the original Maya. Such vases were often placed in the tombs of the former owner and filled with a beverage made of cocoa beans as an offering to the gods. Cocoa was prized by all ancient Mesoamericans both as an edible delicacy and as coins. In the public marketplaces of ancient Mesoamerica one could buy merchandise with cocoa beans just as we do today with half-dollars and quarters. While the Maya language supplied the word we still use for the plant, the later Nahuatl-speaking Aztecs provided the name for its most habit-forming derivative—chocolate.

This vase bears an emblem glyph, *P*, that reads "Naman," thought by archaeologists to be the ancient site now called La Florida, between El Peru and Piedras Negras near the Usamacinta River, which flourished about A.D. 550–700. It is a gift of Herbert Jones (Williams 1914), who claimed it was dug from a "mound" on his father's farm in "southern Campeche [Mexico] at a point about twenty-five to forty miles north of the Guatemala line."

—Samuel Y. Edgerton, Amos Lawrence Professor of Art. Adapted from *The Art of Mesoamerica: Before Columbus*, 1992. [Drawing of the glyphs by Ivar Kronick (Williams 1991), translation by Marc Zender]

INDIAN, BIHAR OR BENGAL

Black Stone Stele of a Crowned Buddha

9th–10th century (Pala Period)

Black chlorite
28 x 14 x 6 1/2 in.
Museum purchase, Anonymous Fund and Karl E. Weston Memorial Fund (96.14)

The image of the Buddha, androgynous, neither young nor old, projects compassion, nonjudgmental acceptance, the sense that God is within us and the path to enlightenment is there for us to choose.

To Max Weber (1864–1920), economic behavior and institutions were derived from religious values. He linked profit seeking and the desire to demonstrate virtue to God external. Buddhists were handicapped by un-Calvinistic values. How ironic: today, societies in which Buddha is revered are among the world's most dynamic, as well as among the most equitable, capitalistic economies.

A capitalist impulse brought this Buddha here. A collector made an offer that poor Indians could not refuse. For one thousand years, they viewed this Buddha on the wall of a temple. We now view it out of context. Does our gain more than compensate for their loss? Buddha teaches us about impermanence and nonattachment. Perhaps this is the way it was meant to be.

—Richard H. Sabot, John J. Gibson Professor of Economics Emeritus. Adapted from *Labeltalk*, 1997

All Buddha statues are equally beautiful.
—Tibetan proverb

The contemplation of this statue raises for me two related questions: What type of practices (religious, aesthetic, commercial) relate to such an object? And, what are the ways in which beauty can figure in these practices? The above proverb reflects a certain understanding of this statue as "sacred," an object of religious practice. Does this mean that beauty is irrelevant to such practice, merely "our" aesthetic vision as opposed to "their" more "authentic" religious way? Probably not, for the proverb is a prescription for veneration, not an aesthetic description. It commands equal respect toward all Buddha statues but also implies that some statues may be more aesthetically pleasing than others. Even in the proverb, sacredness and beauty do not necessarily correlate, though they may.

—Georges B. Dreyfus, Professor of Religion. Adapted from *Labeltalk*, 1997

22, 23

CAMBODIAN, KHMER, KOH KER

Female Divinity
early 10th century

Sandstone
42 1/8 x 15 x 8 1/16 in.
Museum purchase, Karl E. Weston Memorial Fund (68.2)

This figure comes to us from a period of tremendous cultural efflorescence throughout Southeast Asia, a time of Indic Hindu-Buddhist empires and god-kings. That the figure is divine is clear: look carefully and you will see a second arm emerging behind the first from her left shoulder in the classic iconography of Hindu deities. That the figure is female is even less in doubt: her body is more than sensuous, it is frankly sexual, the crescentlike spread of her folded-over sarong hinting at pregnancy and fertility. How different the Indic notions of divinity from European ones. Compare this figure with the angels in Piero della Francesca's *Virgin and Child Enthroned with Four Angels* (Sterling and Francine Clark Art Institute, Williamstown, Massachusetts): the divine figures from fifteenth-century Italy—and it would take Europe five hundred years to reach a cultural flowering like that of tenth-century Koh Ker—are purposely androgynous, "sinless, sexless, and deathless." But in Southeast Asia the divine world and this world mirror each other, the fecundity of the latter depending on the fecundity of the former, and a ripe sexuality is as much to be looked for in Heaven as on Earth.

—Peter Just, Associate Professor of Anthropology. Adapted from *Labeltalk*, 2001

24, 25

CHINESE, YÜAN DYNASTY

Seated Vairocana
ca. 1280–1368

Gilt bronze
12 5/8 x 9 1/4 x 5 1/2 in.
Gift of Professor Willis I. and
Betsey M. Milham (55.22)

Students in my Japanese Art and Culture course were asked to write a paper about this sculpture. The assignment read as follows:

> A Chinese Buddhist figure in bronze is on display in the Stoddard Gallery at the Williams College Museum of Art. Write an essay of 3–4 pages about this work. This is not a research paper; what you have learned about Buddhism and Buddhist art from class should be sufficient as a basis for your analysis. First, look at the artwork carefully and then generate ideas by asking these questions:
>
> • Whom does the sculpture represent? What are the identifying marks or iconographic traits?
> • How effective is the artist in suggesting volume or three-dimensionality, movement of the human form, and drapery? Does the medium dictate or affect the final artistic form, and, if so, in what ways?
> • What was your first response to the work? What feelings or sentiments does it evoke in you?
> • What ideal does this form of the Buddha represent? How successful is the artist in conveying this ideal?
> • Where was the sculpture meant to be seen? (Imagine its original physical context and take into consideration its size.) What purpose did the work serve? To teach, to fulfill a service, to delight the eye, to express a feeling, to convey certain ideals, or to illustrate a story? Keep in mind that these are not mutually exclusive.
> • What purpose does the work serve now? Do its current physical location in the museum, the way it is displayed, its new function, and its current audience affect your appreciation of the sculpture and the ideals it represents, and, if so, in what ways?

My intent for this assignment is clear. I want my students first of all to use their eyes, then their hearts, and finally their minds when studying a work of art. This assignment illustrates a method of studying religious art—or any artwork, for that matter—that combines iconographic and stylistic analyses with a contextual approach. "Context" refers not only to a religious artwork's original physical location, function, audience, and patronage but also to its present physical location, function, audience, and patronage. It encourages students to develop a modern sensibility and sensitivity in considering such questions as: Should religious art be exhibited in the museum as a work of art or as a religious testimony? How should modern museum-goers approach religious art made in the distant past in foreign lands?

The image of Vairocana, the Buddha of Infinite Light, who is central to Vajrayana (Esoteric) Buddhism, provides a prime example for the teaching and studying of religious art.

—Ju-Yu Scarlett Jang, Professor of Art

Vairocana is Sanskrit for the cosmic Buddha, or the quintessential Buddha who presides over all Universes and lesser Buddhas. Unlike many deities of the Shingon sect, which are phenomenal Buddhas invoked for immediate benefit or to resolve a specific problem, Vairocana embodies the essence of Buddhahood, or that which makes lesser Buddhas divine.

The seated Vairocana now on display at the Williams College Museum of Art possesses many of the standard iconographic traits of the Buddha. These include the snail-shaped hair and the fact that the figure is seated in the lotus position. Other identifying marks are the *urna*, or tuft of hair between the eyes that represents wisdom and augmented vision; the *mudra*, or hand gesture, which, in this case, also signifies wisdom; the elongated earlobes, which represent the Buddha's pre-enlightenment life as a prince accustomed to wearing heavy jewelry from a young age; and the *ushishina*, originally a topknot for fastening a turban, which now represents the Buddha's infinite intelligence.

The Buddha appears smooth and flawless; this smoothness helps shape the viewer's visceral reaction to the piece. The unblemished firmness of the bronze and the figure's straight-backed posture give the Vairocana an aura of detachedness, calm, and poise. Its smile, wide and welcoming, reassures the viewer and conveys the Buddha's benevolence. After a longer period of observation, one also senses the Buddha's power: its bronze surface gives the lone, composed figure an abstract, otherworldly elegance. Behind the smile, one can sense the strength of a being at peace.

—Oliver W. Sloman (Williams 2005). Adapted from Assignment no. 1, student paper for Ju-Yu Scarlett Jang, Professor of Art

GIOVANNI DA MILANO
Italian, active 1346–69

St. Anthony Abbot
ca. 1365

Tempera on panel
36 x 17 ⅝ in.
Gift of the Samuel H. Kress Foundation (60.12)

The panel, otherwise in excellent condition, has been cut from the bottom; this is corroborated by comparison with another panel depicting St. Francis that once belonged to the same polyptych altarpiece.

It is the eyes that draw the eye. Eyes that are haunting because haunted. Haunted because of what they have seen and what they now see through. These are not eyes of certainty but of suspicion—deep, dark suspicion. Suspicion bred of temptation. Temptation born in the desert where the beasts dwelling within suddenly approach from without to render the unreal real and the real unreal. Where, then, is the desert? And what is temptation? For one who has seen what Anthony has seen, the crozier—the staff with gilded church and lamb—seems hollow. The church has become the desert and belief the last temptation.

—Mark C. Taylor, Cluett Professor of Humanities and Religion. Adapted from *Labeltalk*, 1995

FRANCO-FLEMISH

St. John the Evangelist
ca. 1430

Alabaster
19 1/2 x 6 1/2 x 2 3/4 in.
Museum purchase with partial funds provided by Lawrence H. Bloedel, Class of 1923 (62.4)

Originally part of an altarpiece ensemble with Christ on the cross in the center and probably Mary, Christ's mother, on the left, this exquisite statue of St. John the Evangelist is one of the museum's true treasures. I like to use it with students as an example of how art can embody paradox—can be two or more contradictory things at once—and how art tends to find its power, its ability to inform and move us, in a tight relationship between form and content. The figure's small scale (19 1/2 in.) engenders in us a sense of intimacy, a desire to protect. This impulse is amplified by John's slim physique, by the delicate, fluid folds of his drapery—in places as thin as linen—and by the decorative braiding of his hair. Together, these features help present John as Christ's most beloved companion, as he is described in the Bible, and as a tender, agonized witness to his friend's death.

John was also famous in the Middle Ages as the author of the most theologically sophisticated Gospel and of the Book of Revelation. In this context, he was celebrated as a man of great fortitude, with the force of belief to see Christ's divinity before anyone else ("In the beginning was the Word") and with the industry to create through his writings the foundation on which Christianity could be built. This contrasting vision of John is also expressed in the statue. The figure, after all, is made of stone, one of the toughest of materials, and on the back of the statue, the folds of his cloak are transformed into parallel vertical ribs, reminiscent of the fluting in a classical column. While these details help characterize John as a "pillar" of the church, his energized drapery and strained gaze upward—the tendons and Adam's apple of the evangelist's neck have been carefully delineated—indicate the source of his strength. He is a spiritual superman, looking not just at Christ on the cross but far beyond, into the high reaches of Heaven.

—Peter D. Low, Associate Professor of Art

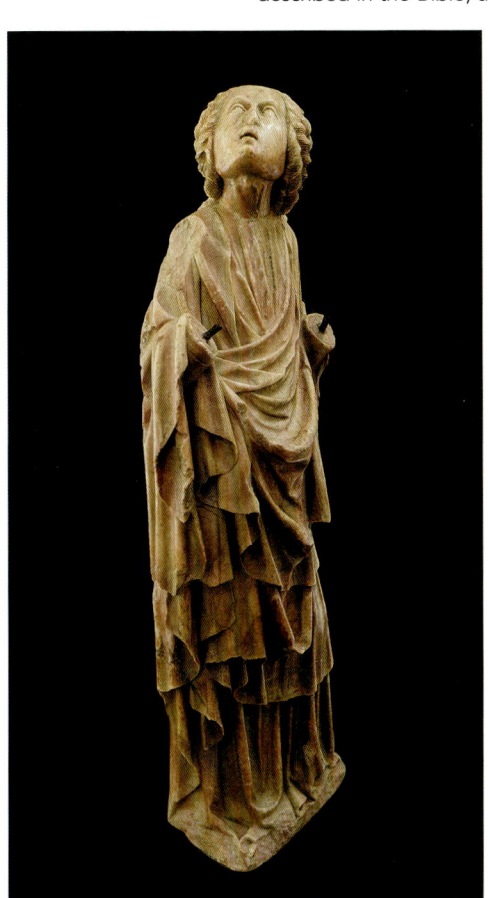

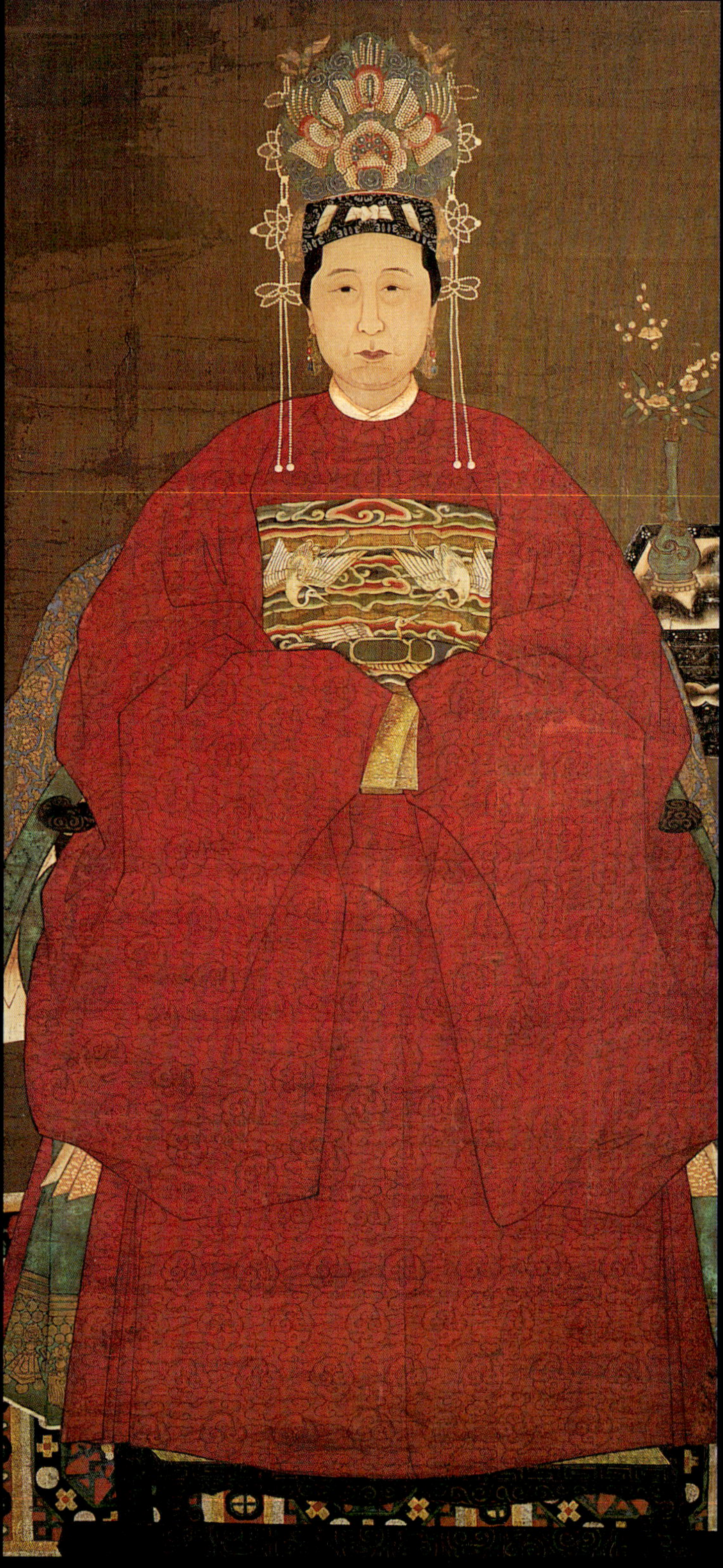

CHINESE, MING DYNASTY

Ancestral Portrait
ca. 1368–1644

Painting on silk
62 3/8 x 31 1/2 in.
Gift of Mrs. Rachel Biddle Raymond, in memory of her son, Ridgeway Miller Cravens, Class of 1914 (PC.63)

The ancestor portraits of the Ming dynasty were exceptionally accurate portraits of important people painted as they approached the end of their lives. Unlike idealizing portraits in Western art, this traditional art form stressed the minute details of facial identity—however unflattering—and adhered to a rigid frontal pose of the head and body. The goal was to make the august personage appear as unlifelike as possible and show him or her inhabiting the powerful world of the dead. The elaborate headdress and robes attested to the high status of the person, both in life and now for eternity. On the woman's chest are the two symmetrical animal designs that would have been separate pieces of cloth sewn onto the robe to denote her rank in the official Chinese hierarchy.

Although the identity of this woman is now lost, her presence (via this portrait) in the homes of her descendants would give them advantages over a less powerful family. In a general sense, in all known cultures, portraits of important ancestors serve to establish family lineage and give social prestige to current generations. But the extreme rigidity of the Chinese ancestor portrait, far surpassing even the most traditional religious icons familiar in Western art, calls to mind the rigidity of the actual human body after death and may echo older traditions of the public display of elaborately dressed mummies. Such practices were recorded among the native Peruvians by the Spanish during the conquest of the sixteenth century and have been witnessed in other traditional cultures as well.

Paintings such as the Ming ancestor portrait are a more practical method of keeping the physical presence of an ancestor in the home while still evoking the tightly sculpted features and eerie stare of a preserved body. The emphasis on the person as *dead* sparks discomfort in the viewer and promotes awareness of an alternative reality, giving these portraits a power beyond mere genealogy.

—Nancy Mowll Mathews, Eugénie Prendergast Senior Curator of 19th and 20th Century Art and Lecturer in Art

ATTRIBUTED TO
PAOLO SCHIAVO
Italian, 1397–1478

Birth Platter (*desco da parto*):
The Story of Diana and Actaeon
ca. 1440

Tempera on panel
27 15/16 x 27 15/16 in.
Bequest of Frank Jewett
Mather, Jr., Class of 1889 (62.3)

Functional objects like this Florentine childbirth tray painted by Paolo Schiavo have recently come to be regarded by scholars as vital windows into Renaissance culture. These trays, originally used to present refreshments to a new mother, were integral parts of the ritual of childbirth during the fifteenth century. Florentines of all classes bought numerous items to celebrate the arrival of a new baby, including ornamented bedding, painted birthing chairs, protective amulets and charms, and impressive clothing for both mother and newborn. The large and elaborately decorated *deschi da parto*, as the trays were called, were considered de rigueur although, like most of these items, they were entirely unnecessary from a practical standpoint. Experiencing the size of such an object and imagining its weight and manageability as an object in use speak volumes about the ritual practices surrounding childbirth during this period. The birth of a new baby was especially important in Florence following the Black Death (1346–53), when childbirth still presented a relatively high risk. The city had lost about two-thirds of its population to outbreaks of the devastating epidemic, and while children were needed to ensure the continuation of family lines, the promotion of procreation coexisted with a sharp awareness of the fragility of life.

The artist has represented the classical, Ovidian story of Diana and Actaeon (*Metamorphoses*, 3.138), a cautionary tale with a tragic ending. Hunting in the forest, Actaeon comes upon Diana, the chaste Roman goddess of the hunt, and her band of virginal wood nymphs in their bath; the young prince's punishment for this glimpse of divine nudity is his transformation into a stag who is promptly devoured by his own hounds, here represented by a single dog. Puzzling out Florentines' motivations for representing this tale on childbirth trays (this is not the only example) is one of the rewards of studying it. Actaeon is the clear outsider in Schiavo's scene, unwelcome to the cluster of women in the bath who, enclosed in its walls, might have evoked the exclusively female world of the Florentine birth chamber (a male presence at a Florentine birth usually indicated that something had gone terribly wrong). Objects commissioned for this space also served a protective function, and a powerful female force such as Diana—goddess of the moon, associated with the menstrual cycle, and considered a protector of pregnant women—may have been chosen with the hope of mitigating the dangers of labor and delivery. In the highly patriarchal society of Renaissance Florence, childbirth was one instance that called for exceptional female strength.

The Actaeon story was malleable in its meaning, however, and the fickle moon goddess's powers of destruction may well have tapped into anxieties about female sexuality and procreative powers. But Diana was also a type for the Virgin Mary, and early modern people spiritually interpreted Actaeon's cruel fate as a transformation, at the hands of a virgin goddess, leading to salvation. Alternatively, Actaeon was read as a purposeful voyeur whose punishment was well justified by his sins of worldliness and lust. Finally, Actaeon's intrusion also raises questions of social propriety, particularly female chastity, which was considered fundamental to the institution of marriage.

Marriage is the appropriate place to conclude, because while childbirth trays such as this one were made as utilitarian serving vessels (albeit elaborate ones), their usefulness continued after the birth of the baby; instead, they remained with the parents, often hanging as a wall painting in the marital bedchamber. This object's many social resonances would have facilitated a lifetime of looking and thinking for its original Florentine audience, and, appropriately, students of the WCMA *desco* find it seemingly limitless in terms of interpretative possibilities. Its physical nature and iconographic richness provide us a glimpse into the lives and values, in all their complexity, of Renaissance Florentines.

—Stefanie Solum, Assistant Professor of Art

GONÇAL PERIS
Spanish, active ca. 1409–d. 1451

St. Lucy (formerly St. Cecilia)
15th century; altered in the
16th century

Tempera on panel
56 1/8 x 32 1/2 in.
Gift of Karl E. Weston, Class of 1896, in memory of Ruth Sabin Weston (54.2)

This fifteenth-century Spanish panel painting was originally believed to be a depiction of St. Cecilia, the saint associated with music. She held a palm frond in one hand and a book in the other, through which, mysteriously, a pair of eyes could be seen. Technical examination later revealed an entirely different head under that of the St. Cecilia figure, as well as a platter bearing a pair of eyes, partially obscured by the painted book. The platter of eyes is a common symbol, not of St. Cecilia, but of St. Lucy, who was said to have had her eyes put out by the emperor Diocletian as part of her martyrdom.

In 1983 conservators at the Williamstown Regional Art Conservation Laboratory (now Williamstown Art Conservation Center) began restoration of the panel painting, removing the layers of repaint that had transformed the figure of St. Lucy into St. Cecilia. The face of St. Cecilia, with its Pre-Raphaelite softness, was stylistically incongruous with the unaltered gilding and punch-work typical of Valencian painting during the fifteenth century. The newly restored image, revealing St. Lucy's platter with eyes, as well as her face, ear, and reddish blond hair, is consistent in style with the other elements of the painting. Its attribution to Gonçal Peris was confirmed through its striking similarity to his other works: the figure of St. Lucy so closely resembles Peris's panel painting of St. Barbara (Museum of Catalan Art, Barcelona) that it is believed he used the same cartoon to create both works.

—Elizabeth Athens (Williams M.A. 2005), The Edith and Herbert Lehman Foundation Publications Assistant

Before treatment 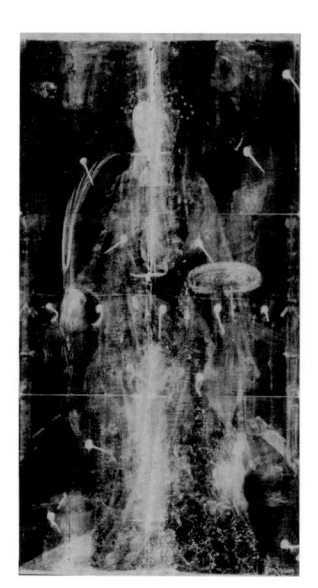 / During treatment  / After treatment

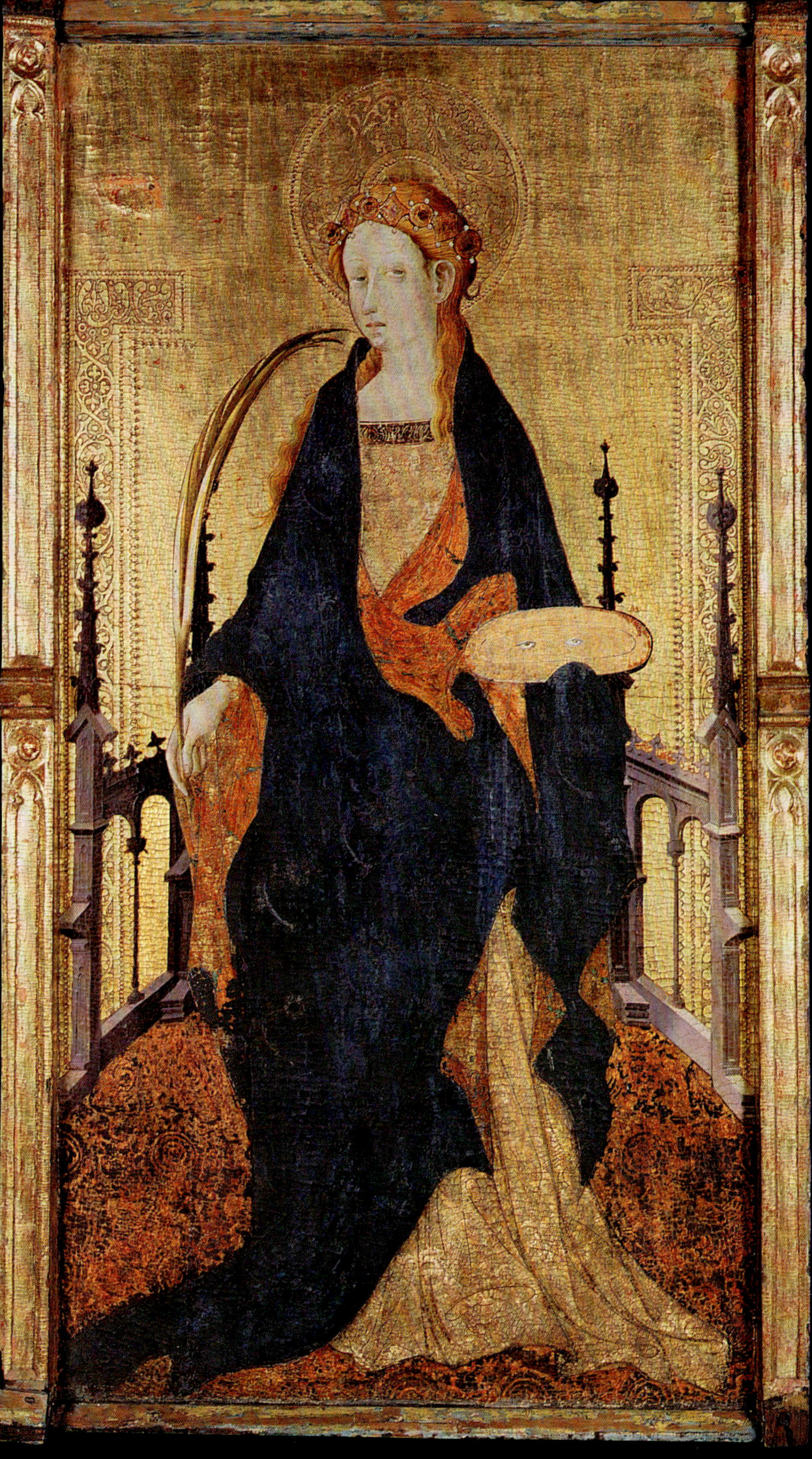

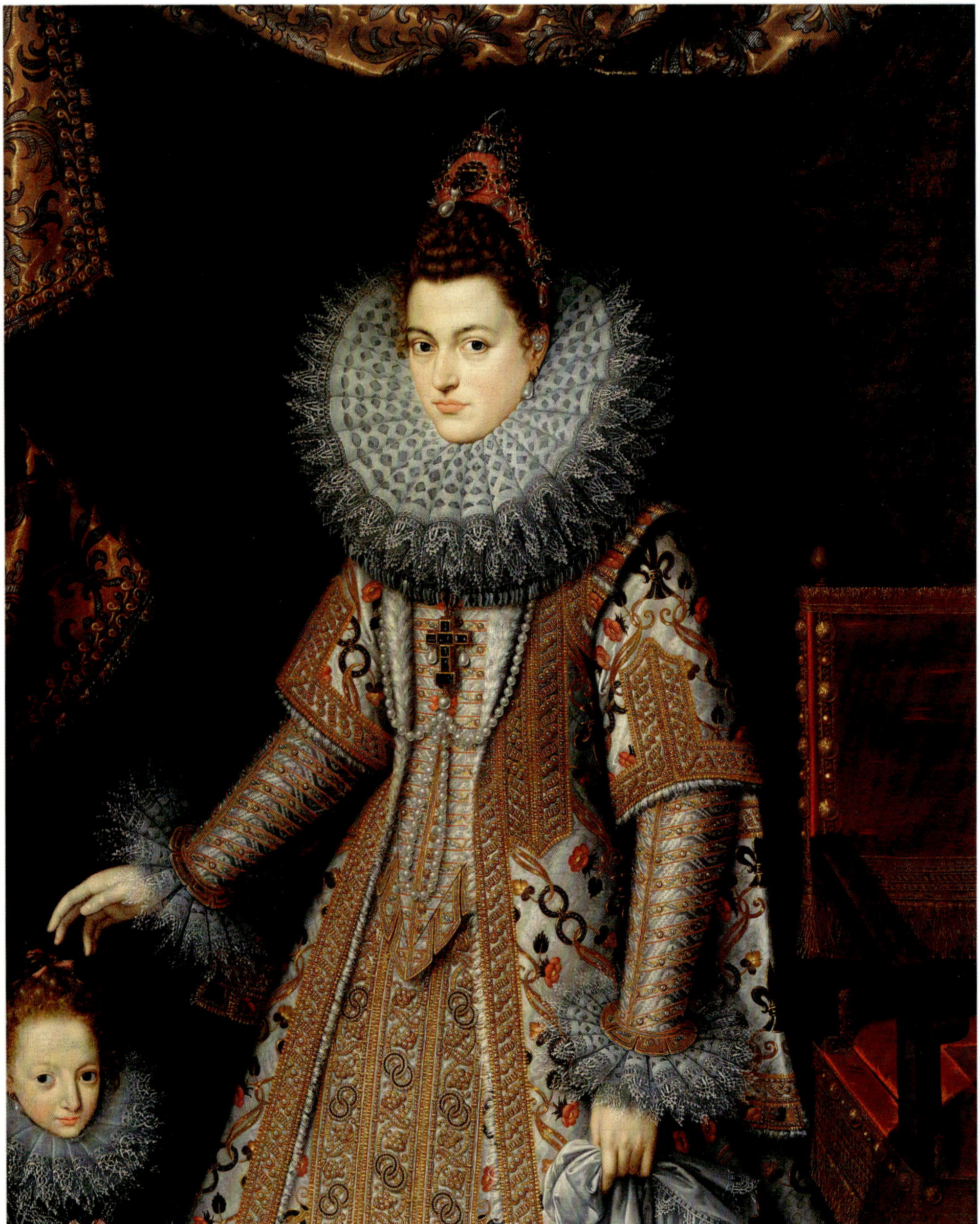

FRANS POURBUS THE YOUNGER
Flemish, 1569–1622

Portrait of Infanta Isabella Clara Eugenia
1599–1600

Oil on canvas
51 x 41 5/8 in.
Gift of Prentis Cobb Hale, Jr.
(64.31)

This court portrait depicts the Infanta Isabella Clara Eugenia, daughter of Elizabeth de Valois and Philip II of Spain, shortly after she had become archduchess of Austria and ruler of the Spanish-controlled Southern Netherlands. The sixteenth century saw a major expansion of Spain's power, which extended—thanks to territorial conquests and interdynastic marriages—through much of Europe and to parts of the Caribbean, North and Central America, and Africa.

The fine detailing of the infanta's costume in this portrait by Frans Pourbus, completed during his year as court painter at Brussels, gives visual expression to Spain's supremacy: the unyielding bodice, splayed ruff, and bell skirt are of typical Spanish style. The stiff, geometric quality of her dress, which flattened the breasts and produced a conelike outline, was in keeping with the moral rigidity of the Counter-Reformation and Spanish Catholicism. Although Spain's strength would decline significantly in the seventeenth century, the elaborate embroidery and rich fabric of the infanta's garment give evidence of the country's powerful legacy.

—Elizabeth Athens (Williams M.A. 2005), The Edith and Herbert Lehman Foundation Publications Assistant

JUSEPE DE RIBERA
Spanish, 1591–1652

The Executioner
ca. 1640–50

Oil on canvas
40 x 34 ¼ in.
Gift of Harry G. Sperling (53.9)

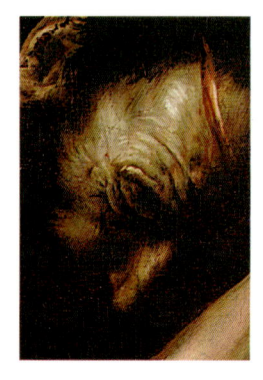

Jusepe de Ribera was born in Játiva, a town near Valencia. After a short apprenticeship with a minor Valencian painter, Ribera left Spain for Naples, which had been ruled by Spanish viceroys since the mid-fifteenth century. There he came under the influence of the great Italian Baroque painter Caravaggio. In 1616 Ribera married a Neapolitan, a daughter of a painter, and had a very successful career with numerous commissions for the viceroy and Spanish nobility of Naples as well as many commissions from Spain.

The Executioner displays a half-figure twisting in space, holding in his right hand a severed head with a huge gash in the forehead. The executioner's face is impassive, and one of his hands rests on his knife, which has been shortened from its original length. The pentiment—or visible evidence of the alteration—gives the sense that the knife is in motion, as though the executioner were, at the moment of the painting, replacing it in its sheath. The dramatic lighting intensifies the painting's dynamism. Blood red eyes stare at the onlooker, while highlights play across the figure's weapons. All these dynamic features are an expression of the Roman Baroque style, yet the vividness of the interpretation and the emphasis on blacks stem from the Spanish tradition.

—Whitney Snow Stoddard (Williams 1935), Amos Lawrence Professor of Art Emeritus. Adapted from *Mostly Spanish*, 1992

ATTRIBUTED TO JOSÉ MORENO
Spanish, 1642–1674

Annunciation
ca. 1660–70

Oil on canvas
53 1/2 x 69 7/16 in.
Gift of George Alfred Cluett, Class of 1896 (54.1)

Since its 1954 acquisition by the Williams College Museum of Art from the family of a German ambassador to Madrid, this painting has, at different times, been attributed to several Spanish Baroque painters. Its initial attribution to Juan de Valdéz Leal was only tentative, as an article written for a 1954 issue of *Art Quarterly* by S. Lane Faison, Jr.—the museum's then director—makes clear. In his article, Faison mentioned that the *Annunciation* was quite unlike Valdéz Leal's early work and expressed his hope that the article might encourage inquiry into the painting, one of the first of its kind to be included in an American collection.

Faison's article was successful; a number of letters came to the museum curious about the work's authorship. Many letters suggested that the painting bore the hallmarks of the Madrid school, and the *Annunciation* is now attributed to José Moreno, a Madrid painter known for the soft color tonalities found in this painting. The loose, dynamic brushstrokes of the *Annunciation* reflect the painterly freedom of Titian and Tintoretto combined with the centrifugal explosiveness of Bernini's sculpture, owing much to the influence of the Italian Baroque artists on their contemporaries in Madrid.

—Elizabeth Athens (Williams M.A. 2005), The Edith and Herbert Lehman Foundation Publications Assistant

Prints

ART COLLECTING AT WILLIAMS started with prints. Although the group of reproductive prints used in teaching from the 1850s to the end of the nineteenth century has not survived, interest in original prints by such contemporary artists as James McNeill Whistler was firmly in place by the 1880s, and today the prints constitute one of the largest and most studied branches of the collection. A highlight of the college's famous yearlong survey of Western art history is the conference devoted to prints wherein students learn the lessons of close looking. Rather than teaching the history of prints, this class is devoted to the identification of printmaking techniques, both historic and modern, and related questions of paper types, inscriptions, and stamps. The demanding study of prints opens our eyes to the identification and interpretation of nuance.

Prints are a paradoxical medium. The product of advances in the twin technologies of printing equipment and paper making in the Renaissance, they are among the most mechanical of arts. Yet prints are also exceptionally intimate and personal. The process of developing the finished design by printing preliminary "states" records the decision-making steps of the artist more precisely than any other medium. And, even though a print by definition is an "exactly repeatable pictorial statement," in the words of print connoisseur William M. Ivins, Jr., each impression has its unique character—produced by variations of ink, paper, inscriptions, and condition. Because prints are multiples, there is a commercial aspect to their production, and they are often the least expensive art objects a collector can buy. Yet the medium of ink and paper has its own expressive qualities, and certain prints are regarded as among the greatest works of art.

Andrea Mantegna
Italian, ca. 1431–1506
Entombment, second half of the 15th century
Engraving on paper
Sheet: 10 ¹³/₁₆ x 17 in.
Museum purchase with funds provided by Mrs. Michele A. Vaccariello in memory of her husband (77.7)

Albrecht Dürer
German, 1471–1528
The Small Horse, 1505
Engraving on paper
Sheet: 6 ⁵/₁₆ x 4 ⅛ in.
Gift of Joseph O. Eaton, Class of 1895 (29.1.9)

Hendrik Goltzius
Dutch, 1558–1617
Urania, late 16th century
Engraving on paper
Sheet: 9 ¹³/₁₆ x 6 ½ in.
Gift of James Bergquist, Class of 1970 (70.31)

Rembrandt Harmensz. van Rijn
Dutch, 1606–1669
Death of the Virgin, 1639
Etching on paper
Sheet: 16 ⅛ x 12 ⁵/₁₆ in.
Museum purchase, with funds provided by Andrew S. Keck, Class of 1924, in memory of Karl E. Weston (57.37)

9
Mueltius Inuent. et sculpt.
anie celi motus, et sydera monstrat,
Quid portendat Hyas, et quid nimbosus Orion,
Jouis, et placide promittat Cypridos astrum
Feraliq coma signum ferale Cometes
F.E.

1505

FRANCESCO SOLIMENA
Italian, 1657–1747

The Miracle of St. John of God
ca. 1690

Oil on canvas
36 3/4 x 29 3/4 in.
Museum purchase, John B. Turner '24 Memorial Fund and Karl E. Weston Memorial Fund
(93.6)

Although this looks like a finished painting by the Neapolitan Francesco Solimena, it is actually a preparatory sketch for a large altarpiece that originally hung in the church of a hospital in Naples, the Ospedalle della Pace. Internationally renowned when he worked on this composition in 1690, the painter made sure its message carried even from a distance. It still does at WCMA.

The dark pile of dead bodies, including an infant being chewed by a dog, evokes the recurrent plagues that swept through Europe, wiping out much of the population. Naples lost half its inhabitants in 1656, the year before Solimena was born there, and plague returned to the city in 1672. Medical remedies proved ineffectual, so people turned for help to the higher power of saints. Because St. John of God had founded and run a hospital in Granada, he became a patron saint of hospitals. Also, since people credited him with stopping the dreadful plague of 1656, he continued to be invoked in Naples for such protection. The sick woman who looks up hopefully to his light-framed figure may symbolize the city's sick, especially the patients in the Ospedalle della Pace.

Unexpectedly, the flying saint holds a painting of himself. Before he founded a hospital, St. John had peddled religious images and books, so this may be a biographical reference. The woman's weakly extended hand also suggests the little picture may depict an ex-voto she presented as part of her appeal for the saint's help.

—Zirka Z. Filipczak, Preston S. Parish '41 Third Century Professor of Art

Here, St. John is celebrated for trying to save the city of Naples from the plague, but, despite the best efforts of the faithful, the Black Death devastated the city. We can only imagine the terror of the survivors, desperate for salvation as they confronted the horrifying physical manifestations of the disease and its mortality rates that approached 50 percent. Chaos and doom, brought on by a near-invisible, microscopic particle, ruled their existence. But there was no miracle, and there was no hope.

Who is to say what the ultimate impact and resulting social dislocation due to HIV/AIDS will be? The socioeconomic cost alone of HIV will be staggering. As countries lose a majority of their population in their prime, the chaos and dislocation of the Middle Ages may be revisited. Due to parochialism and desperation, the world may again turn to faith in the face of tragedy, as scientific knowledge and the necessity of education about HIV/AIDS are routinely ignored. It tries the imagination to think that something so biologically simple —a bacterium or virus—can so dramatically alter the course of human history.

When confronted with tragedy we cannot comprehend, we often turn to those we empower owing to their knowledge or spirituality, such as a physician or a priest. Though the white coat has now replaced the black frock as a symbol of power and salvation, I fear that even St. John of God would have as little success in today's world as he had in Naples in 1656.

—Nancy A. Roseman, Dean of the College and Professor of Biology

42, 43

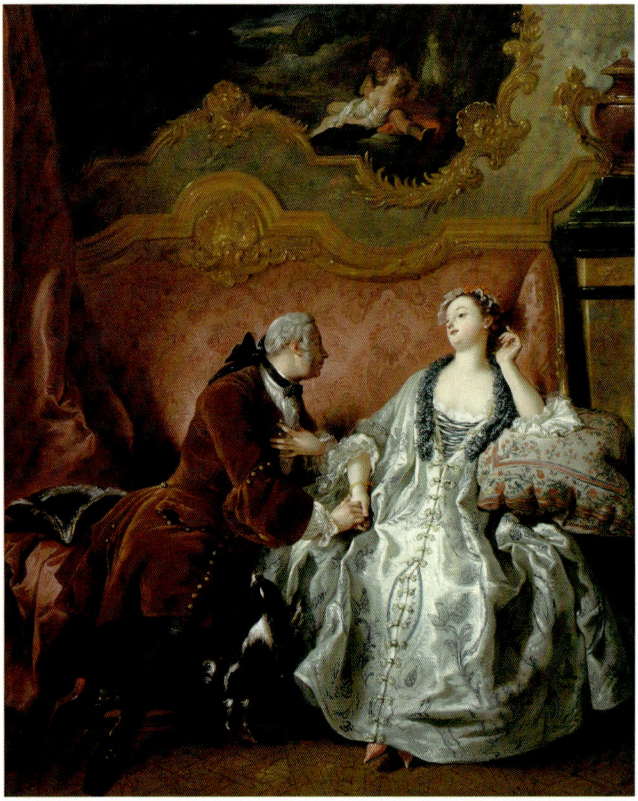

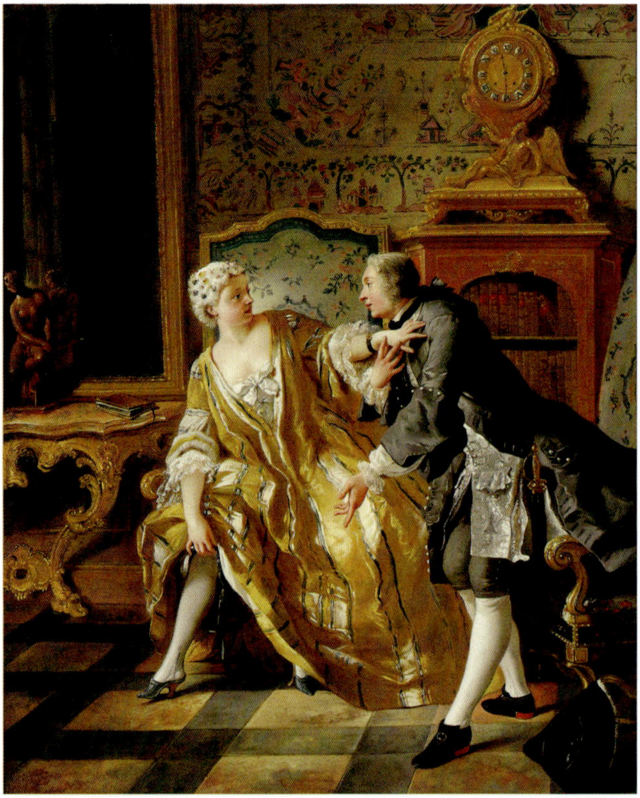

JEAN FRANÇOIS DE TROY
French, 1679–1752

La Déclaration d'amour
ca. 1724

La Conversation galante
ca. 1724

Oil on canvas
25 9/16 x 21 7/16 in.
Gift of C. A. Wimpfheimer,
Class of 1949 (80.17.2)

Oil on canvas
25 9/16 x 21 5/16 in.
Gift of C. A. Wimpfheimer,
Class of 1949 (80.17.1)

Jean François de Troy was the son and student of the popular Parisian portrait artist François de Troy (1645–1730). In 1699 his father sent him to study painting in Rome but cut off support when he refused to come home. The young de Troy, however, found a patron and continued to live in Italy, traveling throughout Abruzzo, Umbria, Tuscany, and the Veneto, returning to Paris only in 1706.

During the decade after his return he devised a new type of genre painting known as *tableaux de mode*, loosely translated as "fashionable pictures," of which the museum's pair is exemplary. These easel-size paintings focus on intimate moments in the lives of the Parisian haut monde, offering a glimpse of their social rituals and interactions while re-creating in great detail and with complete fidelity the look and feel of contemporary costumes and interior decor. In addition to merely chronicling the life of the upper classes, these works often convey an undercurrent of sexual intrigue.

La Déclaration d'amour and *La Conversation galante* are pendants with complementary subjects on the theme of seduction. In the former, a suitor on bended knee shows restraint as he gently holds the hand of a reclining young woman and earnestly pleads his case. Elaborately garbed in a *sacque*, or morning dressing gown open to the waist with a white bodice revealed beneath, the young woman indicates with her body language that she is receptive to the young man's heartfelt declaration. By contrast, the suitor in *La Conversation galante* meets with a stern rebuke as he audaciously rises to retie the garter of the seated woman, also wearing a *sacque*, who has pulled the skirts of her gown up to reveal the lower part of her right leg. She holds the unfastened garter in her right hand while pushing the man aside with her left.

Possibly meant as a reserved "right way" versus an aggressive "wrong way" to pursue love, the meaning of the little dramas is reinforced by objects in the rooms. For example, the landscape painting on the wall in *La Déclaration d'amour* shows the figures of Mars and Venus embracing, implying the successful conclusion of the gentle suitor's wooing. By contrast, the nudity of the statuette on the console table in *La Conversation galante* emphasizes the lustful nature of the suitor, but, in turning away, the statue parallels the action of the woman.

WCMA's de Troys are faithful replicas of the pair exhibited in the Salon of 1725 now in the collection of Jane Wrightsman in New York. The pendants are identical with the originals and reproduce faithfully every detail, save the artist's signatures and the date. They were painted either by de Troy or by an assistant in his atelier.

—Deborah Rothschild, Senior Curator of Modern and Contemporary Art

GIOVANNI PAOLO PANNINI
Italian, 1691–1765

Composition of Roman Ruins
1734

Oil on canvas
44 3/4 x 59 9/16 in.
Museum purchase, Mather Bequest Fund (54.20)

Giovanni Paolo Pannini was one of the most successful artists in Rome in the middle decades of the eighteenth century, a time when that city was still the artistic capital of Europe. Young artists flocked there to study the monuments of antiquity and the works of the great masters of the Renaissance, such as Raphael and Michelangelo. Along with the artists came wealthy tourists, especially young English gentlemen completing their education by making the grand tour. Pannini specialized in views of the city, some painstakingly realistic, others montages of the marvels of Rome, as is the case with our picture, which presents buildings and statues in a relationship they never had in reality. The painting was doubtless intended to be taken home by a visitor as a memento of Rome, something like a modern postcard with photos of many aspects of a city visited. Pannini painted a number of variants on this picture, with a changing cast of statues and ruins. Ours, signed and dated 1734, is the earliest of the series; the latest, in Prague, dates from 1764, the year before Pannini died. We know that he showed pictures like this at public art sales and that there were art dealers in Rome who sold such works to travelers. Like many other artists of his day, Pannini made a living by painting pictures aimed at the tastes of wealthy collectors.

At the left of the picture, poised in front of the Colosseum, the Borghese Warrior, with his left arm extended, leads us simultaneously into the picture space and across the picture plane. His gesture carries us to the lower and slightly recessed figure of the Dying Gaul. The two nude males, on angled podia that visually rhyme with the Pyramid of Cestius in the background, form a triangular group that is reinforced by the raised right arm of the seated man who is pointing up at the Gaul. The man's gesture calls both the attention of his standing companion to the statues and our attention to the companion's head, which is turned over his left shoulder to look at the Warrior. This gazing head—by extension, the act of looking—is actually the focus of the picture. Pannini had been trained in the practice of one-point perspective in his native Piacenza, where he had grown up surrounded by perspectival marvels created by one of the great masters of perspective, Ferdinando Galli Bibbiena. Pannini used his knowledge of perspective to aim the receding lines of the buildings at the right of the picture, particularly the cornices of the Arch of Constantine and of the three-columned ruins of the Temple of Castor and Pollux, at the standing man's head, which is framed by dark tones to give it prominence. Lest our own gaze wander too far afield, Pannini has a little dog charge in at the far right to herd us back into the center of the picture, past the heads of two conveniently placed figures who also gaze at the one who is gazing.

The gazing man is at our level. He stands for us; we contemplate his contemplation. The picture is about pondering antiquity for the moral lesson that can be learned from such action, to say nothing of the aesthetic pleasure thereby acquired. Back home in England, the picture would remind us not only of what we saw, but also of how we saw it. While the Warrior and the Gaul suggest the violent combat that took place in the Colosseum, the Gaul in particular establishes a theme of death that is echoed in the ruins surrounding the central human figures. Vegetation grows from the decaying structures, while fragments of broken architecture are strewn across the ground. The whole is bathed in a tender Roman light. This is not the light of high noon. Rather, it can evoke nostalgia for the evenings a visitor had spent in the city, as well as a melancholic sense of the passage of time.

—Eugene J. Johnson (Williams 1959), Class of 1955 Memorial Professor of Art

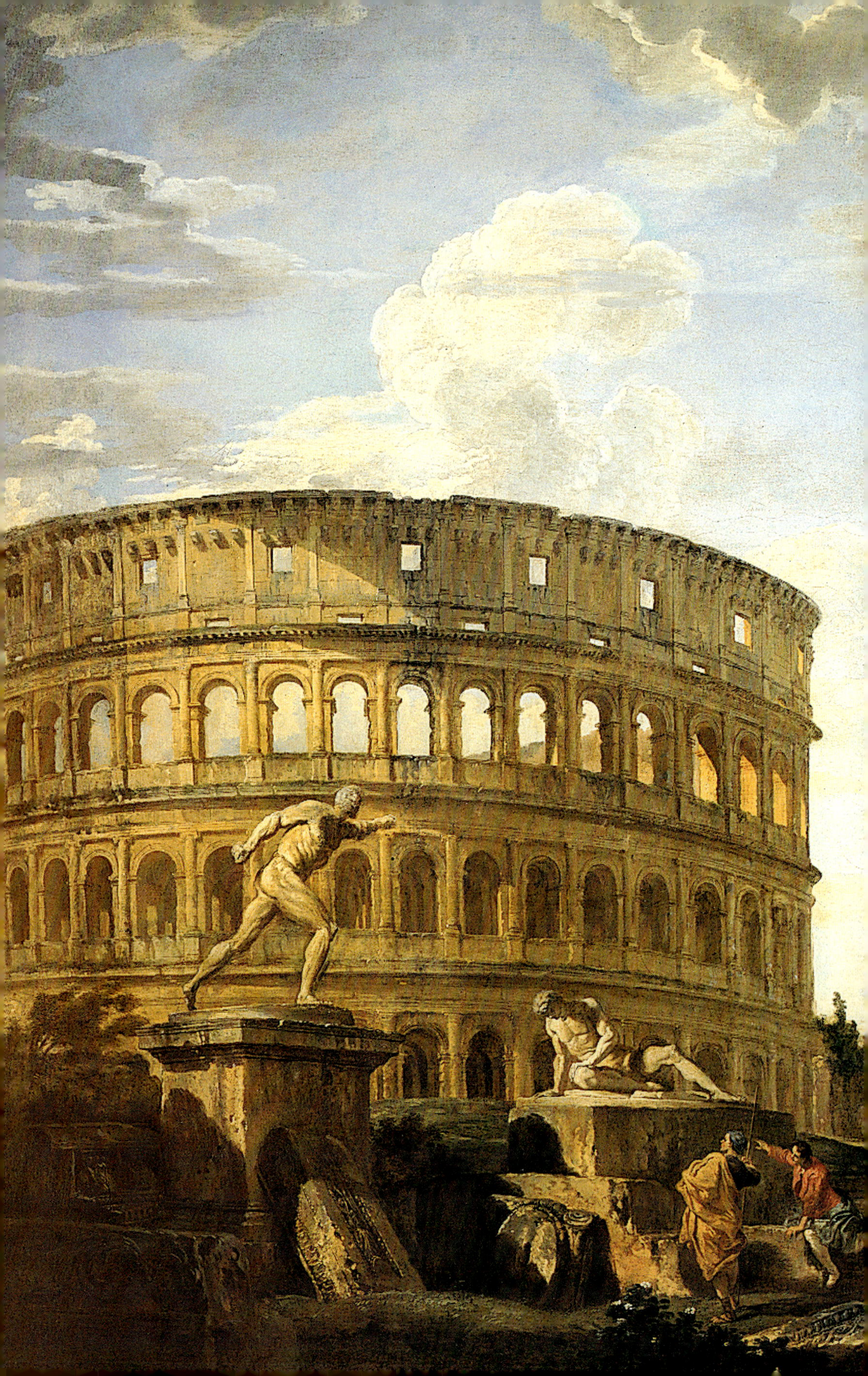

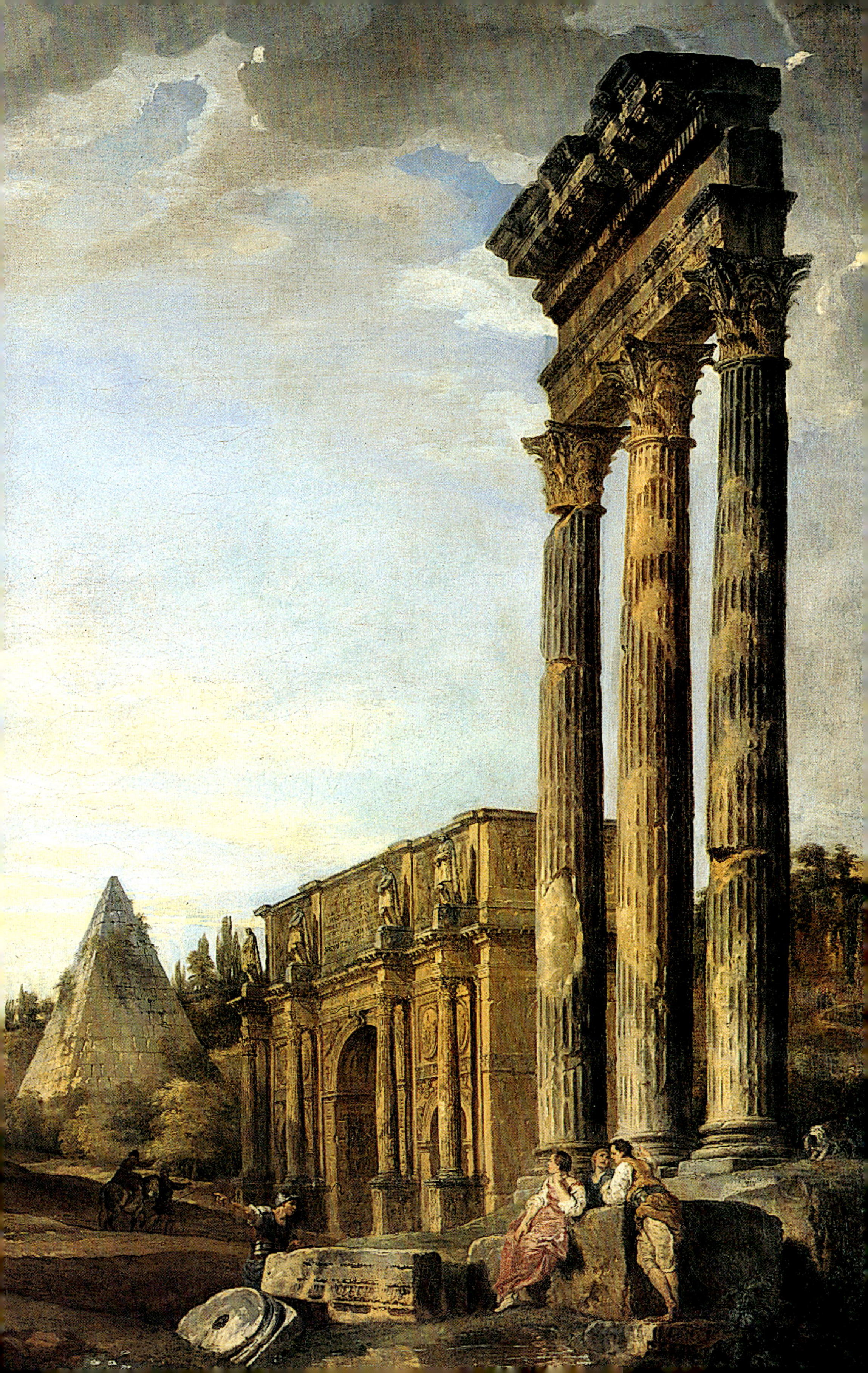

NORTH INDIAN, MUGHAL

A Prince with Ladies
on a Terrace
ca. 1735

Opaque watercolor on paper,
heightened with gold
9 1/2 x 13 5/16 in.
Bequest of Mrs. Horace W.
Frost (91.15.36)

Something is missing or has come to an end in this dazzling late Mughal painting. Hindustani (north Indian) musical performance requires three fundamental units: a supporting drone, rhythmic accompaniment, and a melodic soloist. The women on the right—one bearing the four-stringed *tambura*, the other a generic drum—satisfy two of these roles. Melody, however, seems absent here. Perhaps the young woman proffered to the prince has just finished singing or dancing for his pleasure. The musical offering is now followed by a silent, sexual one. In all Indian art forms, the erotic is one of several legitimate expressive modes, and the goal of painter and musician alike is to arouse such mental states, or *rasas*, in their audience. (Music and art are even more explicitly linked in Indian *ragamala* paintings—a genre that presupposes the synesthetic ability to hear music by contemplating an image.) This painting looks back on the heyday of the Mughal court, when refined courtiers were expected to perceive the *rasa* expressed in any art form.

—W. Anthony Sheppard, Associate Professor of Music. Published in *Labeltalk*, 2001

WILLIAM HOGARTH
English, 1697–1764

Strolling Actresses
Dressing in a Barn
1738

Engraving on paper
Image: 16 7/8 x 21 3/16 in.
Gift of Sam Hunter, Class
of 1944 (80.48.2)

Like the Peeping Tom gazing through the tattered hole in the roof, we are voyeurs engrossed in this bustling backstage scene. The playbill and broadsheet lying on the bed tell us that these actresses are about to perform an imaginary play, "The Devil to Pay in Heaven," with a cast of characters drawn from classical mythology. But Hogarth emphasizes the comic incongruities between the divinities and the earthy, all-too-human actresses who play them, creating a new spectacle before their intended performance. Center stage a disheveled "Diana" practices her poses, while "Flora," one breast exposed, carefully arranges her hair before a broken looking glass. On the left, a siren offers a drink to a half-dressed "Ganymede," while "Juno," far right, looks heavenward as she rehearses her lines, oblivious of the monkey urinating into a helmet on the other side of the trunk. Behind her a woman cruelly snips off the tip of a squirming cat's tail to collect blood for an upcoming scene. But this roaring chaos is about to come to an end: the broadsheet also tells us that this is the troupe's last performance before the Theatre Licensing Act goes into effect, a draconian law that effectively closed down all theaters except those with a royal patent. With this image, Hogarth serves up an exaggerated display of the "lowly" characters targeted by the law. Yet our persistent gaze, returned by that of "Diana," affirms that, regardless of an act of Parliament, these performers will always have an audience.

—Stefanie Spray Jandl (Williams M.A. 1993), Andrew W. Mellon Foundation Associate Curator for Academic Programs

WILLIAM HOGARTH
English, 1697–1764

Credulity, Superstition, and Fanaticism: A Medley
1762

Etching and engraving on laid paper
Image: 14 7/8 x 12 15/16 in.
Museum purchase, John B. Turner '24 Memorial Fund
(M.2003.21.2)

William Hogarth's 1762 engraving *Credulity, Superstition, and Fanaticism: A Medley* is a splendid satire. Hogarth's carnivalesque scene depicts a medley of reprehensible enthusiasms, especially the strange effects of Methodism, and other strange beliefs depicted as ridiculous, dangerous follies.

The preacher on high is a flamboyant charlatan, "St. Money-trap," wearing the jester's motley, flipping his wig in histrionic exuberance, displaying puppets of a witch and a devil and discoursing on the text "I speak as a fool." Under his fake aura, ominously exposed, is a Catholic tonsure.

The preacher's church is more of a music hall than a holy place; front and nearly center, the unused poor box is covered with cobwebs. Nearly every figure is a weird performer or fanatic—except for the outsider, an Arab onlooker quietly smoking hookah. The vile congregation, many of whom carry icons, view bizarre spectacles or carnival acts: a woman gives birth to a litter of rabbits; a boy spews nails; a cleric diddles a woman with a phallic-shaped idol. John Wesley himself is attended by disembodied cherubs.

Hogarth's hugely popular images of fools and knaves, con men and gulls, are often moments in larger narratives. Though this piece stands alone, it flaunts its contingency and textuality, like the satires of Alexander Pope, Jonathan Swift, and Henry Fielding. There is a biblical inscription and several titled texts (Whitfield's *Hymn*, Wesley's *Sermon*, King James's *Demon-ology*). Other items are tagged or labeled: the "Bull Roar" meter and the "Raving" thermometer above a metastasized brain; the grotesque chandelier identified as the "globe of Hell."

All are part of Hogarth's infernal medley, a frenzied jumble, over the top,

CREDULITY, SUPERSTITION, and FANATICISM.
A MEDLEY.

Believe not every Spirit, but try the Spirits whether they are of God: because many false Prophets are gone out into the World.
1. John. Ch. 4. V. 1.

Design'd and Engrav'd by Wm. Hogarth.   Publish'd as the Act directs March 5th 1762.

AMERICAN, SOUTHERN NEW ENGLAND

Bonnet-top High Chest of Drawers
ca. 1765–85

Cherrywood
81 1/2 x 38 x 19 1/2 in.
Bequest of Charles M. Davenport, Class of 1901
(43.2.117)

The high chest of drawers was an English innovation of the late-seventeenth century, which was quickly adopted by the American colonies. Due to their relatively complex construction, high chests, or highboys, were one of the most expensive items of furniture in eighteenth-century America and, as a result, were proudly displayed in prominent places within the home. Placed in either the bedroom, which was a much more public space during this period than it is now, or the living room, the chest would have been used to store linens and other household goods.

The museum's high chest is typical of those made in Connecticut in the second half of the eighteenth century. The case is constructed of cherry, a native wood that would have been readily available to rural craftsmen, as opposed to imported mahogany, which was used more frequently by cabinetmakers in urban centers such as Boston. The use of carved fans on the central drawers, spiral-turned finials, and a robust architectural bonnet top terminating on either side in pinwheels or floral motifs is indicative of highboys made in Connecticut, which tended to be more whimsical and idiosyncratic in design than their urban counterparts. The bonnet tops of New England high chests were probably adapted from doorway designs such as that of the Elijah Williams House in nearby Deerfield, Massachusetts.

—Jamie Franklin (Williams M.A. 2005), Curator of Collections, Bennington Museum, Bennington, Vermont

CHATERI GUMANI
Indian, active late 18th and early 19th century

The Lion Hunt of Maharao Umed Singh of Kota
1779

Opaque watercolor on paper
21 3/4 x 26 3/4 in.
Museum purchase, Michele A. and Georgeann Vaccariello Fund and Karl E. Weston Memorial Fund (83.6)

The Lion Hunt of Maharao Umed Singh of Kota is a remarkably informative picture. Not only is the drama of the hunt clear and exciting, but we can see the arrangements that were made to assure its success. It is not an ordinary hunt, for the ruler of Kota, Umed Singh, is not the man at the left, toward whom the lions are being driven. Instead, he is the almost unnoticeable figure perched in a tree at the bottom right. (His features are recognizable from other paintings, and he is haloed.) Besides being routine sport, a hunt was often a way of honoring distinguished guests or celebrating particular festivals—and this is what we see here. Because the most important men are dressed in green (even the subsidiary figures at the right are wearing something green: a cloak, perhaps, or a turban), this is certainly the *ahaireya*, or Spring Festival, always celebrated by a ritual hunt and green clothing. What may be artistic license is the presence of the lions, rather than the more usual tiger. Long an imperial symbol—the Buddha sat on a lion throne and a rampant lion was the Mughal imperial standard—lions were, in fact, virtually extinct in Rajasthan by the eighteenth century. They appeared in paintings far more often than they stalked the scrub jungles of Kota.

—Milo C. Beach, Director (1987–2001), Freer Gallery of Art and the Arthur M. Sackler Gallery of the Smithsonian Institution. Adapted from *Art of India*, 1994

Animalier

ESTABLISHED IN 1635 during the reign of the French monarch Louis XIII, the initial aim of Le Jardin des Plantes was to provide medical students access to plant life and an opportunity to study their medicinal properties. By the mid–nineteenth century, however, the garden's greenhouses and popular zoo proved a mecca for artists. Its resources beckoned some of the leading proponents of the French Romantic movement—Antoine-Louis Barye (1796–1875) and Eugène Delacroix (1798–1863) among them—who came to examine, study, and draw the exotic animals and plants in the facility's varied collections.

Antoine Barye widened the range of French sculpture during the mid–nineteenth century with his skilled manipulation of bronze, realizing work of a quality not matched since the Renaissance. He became known for his ability to capture musculature and bone structure, as well as the attitude of the subject, creating sculpture combining anatomical correctness with a high degree of visual and sensual beauty. His attention to broad modeling resulted in massive compositions illustrative of the force and strength of the noble animals he assiduously observed at the gardens. Capitalizing on the then-current fascination with things "oriental," he gave an energetic nod to the exotic but responded with works in a full-blown realist tradition—for instance, his big cats triumph in vicious and passionate combat. They are keen, ferocious predators with teeth bared and claws extended, devouring their quarry, skin ripping, the prey suffering, dying, or dead.

Eugène Delacroix often accompanied his friend Barye to the gardens, where both sketched the caged creatures. Both attended the dissection of dead animals and clearly had a near-scientific understanding of animal anatomy and behavior as developed through their studies of scholarly texts and skeletal specimens. A fascination with themes of violent passion linked the two artists, but unlike Delacroix, Barye chose to focus primarily on subject matter—the animals themselves—that ran counter to the prevailing prejudices of academic art.

Eugène Delacroix
French, 1798–1863
Lion Devouring a Horse, 1844
Lithograph on paper
Image: 6 11/16 x 9 5/16 in.
Museum Purchase, John B. Turner '24 Memorial Fund (M.2003.21.1)

Eugène Delacroix
Sheet of Studies, first half of 19th century
Pen and ink
9 1/16 x 13 3/4 in.
Gift of Karl E. Weston, Class of 1896 (38.10)

Antoine-Louis Barye
French, 1796–1875
Horse Attacked by a Lion
ca. 1835
Bronze
14 3/4 x 10 5/8 in.
Museum purchase, Karl E. Weston Fund (63.18)

Eugène Delacroix
Lion, first half of 19th century
Pen and brown ink on paper
8 x 10 5/8 in.
Gift of Mrs. John W. Field in memory of her husband (1887.1.9)

Eugène Delacroix
Lion de l'Atlas, 1829
Lithograph on paper
Image: 12 3/4 x 18 in.
Gift of Elizabeth and David P. Tunick, Class of 1966, on the occasion of his Twenty-Fifth Reunion, in honor of S. Lane Faison, Jr., Eugene J. Johnson III, William H. Pierson, Jr., and Whitney S. Stoddard (91.21)

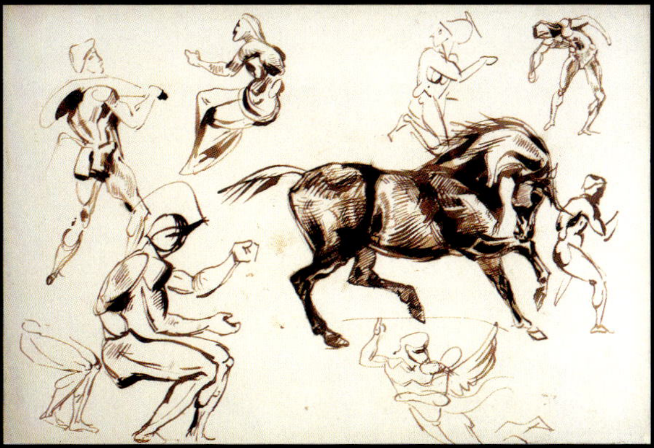

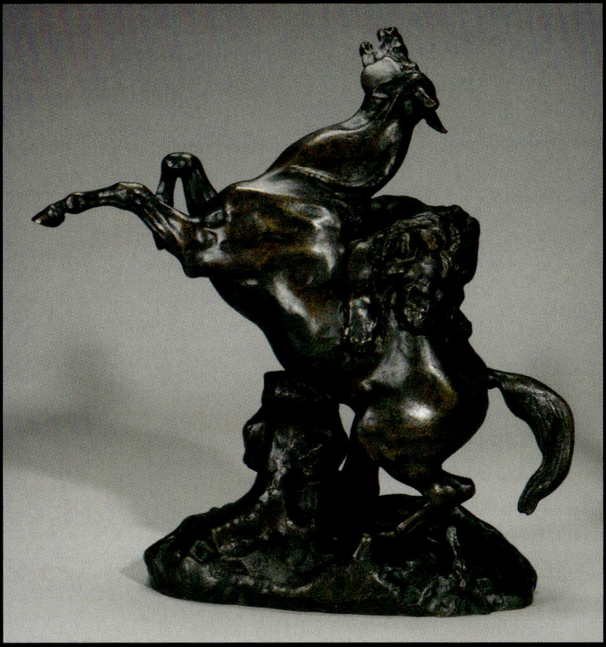

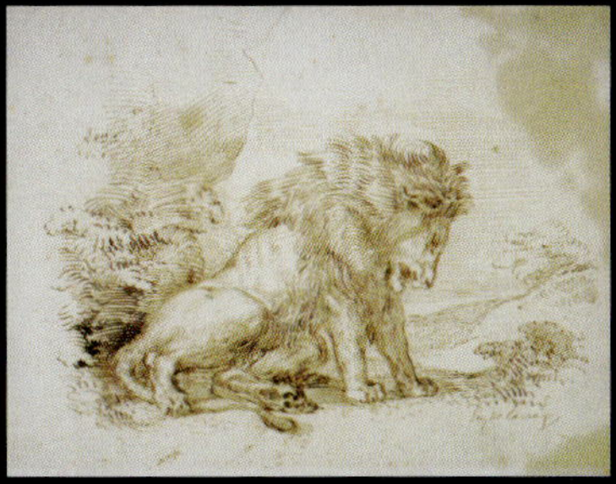

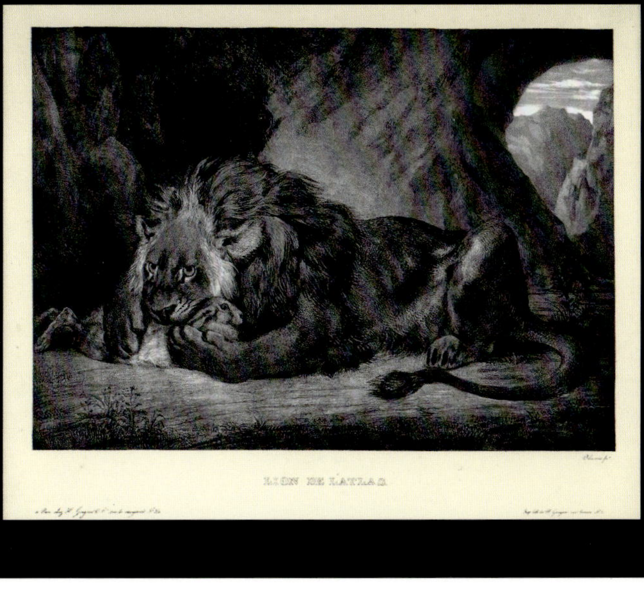
LION DE LATLAS

GEORGE INNESS
American, 1825–1894

Twilight
1860

Oil on canvas
36 x 54 1/4 in.
Gift of Cyrus P. Smith, Class of 1918, in memory of his father, B. Herbert Smith, Class of 1885 (79.66)

George Inness changed his artistic ideals and consequently his style many times in his career, sometimes in directions that took him away from the dominant taste of the times and practice of his colleagues. In the late 1840s and early 1850s, for example, an allegiance to old master styles lured him from the nature studies of his fellow artists. Later in the 1850s, however, Inness shared with the majority of American painters a taste for detailed realism based on close study of nature.

Like his leading contemporaries, Inness was approaching landscape in the spirit of scientific study of natural forms, which is reflected in the very specific cloud formations in *Twilight*. Whereas in the 1840s Inness painted generalized, fluffy, conceptual clouds, by the 1850s he had made careful cloud studies, informed by a knowledge of cloud classifications. In *Twilight*, Inness painted an extensive pattern of classic stratocumulus, in which the thick-thin appearance of the clouds indicates the presence of some convective motion, demonstrating a conspicuous knowledge of natural science. Also in its overall approach to landscape as spectacle, *Twilight* represents Inness's fullest participation in the aesthetic of his contemporaries in the second generation of the Hudson River School.

—Michael Quick, Director, George Inness Catalogue Raisonné. Adapted from *American Dreams: American Art to 1950 in the Williams College Museum of Art*, 2001

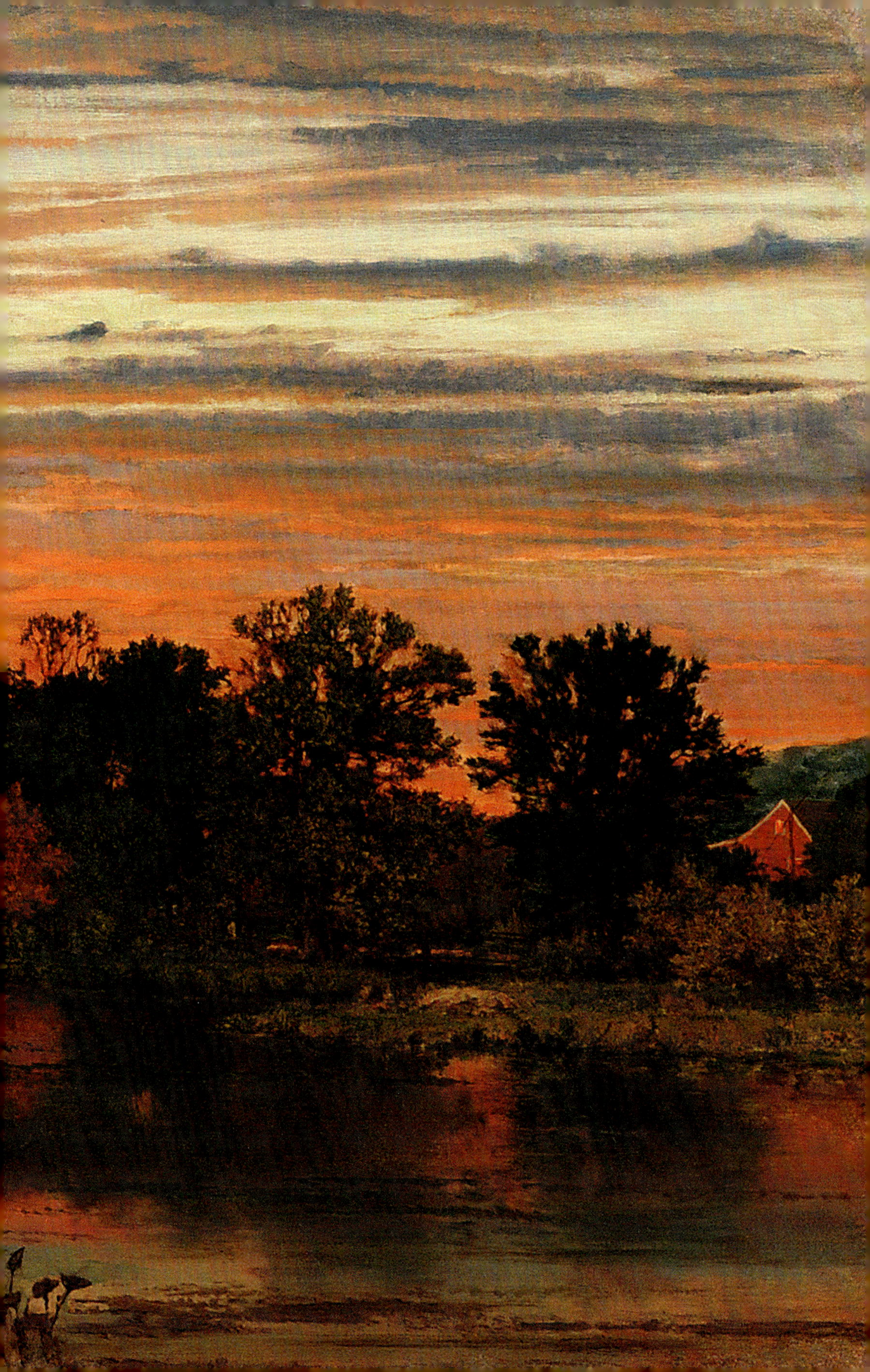

Page 20
112
Topsy
Page 31
first appearance 113
Topsy
48
Page
Topsy bed making
119
Page 58
121
Page 33
Topsy
Accomplishment
114
Page 34
115
Page 61
The letter from George
123
Page 62
124
Page 40
Topsy first Lesson in bed making 116
117
118
Page 63
Sunday Evening
125
Page 67
126
Page 68
The Jewel Box
127
Page 71
128

THOMAS NAST
American, 1840–1902

Drawings for "Uncle Tom's Cabin"
ca. 1867

Pencil and crayon on paper
Sheets: 9 7/8 x 13 1/8 in.
Gift of Mabel Nast Crawford and Cyril Nast (49.17.40a-f)

New versions of the novel *Uncle Tom's Cabin* were published every year from 1852 to 1930. Many of these have been collected in the Barrett Collection at the University of Virginia and at the Harriet Beecher Stowe Center in Hartford, Connecticut.

The illustrations on the covers and inside these multiple editions are steeped in nostalgia for a South before the Civil War. That South was bucolic, timeless, elegant, and a place of containment and contentment. In the plantation South, everyone knew his or her place, status, and purpose. Because of the clearly defined hierarchy, there could be and was close contact between blacks and whites. Indeed, a common element in most editions of *Uncle Tom's Cabin* is that blacks and whites touch each other. Eva teaches Tom to read, with a hand on his knee. Topsy and Eva hold hands, laughing. The mixed-race Eliza helps her white mistress to dress. It is clear that several illustrators picked up on Stowe's use of the white child Eva and the mixed-race Eliza as the conduits between white and black.

In her essay on Thomas Nast's drawings for *American Dreams: American Art to 1950 in the Williams College Museum of Art*, Karen Binswanger (Williams M.A. 1997) comments on a published frontispiece for Stowe's novel that Nast drew as a woodcut in 1868. In that piece, the central vignette is of Eva teaching Uncle Tom to write the alphabet. Binswanger describes Eva at a "cool remove, her arm slack at her side, a far cry from the picture of intimacy that Stowe herself described." The WCMA sketches are segmented, drawn by Nast for a children's version of Stowe's novel that was never published. However carefully segregated, Nast's markings bleed through the pages. The pencil and crayon imprint and darken the recto and verso sides of the page. Visual statements Nast makes in his representations of black bodies (Uncle Tom, Topsy, Cassie), white bodies (St. Claire, Eva), and those of mixed race (Eliza, George, and Harry Harris) all blend into the other because of the thinness of the paper, the result being that a recto drawing of Topsy superimposes over a verso drawing of Eliza.

Contrary to Stowe's intentions in her novel, in Nast's illustrations we see very few examples of physical contact between the white and black characters. Even the central drama of the first part of the novel, when Tom rescues Little Eva from the Mississippi River by carrying her wet, prone body back to the steamboat, is shown as Tom swimming near Eva, but not carrying her. Nast's drawings were never completed or published because, as the Nast family lore goes, he felt he could not draw African Americans "sympathetically." For me, what Nast could not bring himself to create was the close contact between those of light, white, and dark skin about which Stowe wrote. Unwittingly, that contact did happen and continues to happen between the sketches themselves through the thin pages.

—Annemarie Bean, Assistant Professor of Theatre and Co-Chair of Performance Studies Program

WINSLOW HOMER
American, 1836–1910

Children on a Fence
1874

Watercolor over pencil on paper
7 3/16 x 11 7/8 in.
Museum purchase with funds provided by the Assyrian Relief Exchange (41.2)

Children on a Fence underscores how synthetic the creative process was for Winslow Homer. Most likely painted in a studio, the watercolor's composition is carefully planned around the vignette of the four children. All the additional elements join to present an image dependent on a delicate equilibrium, where form and void, light and dark echo those of the children on the fence. For instance, the more carefully delineated, boldly colored, and narrative foreground is balanced within the whole sheet, not only by the golden-colored field that serves as its immediate backdrop but also by the relationships of the masses of trees and buildings, which alternate in weight and from foreground to background and from left to right. The considered balancing act of the composition visually supports the relationship of the children on the fence. The larger, older boy on the right sits apart from the three younger children. This grouping suggests the changing status of a youth's life as he matures. Growing toward adolescence, he does not mix as comfortably with the opposite sex as does the little boy to the left, and his bare feet, in contrast to the fully shod younger ones, give him an air of independence. A charming glimpse of youth on a summer's day, *Children on a Fence* evokes the rites of passage that often accompany the season.

—Margaret C. Conrads, Samuel Sosland Curator of American Art, The Nelson-Atkins Museum of Art, Kansas City, Missouri. Adapted from *American Dreams: American Art to 1950 in the Williams College Museum of Art*, 2001

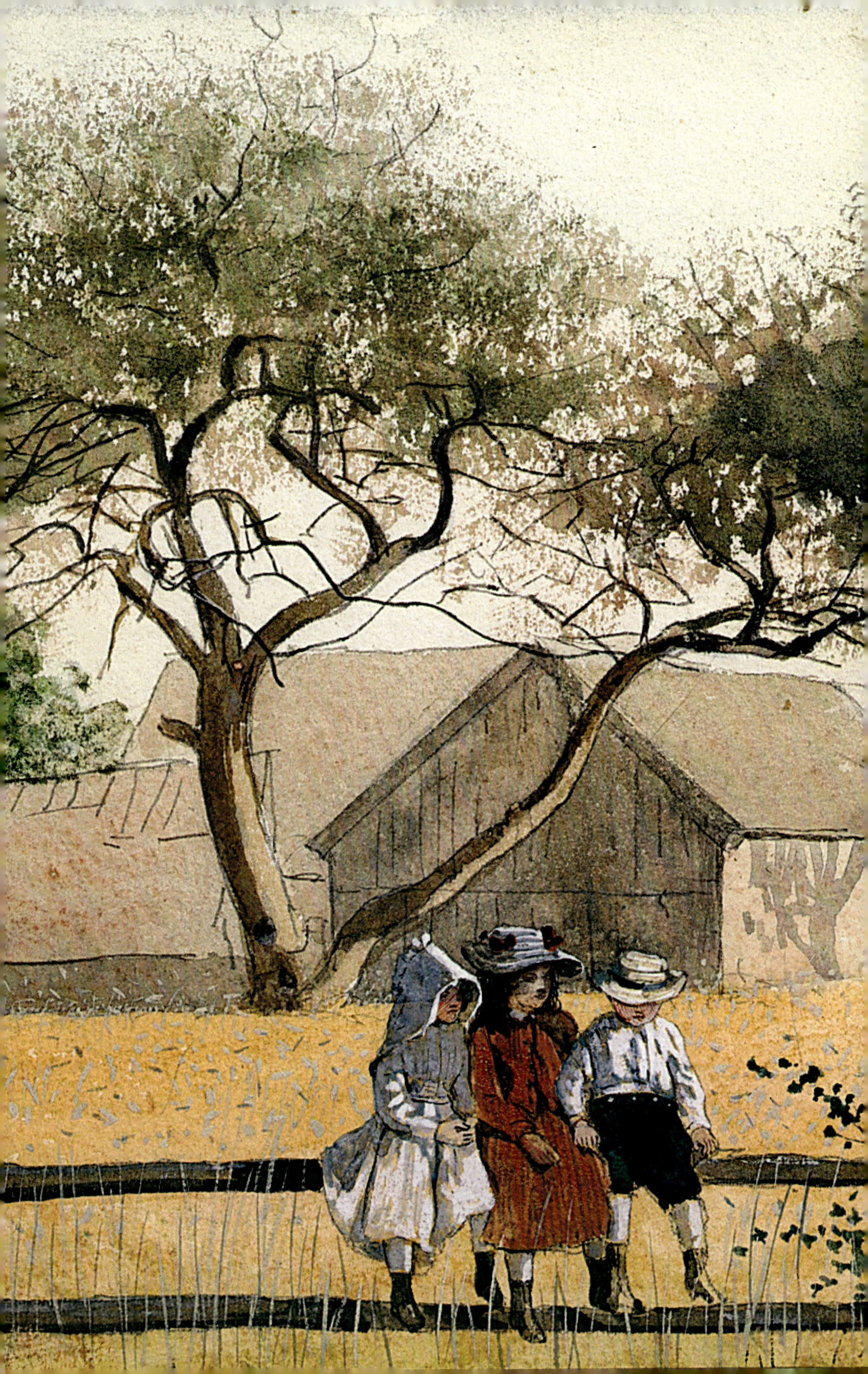

WILLIAM MORRIS HUNT
American, 1824–1879

Niagara Falls
1878

Oil on canvas
66 3/16 x 99 3/16 in.
Gift of the Estate of
J. Malcolm Forbes (61.7)

William Morris Hunt's *Niagara Falls* began amid a failed vacation. In 1878 the artist still had not fully recovered from several crises, including the loss of his studio by fire and estrangement from his wife. In late May he traveled with his sister Jane for a rest cure to Niagara Falls, where the landscape reinvigorated him. He promptly sent to Boston for canvas and oils. On June 1 he received a letter from Leopold Eidlitz, one of the architects of the New York State Capitol, asking for advice about paintings for the Assembly Chamber. A more definitive request came later from Lieutenant Governor Dorsheimer, asking him to paint two massive murals.

Hunt seized on the falls as a fitting metaphor for the churning commercial and intellectual energy of the state, and returned to Boston to work up his sketches into two monumental canvases (the other is now in the collection of the Museum of Fine Arts, Boston). Each was about 62 by 100 inches, a scale on which he had never before worked. WCMA's painting was the more panoramic view; the composition placed the viewer's feet virtually in the water, on rocky banks that traced a long arc to the right toward the far shore.

In the end, however, Albany rejected the falls as a theme, insisting instead on colossal figural allegories. Hunt never returned to the painting; a year later, he was dead, drowned under circumstances that still have not been explained.

—Michael J. Lewis, Professor of Art. Adapted from *American Dreams: American Art to 1950 in the Williams College Museum of Art*, 2001

WILLIAM MICHAEL HARNETT
American, 1848–1892

Deutsche Presse
1882

Oil on panel
7 1/2 x 5 11/16 in.
Gift of Mrs. John W. Barnes, in memory of her husband, Class of 1924, on the fifth anniversary of his death (69.50)

In an interview, William Harnett revealed that, limited by poverty, he could not afford to hire models and so came to still-life painting. The subjects for his first painting were "a pipe and a German beer mug." This painting was accepted for exhibition at the National Academy of Design and sold for fifty dollars, which, he stated, "seemed a small fortune to me."

Harnett went on to paint a great many pictures of just this type, depicting a beer mug, smoking materials, and a newspaper. These pictures earned him only scant critical attention, and nearly all of that was derisive. The paintings were scorned in part because of their low subjects, and the painstaking rendering of such subjects only aggravated the offense.

But the sales of such pictures enabled him to travel to Europe for study. By 1881 his fortunes would appear to have changed; champagne bottles outnumber beer mugs, pipes give way to boxes of fine cigars, and dry biscuits are replaced by cooked lobsters. Yet, at the same time, Harnett's application for membership in the Munich Academy was rejected.

The primary subjects of *Deutsche Presse* return to Harnett's austere, mug-and-pipe formula. In the background, however, he shows the corners of two framed paintings on the walls; this is probably the only occasion on which Harnett does so. Also, despite the miniature scale, the treatment, most notably in the background, shows a brushier handling than Harnett's usual smooth, flat finish. This was a step closer to the prevalent painterly style of the Munich School.

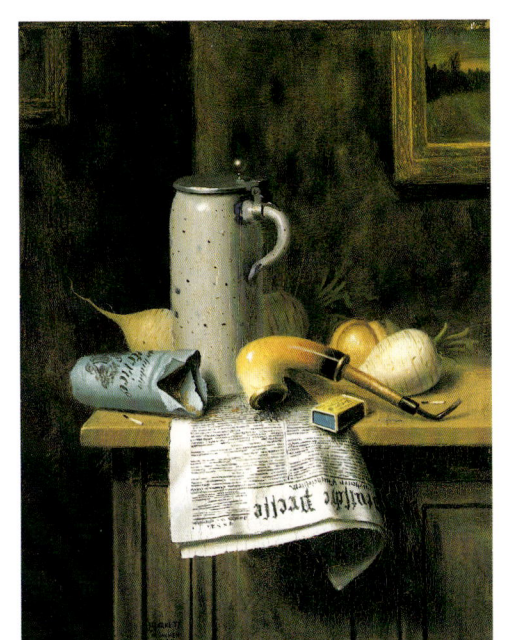

Was this picture partly a response to the critical rejection? By bracketing his still life between gilded frames, perhaps Harnett was asserting that his paintings, even with the most humble subjects, were no less worthy than the productions of the academy.

—Steven P. Levin, Professor of Art

EADWEARD MUYBRIDGE
American, 1830–1904

"Lizzie M." trotting, harnessed to sulky, Animal Locomotion, plate 609
1884–86

Collotype
Image: 7 3/4 x 14 3/8 in.
Gift of the Commercial Museum, Department of Commerce, Philadelphia, Pennsylvania
(62.41.42)

The Williams College Museum of Art owns eighty-two prints from Eadweard Muybridge's massive portfolio of almost eight hundred photographic studies of the movement of men, women, children, and assorted animals, called *Animal Locomotion*. Published in 1887, the set is the capstone of Muybridge's career as a photographer. English by birth, Muybridge had established a photographic practice in San Francisco by 1860 and by 1872 was attempting studies of the moving horse under the patronage of Leland Stanford. These studies brought him international recognition and the commission to carry out the *Animal Locomotion* project at the University of Pennsylvania, which he began in 1884. The photographs themselves were taken either at Muybridge's specially designed outdoor photo set at the university or at such sites as the Zoological Gardens or the Gentlemen's Driving Park outside Philadelphia.

After spending two years photographing his subjects, Muybridge arranged the negatives from the multiple cameras on large single sheets so that each movement could be followed from beginning to end and from various angles. The photographs were printed in this format and the photographic prints were used to create collotypes—lithographic impressions that could be mass-produced. Complete sets of the collotypes were then sold by subscription as well as by advertisement, and many smaller sets, such as the one at Williams, were created as gifts or for special sale.

The impact of Muybridge's motion studies on the art of the late-nineteenth century cannot be overestimated. Although only one of several photographers doing studies of this sort, Muybridge attracted attention through important publications, such as *Animal Locomotion*, and by carrying out a rigorous lecture itinerary in the United States and abroad. He challenged artists to come into the modern age by studying his photographs, which allowed them to see for the first time phases of movement not apparent to normal human sight and now made visible by stop-action photography. The idea that nature held surprises that only modern technology could reveal became commonly accepted, and the belief that artists should explore what lies beyond observable reality formed the basis of modern art.

—Nancy Mowll Mathews, Eugénie Prendergast Senior Curator of 19th and 20th Century Art and Lecturer in Art

66, 67

MARY CASSATT
American, 1844–1926

Reflection
1889–90

Drypoint on Japan paper
Image: 10 3/8 x 7 1/8 in.
Museum purchase, Karl E. Weston Memorial Fund
(M.2003.7)

Mary Cassatt's drypoint *Reflection* makes use of one of the most curious themes in her art: the visitor, or the woman in the hat. In more than thirty major paintings, pastels, drawings, and prints, Cassatt explored the theme of the woman who wears a hat in the house—signaling her association with the outside world and her imminent return to it. In Cassatt's interpretation, the visitor is oddly detached from her temporary social interior, that is, the home of the hostess. In some works, the visitor sips tea and listens politely but without response to the conversation around her; in others, such as *Reflection*, she stares absently into space, the elaborate hat suggesting the weight and complexity of her thoughts.

According to Realist and Impressionist theory, artists should explore the world around them, acting as voyeurs of their own lives. Hence, in this remarkable period of art history we have come to know, through Impressionist portraits and genre scenes, the friends, servants, and favorite models of the artists; we can recognize their parents, siblings, cousins, children, nieces, and nephews. We know their apartments and their furniture; we visit their favorite restaurants, theaters, and resorts; and we can tell stories about their dogs, cats, birds, and horses. It is the nineteenth-century version of a reality show.

This is especially true of Mary Cassatt, who turned her detached eye on the inhabitants of the Cassatt world. Her living room thus was transformed from a personal space for friends and family into her personal art academy, where she drew repeatedly the scenes that unfolded in front of her—quiet pursuits like reading, sewing, and gazing into the fire, or the daily social rounds of visits and tea. Forcing herself into the role of objective witness, a type of surveillance camera *avant la lettre*, she caught the boredom and isolation of such scenes and even the lethargy of her dying sister. But the attention she paid to such scenes ("That's what teaches you to draw!" she told her biographer) and the respect for these people that she conveyed through solid bodies and subtle facial expressions ennobled even their isolation and self-absorption. And since the only two known self-portraits show the artist wearing a hat (even indoors in front of her easel), it is possible that Cassatt thought of herself as the visitor—detached but watchful, with a hat (I mean head) full of thoughts.

—Nancy Mowll Mathews, Eugénie Prendergast Senior Curator of 19th and 20th Century Art and Lecturer in Art

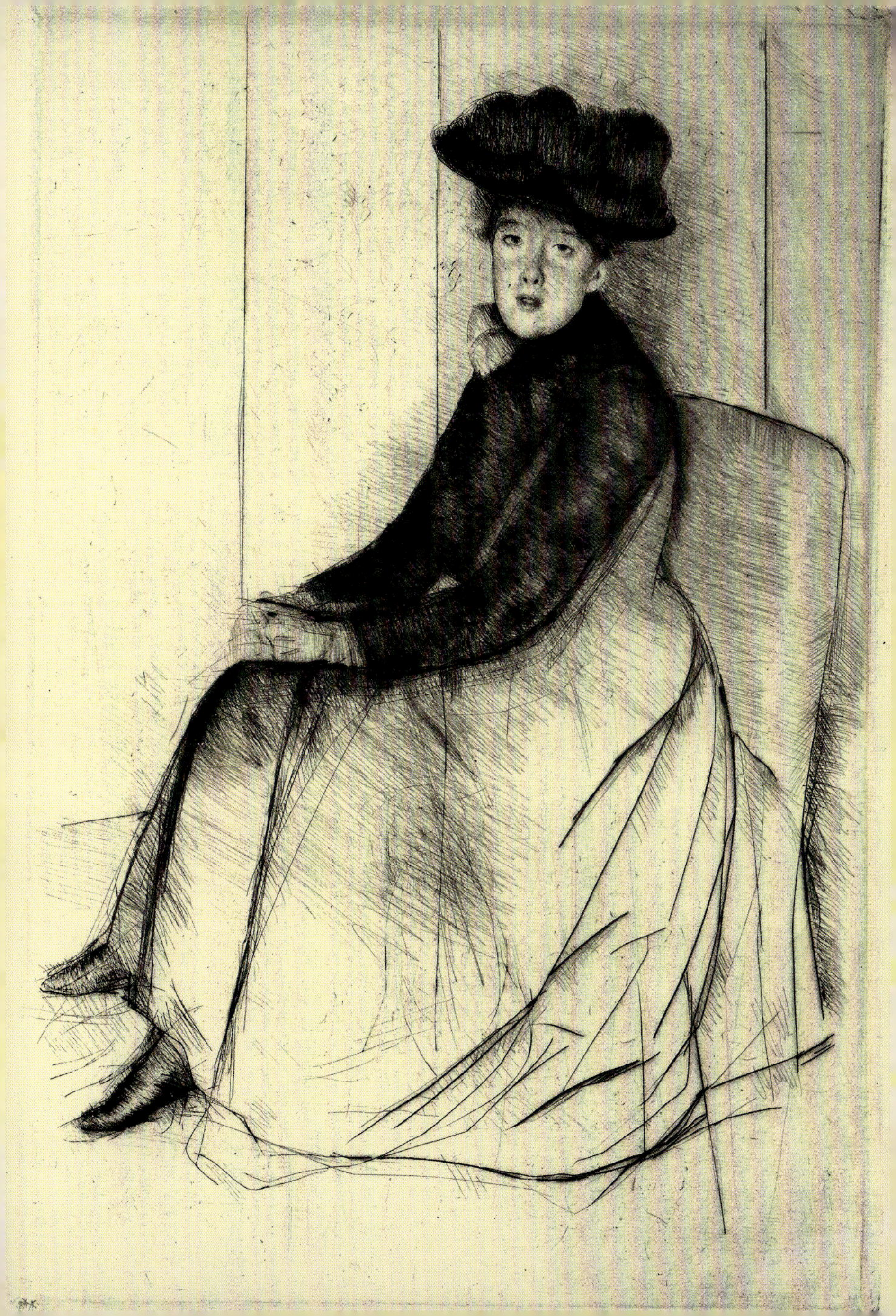

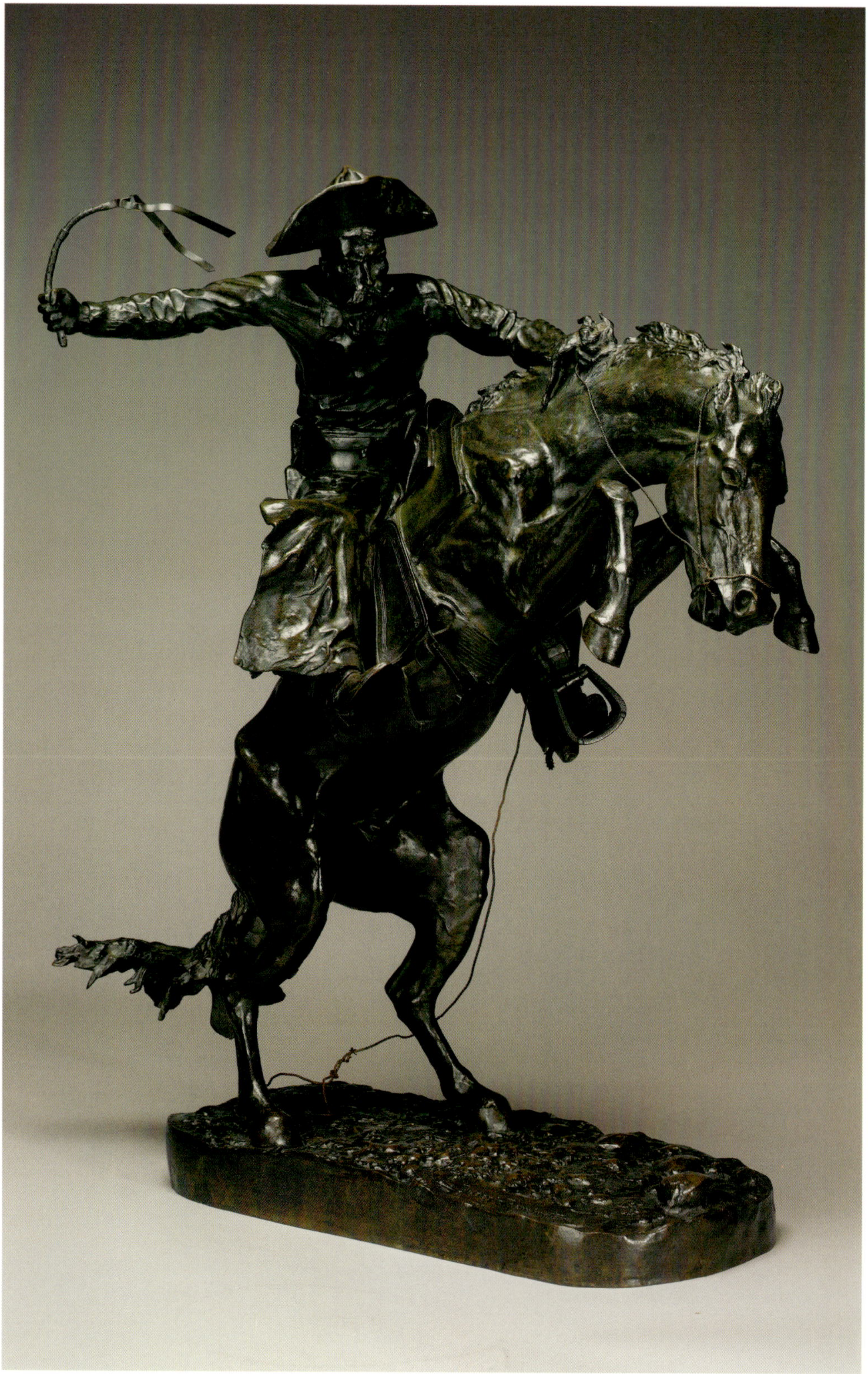

FREDERIC REMINGTON
American, 1861–1909

The Bronco Buster
1895

Bronze (sandcast by the Henry-Bonnard Bronze Company, New York, R11)
23 7/8 x 22 1/2 x 11 in.
Gift of James Rathbone Falck, Class of 1935 (95.10)

Before 1895 Frederic Remington had made his reputation mainly as an illustrator, creating drawings for periodicals and novels that helped forge a popular image of the American West. Remington's foray into sculpture was instigated by his friend the playwright Augustus Thomas. Noticing how easily Remington could reposition figures within his drawings, Thomas stated that he had "the sculptor's degree of vision." *The Bronco Buster*, the artist's first attempt at sculpture, not only boosted Remington's artistic reputation, proving he could create high-quality work beyond black-and-white illustration, but it also became an icon of the American West's rough-and-tumble past.

Depicting a cowboy breaking in a wild horse, *The Bronco Buster* is a technical triumph with its intricately finished surface and its conveyance of dynamic action, which was achieved by balancing the statuette on the horse's rear legs. During the late-nineteenth and early-twentieth centuries America's western frontier was an extremely popular subject among easterners nostalgic for a "lost" American past. This phenomenon was undoubtedly influenced by Frederick Turner Jackson's seminal essay, "The Significance of the Frontier in American History," written in 1893. In this essay Jackson declared the American frontier officially closed and wrote, "Up to our own day American history has been in a large degree the history of the colonization of the Great West." *The Bronco Buster* recorded an integral aspect of American history that was believed to be quickly disappearing. In the end, it became one of the most successful single statuettes produced in America during the nineteenth and twentieth centuries, forever influencing the way we conceive of the American West.

—Jamie Franklin (Williams M.A. 2005), Curator of Collections, Bennington Museum, Bennington, Vermont

Prendergast

Maurice Prendergast
American, 1858–1924
Rocky Shore, Nantasket
ca. 1896–97
Watercolor, pencil, and ink on paper
17 x 12 1/2 in.
Bequest of Sophia W. Brumbaugh (M.2004.13.1)

Maurice Prendergast
Festa del Redentore
ca. 1899
Watercolor and pencil on paper
11 x 17 in.
Gift of Mrs. Charles Prendergast (91.18.5)

Charles Prendergast
American, 1863–1948
Man Dancing, ca. 1917
Watercolor and gold leaf on wood
8 x 3 7/8 x 2 1/2 in.
Gift of Mrs. Charles Prendergast (86.18.23)

Charles Prendergast
Circus, 1940
Tempera and gold leaf on incised, gessoed masonite
24 7/16 x 23 3/4 in.
Gift of Mrs. Charles Prendergast (86.18.34)

IT IS RELATIVELY UNCOMMON for two siblings to become recognized artists of similar stature. Many start out along the same path, but few achieve the recognition in their lifetimes and afterward that Maurice and Charles Prendergast have attained in the history of American art. Five years apart in age, they were the sole surviving children in a family that produced three more, including a twin sister of Maurice. By the 1890s both were well established in the Boston art world—Maurice as a painter and Charles as a frame maker and woodworker in the Arts and Crafts style. They gravitated toward modernist art circles and eventually moved to New York. Charles joined his brother as a pictorial artist about 1912, and the two became active in the independent artists' associations and exhibitions that drove the American modern art scene of the 1910s. They lived and worked together without marrying until Maurice's death in 1924. Soon after, Charles met and married Eugénie Van Kemmel, a woman some thirty years his junior, who encouraged him to continue his artistic career until his death in 1948.

Eugénie Prendergast was an active guardian of the work and reputations of both brothers during the decades that followed. In 1983 she and the Prendergast Foundation formed an association with the Williams College Museum of Art to sponsor the Prendergast catalogue raisonné project, which has since become the Prendergast Archive and Study Center. A generous patron of the museum as a whole, she also donated or bequeathed approximately four hundred works by the Prendergast brothers and established funds for ongoing research, exhibitions, and publications on the Prendergasts and their artistic era, as well as operating support for the museum and its education and outreach programs. This largesse is supplemented by letters, documents, books, and other archival materials that support the original research.

The collection of art by the Prendergasts at Williams is the largest in the world and represents all periods, styles, and media. Since it constitutes the "estate" of the artists (works remaining in the studio after their deaths), it has all the strengths and weaknesses of such bodies of work. Because works by both artists sold well during their lifetimes, many had entered important private and museum collections early on. What remained in their studios were personal favorites, sketches and works in progress, experiments (both successful and unsuccessful), and "multiples"—works they produced more of than they could sell. Overall, this body of work offers an unusual resource for the study of the creative process, especially over an artist's lifetime, and opens a window into the changes that occurred in early-twentieth-century modernism from the point of view of two brothers who were at the heart of it.

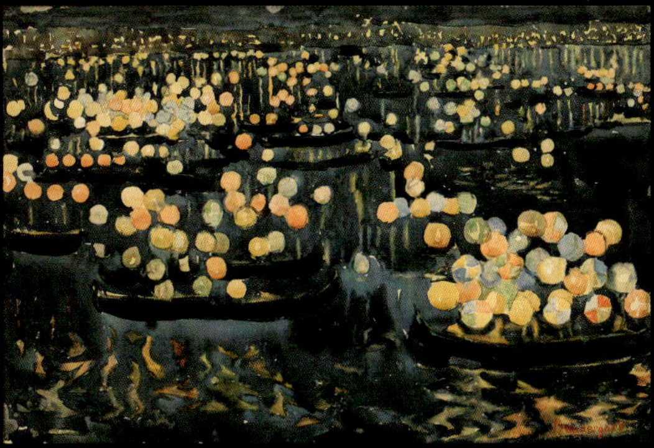

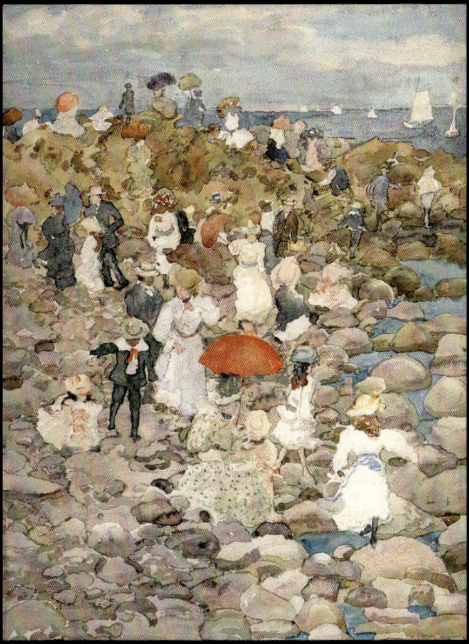

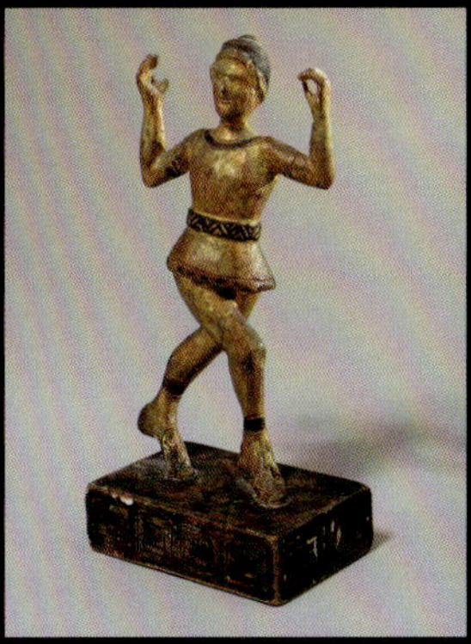

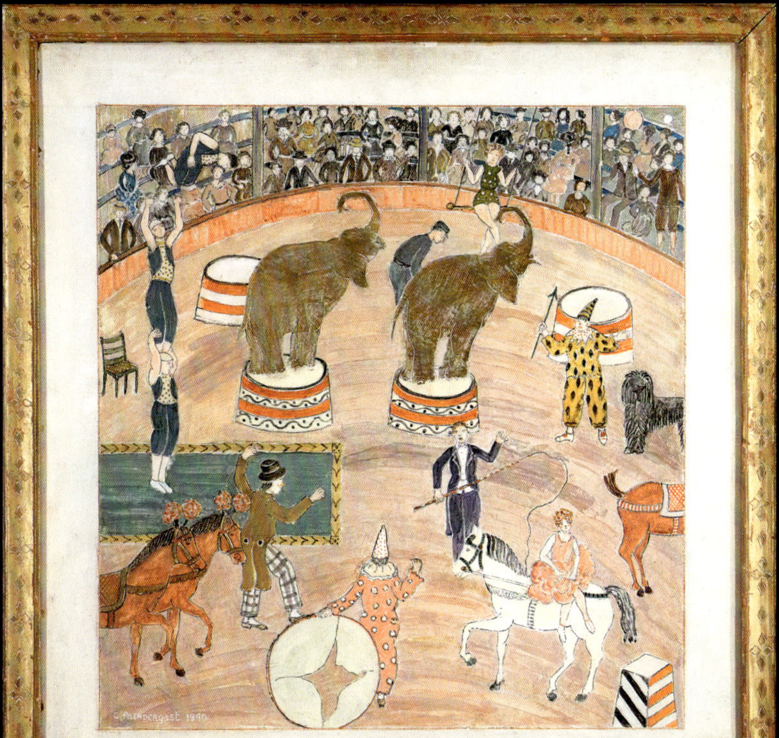

AFRICAN, NIGERIA, IGBO

Helmet Mask (Mgbedike)
20th century

Wood and pigment
34 1/4 x 15 3/8 x 16 3/4 in.
Gift of Albert F. Gordon
(91.44.4)

This horned *Mgbedike* helmet mask embodies the spiritual power and potent male forces necessary to rid the community of harmful spirits. Throughout the Niger Delta region, horns symbolize virility and supernatural strength. This power imagery is echoed by the male figure that clasps the horns and whose controlled stance is similar to that of protective *Ikenga* statues. Today, *Mgbedike* maskers are important titled men of middle age considered to possess both physical and spiritual strength. In earlier times, these spirit masks would have been danced by warriors. A voluminous costume completes the awesome effect by giving the dancer superhuman size. *Mgbedike* masqueraders perform energetic feats of agility and endurance during agricultural festivals and burial celebrations.

The aura of power is created by the dark patina, bold facial planes, and exaggerated features such as the large jagged-toothed mouth. This particular *Mgbedike* helmet is surmounted by two pairs of horns: curved horns projecting forward from the crown and upswept bush spirit horns embellished with rows of incised scarification.

—Suzanne Bach. Adapted from *Assuming the Guise: African Masks Considered and Reconsidered*, 1991

PABLO PICASSO
Spanish, 1881–1973

Dance of Salome
1905

Etching and drypoint on paper
Image: 15 3/4 x 13 3/8 in.
Gift of Mr. and Mrs. Gordon B. Washburn, Class of 1928 (76.14)

In 1905 Pablo Picasso deviated from his Rose-period theme of saltimbanques, poor itinerant circus players, to create this etching whose subject is taken from the New Testament. The acrobats and harlequins who populate the Rose period are based on a traveling troupe from Spain with whom Picasso became friendly beginning in 1904. He recycles some of these people in the *Dance of Salome*. The strongman, known as El Tio Pepe in real life, is recast as King Herod seated with a large mitered hat at left. Queen Herodias stands beside him. The lithe young acrobats who populate the Rose period are the prototypes for the agile Salome.

At once delicately beautiful and powerfully disturbing, *Dance of Salome* is exemplary of the mystery certain works by Picasso evoke. Each of the characters in the drama appears detached from one another as they float in a space so empty it is devoid of even a ground line. Picasso further augments a sense of disconnect in the way he varies the finish of the figures—from the highly articulated severed head of John the Baptist and the attendant who holds it to the unfinished form of King Herod whose body is indicated with only a few lines.

Salome is depicted dancing nude with her legs open to Herod's stare. It is an effective strategy for heightening eroticism as the viewer of the artwork fills in mentally what is hidden from his gaze. We feel the power of female sexuality and understand the king's acceptance of the young siren's bargain —her "dance" in exchange for the Baptist's head—even as the martyred saint reproaches with his soulful and tragic face.

—Deborah Rothschild, Senior Curator of Modern and Contemporary Art

EUGÈNE ATGET
French, 1857–1927

Cabaret de l'Enfer [et du ciel], Boulevard de Clichy 53
1910

Vintage albumen print
6 7/8 x 8 3/8 in.

Museum purchase, Wachenheim Family Fund (M.2002.7.1)

Eugène Atget's photographic work, more than ten thousand views of Paris taken from the 1890s to the 1920s, remains a lively area of debate for scholars of art. The issues range from the philosophical—is his work art?—to the more pragmatic—how did he organize his mammoth archive? Though much is known about him now, some of these questions remain largely insolvable.

Atget specialized in close-ups of the buildings and monuments that lined the streets of Paris, rather than the long views that characterized the work of his predecessors. He had a fairly steady clientele for his photographs, especially for those showing structures that remained after the huge urban renewal programs carried out under Napoleon III in the mid–nineteenth century. Working with a view camera that produced glass-plate negatives, he made albumen prints for sale (a technique that literally involved using egg whites as the binder for the light-sensitive chemicals). In 1920 he sold approximately five thousand of his glass-plate negatives to the French government.

This may have been the whole story of Atget's contribution to the history of photography, a documentarian of Paris, but for the accident of his address. The American expatriate artist Man Ray lived on the same street. For him, discovering Atget's scenes of Paris was an act of Surrealist discovery because the images were rife with literary implications for those sensitive enough to discern them. Thus began the transformation of Atget's archive from documents to art. Man Ray included photographs by Atget in a Surrealist journal, claiming him as an unwitting forebear to the Surrealist movement. During this time, Berenice Abbott, Man Ray's onetime assistant who now had her own photographic career, likewise became entranced by Atget's work. Abbott bought all the photographs and negatives she could from the estate when Atget died and brought them to the United States. She eventually sold them to the Museum of Modern Art in New York, thereby completing Atget's apotheosis from journeyman photographer to progenitor of modern photography.

—John Stomberg, Associate Director

E. J. BELLOCQ
American, 1873–1949

Storyville Portrait
ca. 1912

Printing out paper, gold toned
8 × 10 in.
Museum purchase, Joseph O. Eaton Fund (95.1.3)

In 1967 the photographer Lee Friedlander found a box of Ernst Bellocq's damaged glass-plate negatives in a New Orleans antique shop and from them began to make prints; he was intrigued both by the beauty of the images and by the questions regarding viewership that they raised. Bellocq was long forgotten by then, though earlier in the century he had been a moderately well-known figure in New Orleans's photographic circles. He kept secret the numerous portraits—such as this one—that he made in Storyville, the city's notorious center for legalized prostitution. The negatives were not even listed on the inventory created at the time of his death. Eventually they were sold discretely as interesting oddities.

This image of Bellocq's remains intriguing, almost defiantly so, even though in many ways it should be a bad photograph. The glass negative cracked before being printed and some of the emulsion was abraded. These technical "problems" interfere with the viewer's contemplation of the image by asserting its primary status as a physical object. This same sequence applies in reverse to the potential reverie of looking at the nude—we are not free to turn her into an object, simply the subject of our gaze, because she looks out at us, individual and human. Rather than a window onto the moment of its creation, this photograph insists that viewers be conscious of their role in constructing meaning through their act of looking.

—John Stomberg, Associate Director

MORTON LIVINGSTON SCHAMBERG
American, 1881–1918

Study of a Girl (Fanette Reider)
ca. 1912

Oil on canvas
30 11/16 x 23 1/8 in.
Bequest of Lawrence H. Bloedel,
Class of 1923 (77.9.11)

Study of a Girl is a terse, enigmatic composition: a woman wearing a blue turban clasps her hands in her lap and faces right in three-quarter view. The face just barely suggests a specific likeness, not quite portrait nor quite the rigid mask that Picasso's portraits were becoming at about this time. Although her posture suggests she is sitting, no chair is visible. She is thrust against a horizon line that conveys not so much the spatial sense of a room as that of an empty landscape, or a barren theater stage. The lighting is similarly unsettling, an unearthly green streak running along her face and neck while a kind of pale spectral aura emanates from her. In fact, she was anything but spectral: she was Fanette Reider, Morton Livingston Schamberg's close friend, favorite subject, and, for a time apparently, his fiancée.

For two years, Schamberg had been painting and photographing Reider, usually seated, her arms clasped before her, a rather tentative expression on her face. These images of Reider record Schamberg's gradual drift from academicism in the direction of Paul Cézanne, and now toward Henri Matisse. This constant reworking of the same subject makes *Study of a Girl* part of a progressive series, an instrument with which Schamberg could calibrate his modernism by the trajectory of his growing abstraction. From Matisse came the black outlines that reduce Reider's body to an affair of contours, describing simplified geometric forms, from the oval mass of the torso to the oversize almonds of the eyes. All these curves are subordinated to the central motif, the heroic arc of Reider's arms, carried through from the neck down to the hand resting on the wrist and back through the oddly lopsided elbows and rounded shoulders. And the result of these cartoon outlines was much the same as in Matisse's contemporary work: a sinuous, languid expression, a quality that is lacking in Schamberg's earlier work.

—Michael J. Lewis, Professor of Art. Adapted from *American Dreams: American Art to 1950 in the Williams College Museum of Art*, 2001

78, 79

MARC CHAGALL
Russian, 1887–1985

The Flying Cow
1912

Gouache on paper
10 x 12 ½ in.
Gift of Sylvia and Joseph Slifka (M.2004.4.2)

"I have brought my subjects from Russia, and Paris has given them light," said Marc Chagall. By 1912 the artist was living in Paris, and that year he painted a series of gouaches titled *Impressions of Russia* that evoked his childhood years in Vitebsk. The realm of memory and the world of dreams collide in these works. In *The Flying Cow*, a transparent, pregnant horselike cow floats across the dark night sky; in the corner, birds take flight from behind a rustic white cabin, while a small blue bird perches precariously on the roof; and a doll-like woman, her arms akimbo, mysteriously lies supine on the yellow ground. The work seems the memory of a childhood dream in its eeriness, highly personal symbolism, and anthropomorphized smiling cow. Visible pregnancies recur within the *Impressions of Russia* series: in *The Cattle Dealer* (1912), the horse pulling the cart is carrying a foal. In *Maternity* (1913), a towering, majestic female points to a window in her skirts that reveals a small boy, standing upright in her womb. Perhaps feeling uprooted and full of self-doubt in Paris, and longing for his fiancée Bella Rosenfeld, Chagall turned to such comforting themes as pregnancy, fertility, and memories of an idealized childhood in Russia.

Sylvia Slifka, a New York City philanthropist, was, with her husband, Joseph, an important collector of twentieth-century European and American art. On her death, she bequeathed sixty-five objects to a wide range of museums in the United States and Israel. This is the first major work by Chagall to enter WCMA's collection.

—Dana Pilson, The Edith and Herbert Lehman Foundation Publications Assistant

ERNST LUDWIG KIRCHNER
German, 1880–1938

Gewecke und Erna
1913

Drypoint on paper
Image: 9 13/16 x 8 in.
Museum purchase, Ruth Sabin Weston Fund (63.9)

Each year hundreds of Williams College students visit the museum's Rose Study Gallery to learn about printmaking. Most of them study Ernst Ludwig Kirchner's striking portrait alongside another drypoint made about 1890 by Mary Cassatt (see page 69). What do Williams students learn about drypoint through this comparison?

Drypoint is a simple process whereby a line is scratched directly into a copperplate with a needle or a sharp metal point. As the needle is drawn across the plate, the metal is displaced and pushed to either side of the line —much the way a field is furrowed while being plowed. Known as *burr*, this uneven accumulation of shaved metal soaks up ink when the plate is prepared for printing, thereby creating drypoint's trademark effect: inky lines with soft, velvety edges. Rembrandt, Whistler, Cassatt, and other artists exploited the subtleties of the technique by using it to add warmth and depth to lines on an etched plate or by creating a rich, slightly blurred composition made entirely of drypoint.

German Expressionist artists, however, revealed drypoint's capacity for a distinctly different line. By cutting deeper and more aggressively into the plate, they created a burr so pronounced that the line sometimes printed with a faint gash along its center. These incisions have a jagged edginess that was equal to the urgency and emotion of their social criticism. For Williams students who have the opportunity to view Cassatt's exquisite, feathery lines alongside Kirchner's slashes, the study of the contradictory range of the simple drypoint line is unforgettable.

—Stefanie Spray Jandl (Williams M.A. 1993), Andrew W. Mellon Foundation Associate Curator for Academic Programs

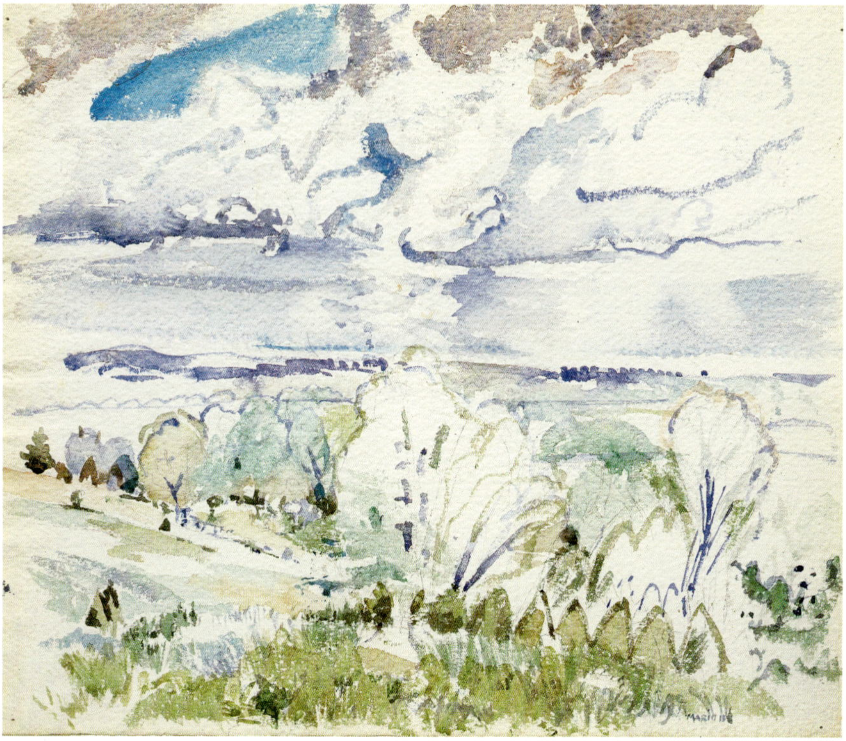

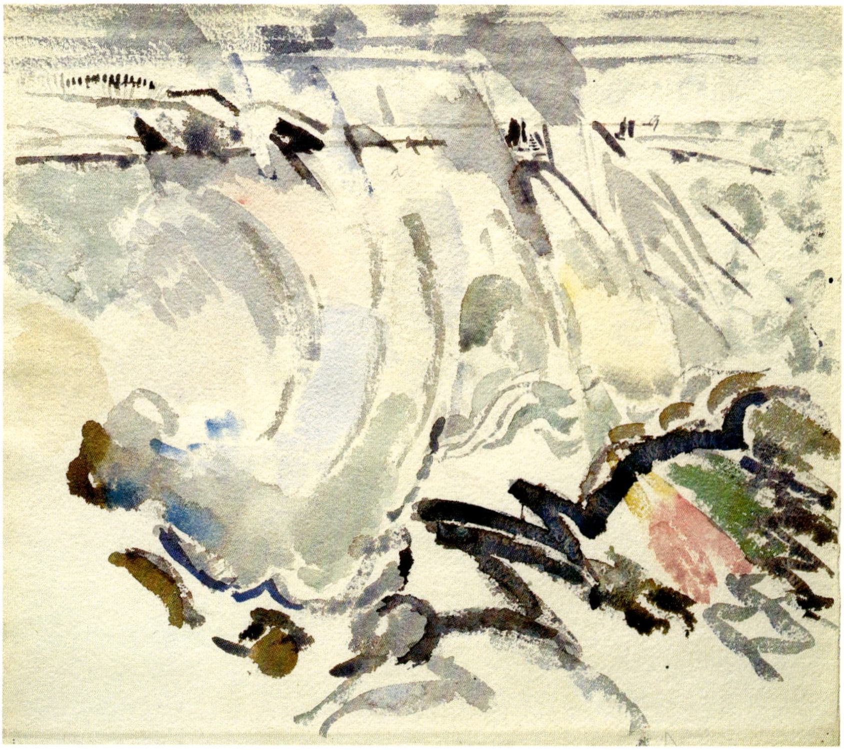

JOHN MARIN
American, 1870–1953

Black River Valley, Castorland, New York
1913

Watercolor over graphite on paper
16 x 19 in.
Gift of Mrs. Walker C. Allen
(79.30)

Harbor Scene
ca. 1914
Watercolor on paper
16 3/4 x 19 1/4 in.
Gift of John H. Rhoades,
Class of 1934 (67.31)

Stonington, Maine
1919
Watercolor on paper
19 x 16 in.
Bequest of Lawrence H. Bloedel, Class of 1923
(77.9.10)

Black River Valley, Castorland, New York was painted in 1913 in upstate New York farmlands on the edge of the Adirondacks. Slow to find himself (and having served four years as an architect), Marin had spent the years 1905–9 in Europe, exposed to the latest avant-garde developments in Paris. On a return trip in 1910, he "broke through" in a series of watercolors painted in the Austrian Tyrol—fluid, with high intensities, very atmospheric, but with little relationship as yet to developing modern art. This early style of Marin's persisted into 1913. The Castorland example is at once conventional—theme and horizon line at center—and daring in its great freedom of washes, intense blue lines drawn with the brush, and the white paper left untouched in the foreground to express objects' forward projection. Marin once stated, "See the white paper and the part it plays. Each touch of color is an instrument. Each uncolored space is an instrument no less."

In 1914 Marin made a leap into new forms when he painted the remarkable *Harbor Scene*. The horizon line is now near the top, color intensities are much reduced for soberer effect, and rolling forms of great power energize the wave that explodes onto harsh, angular shapes not found in the artist's earlier work. These will become major elements in watercolors of the vintage years.

By 1919 Marin's style had taken another direction. Here the theme is sailboats in the busy little harbor of Stonington, Maine, on the southern tip of Deer Isle. Tones are now applied as flat planes with well-defined edges. Strong black lines suggest the stays of the boats. A prow appears prominently at lower left; a second prow above parallels it. A geometric grid seems to hold this bristling array in order. It is as close to Cubism as Marin ever came.

—S. Lane Faison, Jr. (Williams 1929), Amos Lawrence Professor of Art Emeritus and Director Emeritus, WCMA. Adapted from ". . . and Gladly Teach," 1989

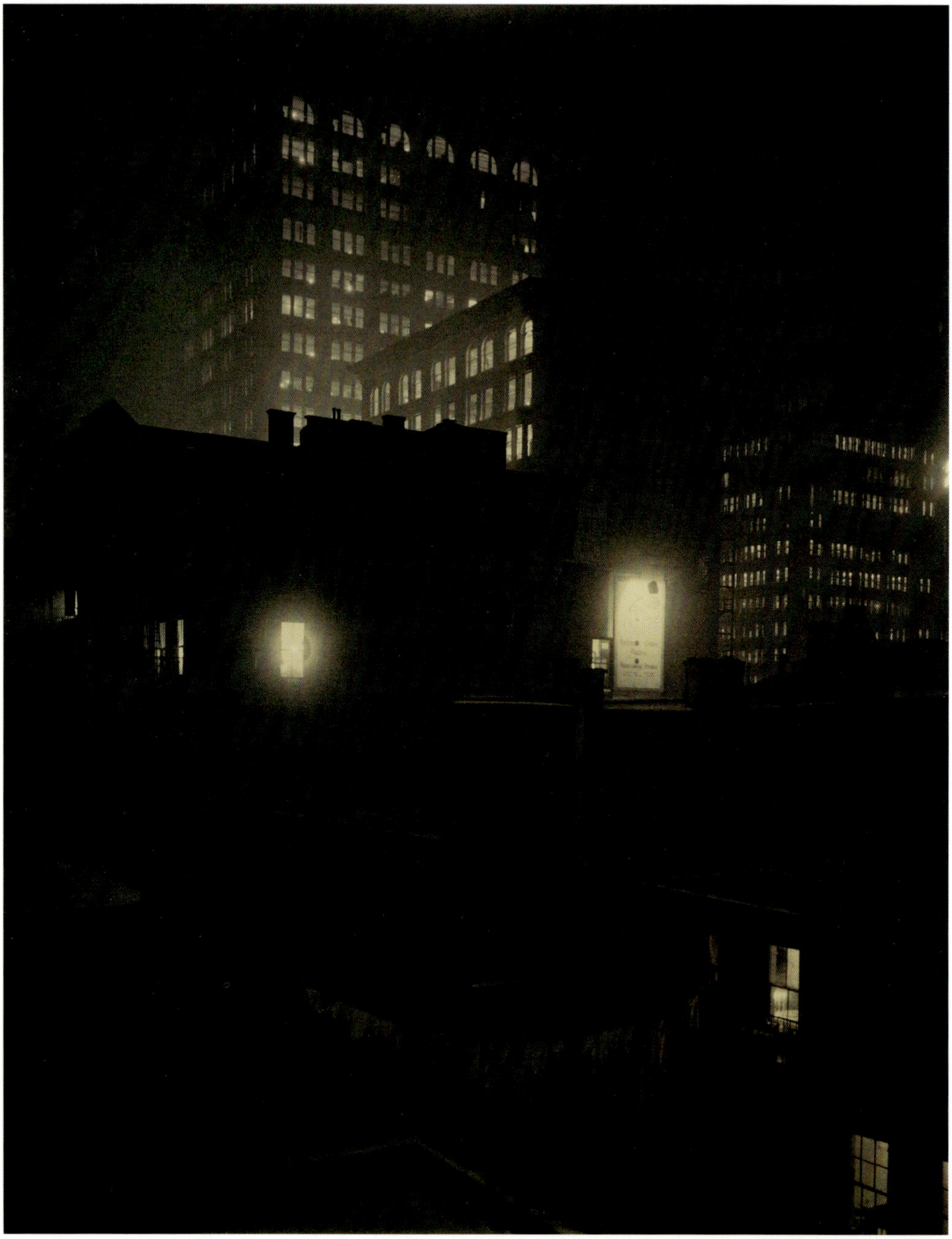

ALFRED STIEGLITZ
American, 1864–1946

View from Rear Window,
Gallery 291, at Night
1915

View from Rear Window,
Gallery 291, Daytime
1915

Platinum prints
10 x 8 in. each
Gift of John H. Rhoades,
Class of 1934 (68:16–17)

Urban vistas offered Alfred Stieglitz an approach to the dilemma that Cubism posed to photographers—how to capture the idea of interpenetrating forms when camera arts were bound to the visual world? The overlapping forms and massing in space of a city scene, when rendered photographically, successfully embodied some of the formal characteristics of Cubism—the buildings appear to emerge from and through one another and appear changeable—and the city itself was an essential icon of modernity.

In these ways, Stieglitz had adapted his personal photography to coincide with the evolving goals of modern art—goals that he helped to define through his Gallery 291 on Fifth Avenue in New York. As a gallerist and the publisher of the art journal *Camera Work*, Stieglitz was responsible for bringing modern art to the United States and for fighting throughout his life for photography's acceptance as art. But the role of impresario can overshadow the remarkable work Stieglitz did in his chosen medium. For him, the image was only part of the art; the print itself had to have individual distinction.

Stieglitz often used the platinum printing technique because it offered subtleties that other approaches lacked and because each print had slight variations that resulted from decisions made during the printing process. WCMA's Stieglitz prints encourage close study. Some of the differences result from printing variations and others from decisions he made when he captured the image. The view in each is essentially the same, but the differing light conditions and how he printed each image have created different effects both visually and emotionally; this is the essential Stieglitz experience of art.

—John Stomberg, Associate Director

PAUL STRAND
American, 1890–1976

Blind Woman, New York
negative 1916, print 1917

Photogravure
Image: 8 11/16 x 6 5/16 in.
Museum purchase, Ruth Sabin Weston Fund (77.20)

Two questions usually surface when we teach with this photograph: did this woman know she was being photographed, and, what is a photogravure? The first is an issue of fairness, and it reveals an uncomfortable truth about the medium: those with the camera have the power. Sometimes in portraiture the sitter has a strong presence—presenting him- or herself and looking at the camera—and in these instances the power seems somewhat shared. But here the woman was the passive subject of the photographer's gaze. The gender roles at play in this work fuel further rumination—he shoots; she's captured.

With this image, Paul Strand seems to ask who is blind. The photograph works as a metaphor for the relationship between those who are subjected to the camera's lens and those behind it. The photographer sees the subject, but the subject cannot see back. The photograph itself is also blind, but not mute; it communicates in a complex language of signs. Strand relishes the play between the sign in the image reading "BLIND," our reading of the damaged eyes as "signs" indicating blindness, and the inherent nature of the photograph as a blind sign.

Alfred Stieglitz published this work in the last issue of *Camera Work*, his handcrafted journal of the arts and modernism. He always used photogravures for his magazine, as they offered connoisseurs of fine photography the best alternative to photographic prints. The technique involved transferring a photograph to an engraving plate so that it could be rendered in printer's ink. The original images made for *Camera Work* were praised for their tonal range and deep blacks. Indeed, today a small cadre of photographers works directly in photogravure, rather than the traditional gelatin silver, as a way of giving their prints the imprimatur of art and connecting it to a lineage that started with images such as this one by Paul Strand.

—John Stomberg, Associate Director

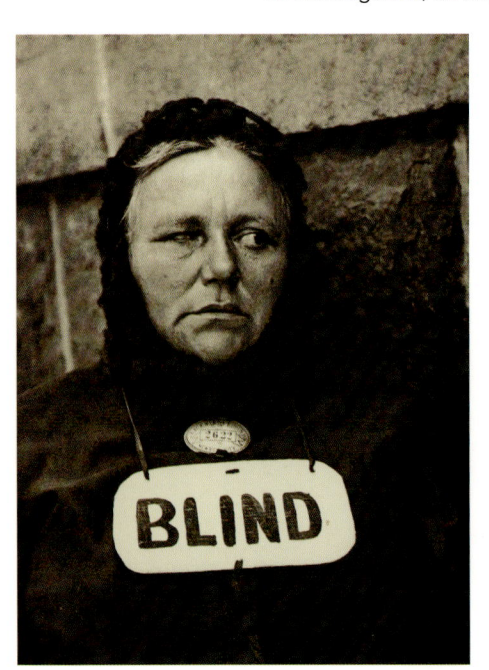

CHARLES DEMUTH
American, 1883–1935

Trees and Barns: Bermuda
1917

Watercolor over pencil on paper
9 1/2 x 13 7/16 in.
Bequest of Susan Watts Street
(57.8)

Trees and Barns: Bermuda marks a turning point for Charles Demuth: the artist's first extensive experimentation with Cubism and the origins of his so-called Precisionist style. He began *Trees and Barns: Bermuda* by laying down a network of lines, using a ruler to pencil in the edges of the buildings. Watercolor was then brushed in between the shapes. Rather than let paint spill over the lines, he carefully blotted the color, giving the painting a marvelous sense of texture. Despite the name given to Demuth's new style by art critics in the 1920s—Precisionism—his use of the ruler was no more precise than the free hand. The artist did not literally measure the barn walls or fix their position in space; rather, the ruled line brought containment and control.

Demuth did not seem anxious about the exact placement of things. As his art progressed, there was a growing certainty about the shapes of objects, but he sheathed everything with glasslike surfaces. As in *Trees and Barns: Bermuda*, he gave objects a clean, light-filled, modern look. But in converting everything into prisms he also suggested the fragility of the world, a fragility that—marginalized by his childhood lameness and his homosexuality—he knew well.

—Jonathan Weinberg, Painter and Art Historian. Adapted from *American Dreams: American Art to 1950 in the Williams College Museum of Art*, 2001

RUBE GOLDBERG
American, 1883–1970

Now you know how to tie a full-dress tie
ca. 1918

Pen and ink on posterboard
8 3/8 x 13 11/16 in.
Gift of George W. George,
Class of 1941 (81.24.63)

How to keep bewhiskered uncle from kissing baby
ca. 1960
Pencil on paper
8 9/16 x 11 in.
Gift of George W. George,
Class of 1941 (81.24.3)

Rube Goldberg's cartoons of ingenious—though counterintuitive—mechanisms reveal his early training in engineering. The artist's contraptions are intricate amalgamations of pulley and lever systems, whose complexity is matched by the prolix titles he gives them. In the sketch *How to keep bewhiskered uncle from kissing baby*, a chain reaction involving a refrigerator door, a tipped garbage can, a sun lamp, and the headgear of a deep-sea diving suit protects the yowling infant from the uncle's abrasive beard. Similarly, dressing up for an elegant evening in *Now you know how to tie a full-dress tie* depends on the length of a growing puppy's tail, a bird's empathy, and pungent Limburger cheese. All of Goldberg's inventions purport to make life easier but in fact do the opposite, revealing the artist's fascination with and distrust of machinery. These fantastic inventions have succeeded in gaining Rube Goldberg a place in the English language—his name is now used to refer to any "contrivance that brings about by complicated means what apparently could be accomplished simply."

How to keep bewhiskered uncle from kissing baby and *Now you know how to tie a full-dress tie* are two of more than five hundred works from the museum's collection of Rube Goldberg material. Given to WCMA by his son, George W. George (Williams 1941), the collection includes both preparatory sketches and finished cartoons that span the artist's prolific career.

—Elizabeth Athens (Williams M.A. 2005), The Edith and Herbert Lehman Foundation Publications Assistant

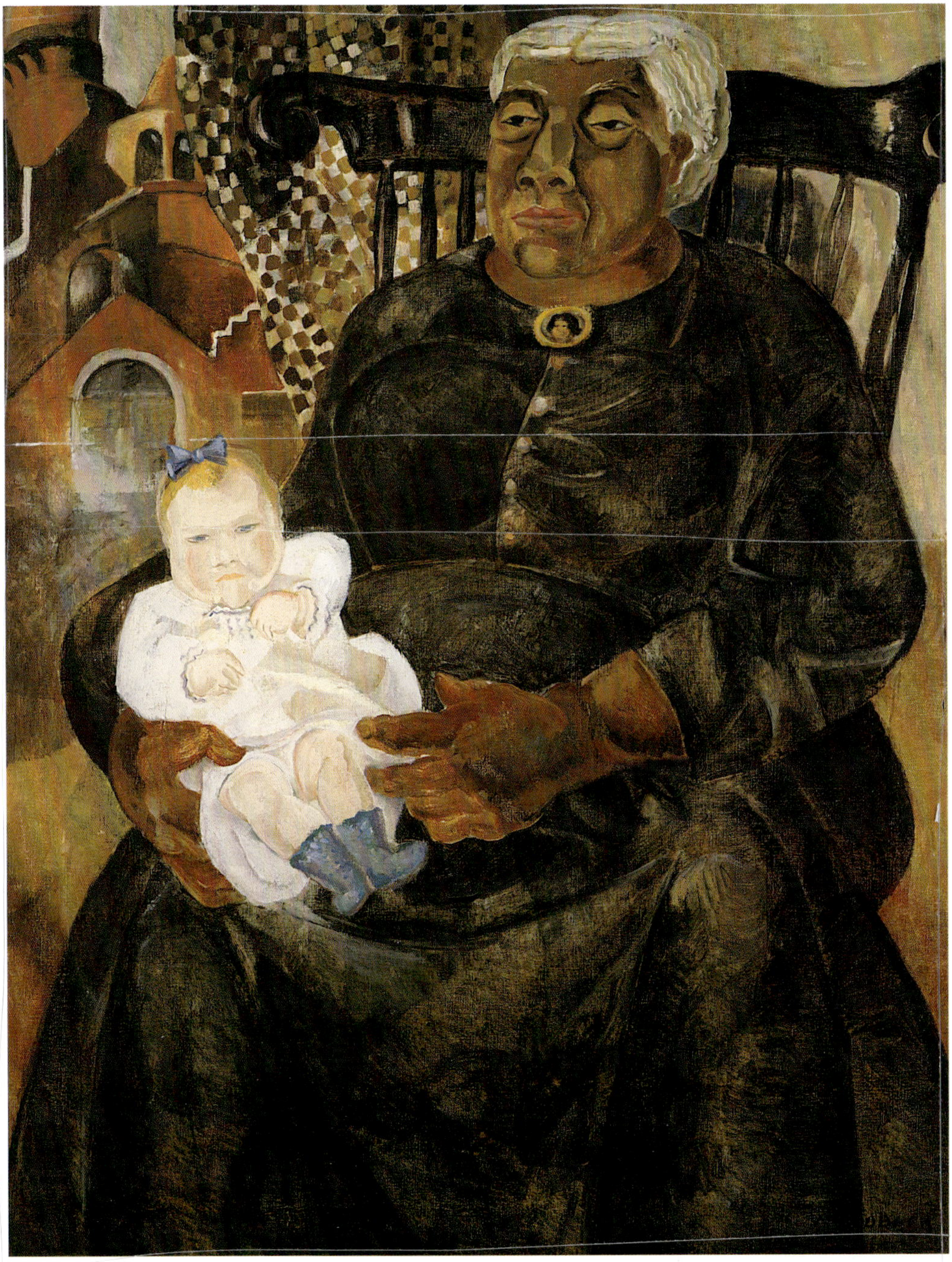

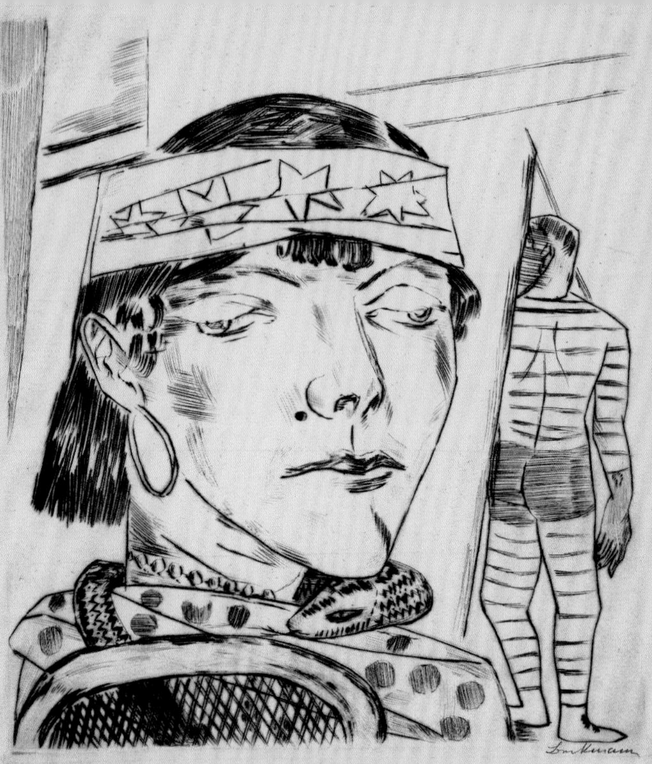

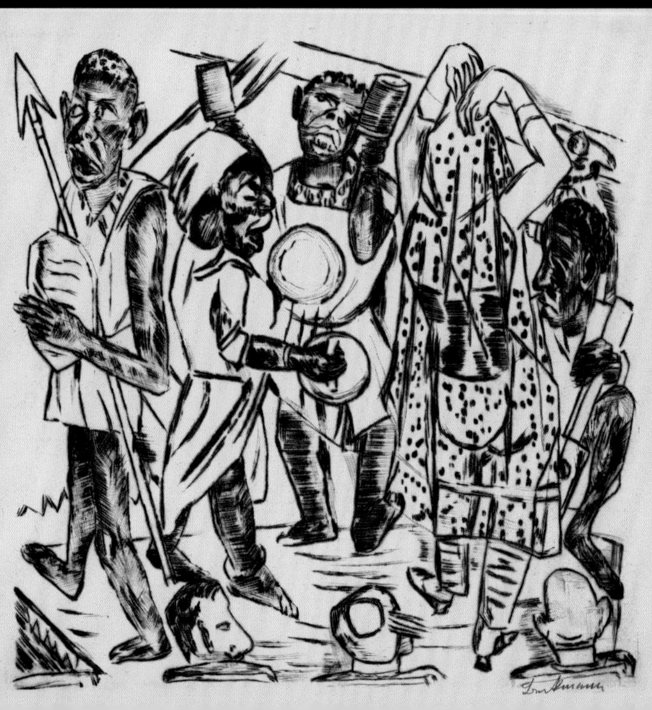

MAX BECKMANN
German, 1884–1950

Jahrmarkt
1921

Drypoints on Japan paper
Sheets: variable 16 1/4 x 9 3/4 in.
to 21 x 15 1/2 in.
Partial gift of David P. Tunick,
Class of 1966, in memory of
J. Kirk T. Varnedoe, Class of
1967, and Museum purchase,
Karl E. Weston Memorial Fund
(M.2003.25a–j)

Performing the role of barker, the artist opens *Jahrmarkt*, summoning the viewer to enter the "Circus Beckmann." Within, we encounter a collection of vulgar, colorful characters, performers as well as consumers, drawn from the world of the fair and the sideshow. Spikily rendered in drypoint, with compact figures crowded into spaces too small to contain them comfortably, these prints are wonders of fierce graphic energy tightly harnessed.

In 1912 Beckman professed that the task of modern art was to extract "from our own time—murky and fragmented though it may be—types that might be for us, the people of the present, what the gods and heroes of past peoples were to them." On the threshold of the 1920s he embraced a new strategy for achieving his goal, developing an imagery and a formal language that allowed him to endow contemporary life with the semblance of pictorial myth, to "make what is timeless contemporary and what is contemporary timeless," as he later formulated it. The circus and the sideshow had already been discovered by other artists, but in Beckmann's hands these subjects, even in their vulgarity, take on an air of the marvelous. The world of the circus, the carnival, and the fair that Beckmann celebrates in his *Jahrmarkt* cycle would permeate his art for the remaining three decades of his life.

—Charles W. Haxthausen, Director, Graduate Program in the History of Art and Faison-Pierson-Stoddard Professor of Art History. Adapted from *Labeltalk*, 2004

The *Jahrmarkt*, or *Kirmes*, is a kind of mini-carnival with music, food and drink, shooting galleries, circus acts, amusement-park rides, and other forms of popular entertainment that even today comes annually to cities and towns in central Europe. The *Jahrmarkt* can be traced back to medieval times; it was and remains part of the annual celebration to mark the dedication of the local church, the annual *Kirchweihfest*. Thus, despite the bawdy entertainment, the *Jahrmarkt* has a religious connotation.

Before 1914 the *Jahrmarkt* had allowed Germans an exciting peek at what was thought to lie beneath the cover of a civilization that they had experienced as increasingly onerous. The war, it seemed, had torn off that cover, damaging it irreparably. Germans, Beckmann's portfolio suggests, had lost their innocence and would never experience themselves or the world in the same way again. Even the pleasures of the *Jahrmarkt* now testified to nearly a millennium of unredeemed human suffering.

—Thomas A. Kohut, Sue and Edgar Wachenheim III Professor of History and Dean of the Faculty. Adapted from *Labeltalk*, 2004

African

African
Ivory Coast, Baule
Portrait Mask, 20th century
Wood, cloth, shells, and beads
32 11/16 x 9 x 7 11/16 in.
Museum purchase, Karl E.
Weston Memorial Fund (75.13)

African
Nigeria, Igbo
Helmet Mask, 20th century
Wood, pigment, and cloth
13 1/2 x 8 x 13 in.
Gift of Robert and Suzanne
Bach (97.12)

African
Mali, Bamana
Kono Cult Animal Mask
20th century
Wood and hair
23 x 7 x 5 1/4 in.
Gift of Oliver E. Cobb,
Class of 1952
(M.2005.16.6)

African
Benin
Figure, 20th century
Wood
18 1/4 x 7 7/8 x 3 1/8 in.
Museum purchase, Karl E.
Weston Memorial Fund (82.4)

SINCE THE 1980S, WCMA has been committed to the presentation of African art, due in part to the growing ethnic diversity of the college's student body and the increasing diversity of Williams's curriculum. New faculty members with expertise in various aspects of African cultures have also prompted the museum to present interdisciplinary and related programming of the highest quality.

Of the total number of objects in WCMA's African collection, 20 percent represent East African cultures; the balance is from West Africa. The works include ceremonial vessels and furniture, articles of personal adornment, ritual and helmet masks, fetish figures, dolls, marionettes, agricultural implements, textiles from the nineteenth and twentieth centuries, and utilitarian objects. The geographic areas represented are encompassed by the present-day nations of Mali, Ivory Coast, Zaire, Nigeria, Cameroon, Liberia, Gabon, Benin, and Kenya.

The majority of items in the collection were made to function within the bounds of religious and political ceremony. Ornamented stools indicate political office and rank, while masks link the world of the living with the spirits of the world beyond. Wooden effigies and zoomorphic figures can honor the dead by summoning spirits, which protect communities from malevolent events or otherwise serve as instruments of social control and symbols of male power.

The African art object has often been presented in Western museums within the framework of tradition, but the same piece and its meaning can also be seen to be in a perpetual state of transition. As a work passes through time from individual to individual and from culture to culture, it is drained of its traditional meanings, only to be imbued with new ones that make it relevant to its present audience. Against this backdrop, WCMA has set out to enable its audiences to better appreciate the complex diversity and creativity of African artists, past and present. Through study of African objects, students can explore the art and religion, philosophy, politics, and history of a given civilization.

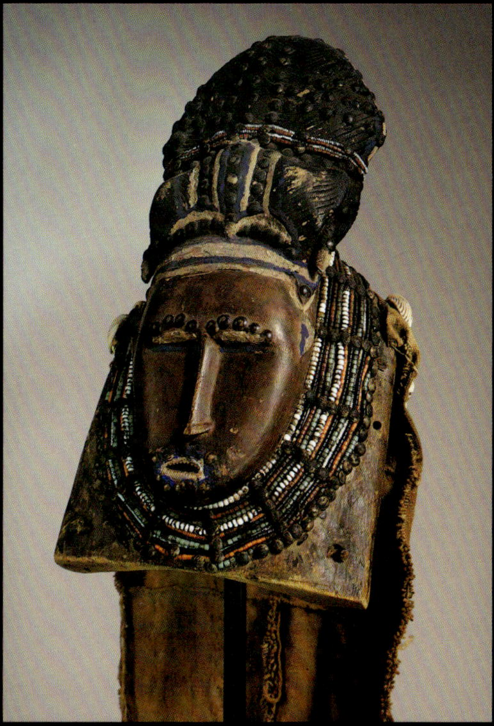
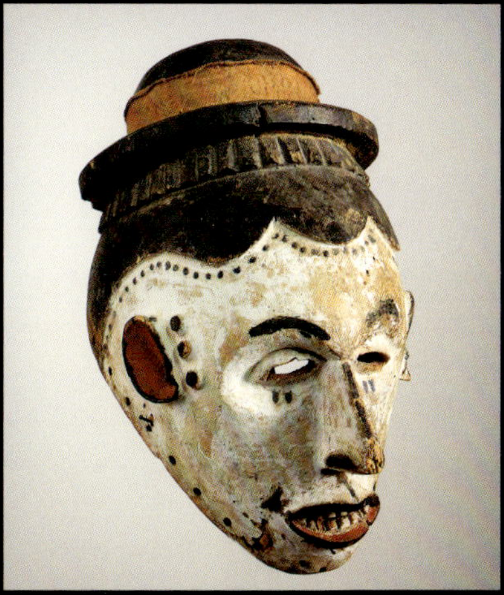
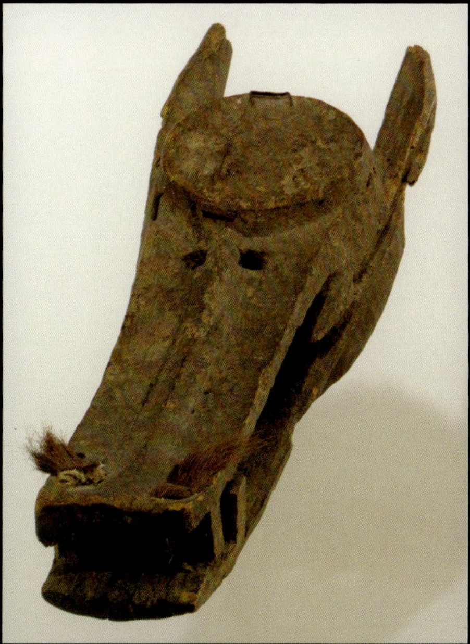
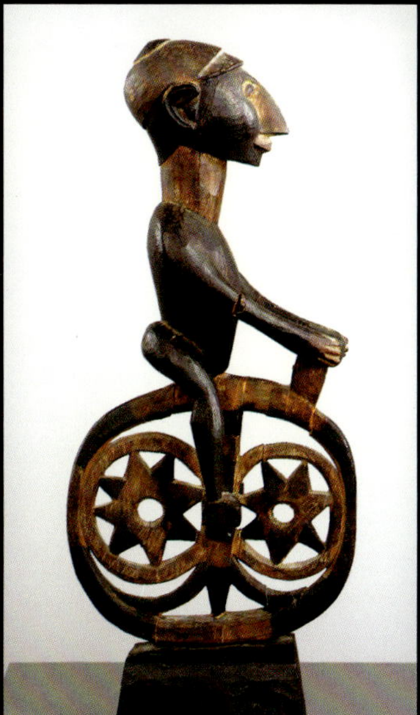

GEORGIA O'KEEFFE
American, 1887–1986

Skunk Cabbage (Cos Cob)
1922

Oil on canvas
23 5/16 x 16 5/16 in.
Bequest of Kathryn Hurd
(82.22.40)

Georgia O'Keeffe was especially drawn to the natural world—from stars and skies and wide open landscapes to closer encounters with plants and flowers. In the early spring of 1922 she was exhilarated to be out of New York City and outdoors in rural Cos Cob, Connecticut. Skunk cabbages are among the earliest plants to appear in the spring, often pushing up through late snow by virtue of the plant's unusual capacity to generate its own heat. O'Keeffe's interest was captured by the odd shape and color of the small swamp plant and, with little else growing so early in the year, she chose it as subject over the cold brown landscape.

WCMA's work is one of O'Keeffe's series of skunk cabbage sketches and paintings, all done in the 1920s before her life-changing travels to New Mexico. Her style within the series moves generally from a naturalistic to an abstracted portrayal of the plant, but in no treatment of the subject does the artist completely abandon the real specimen. The Williams painting is naturalistic in color and shape but extremely abstracted in its close, ground-level viewpoint and fiery atmosphere. The accompanying photo by Henry W. Art, Samuel Fessenden Clarke Professor of Biology, serves to remind that O'Keeffe's portrait of a living plant, the skunk cabbage, pulses with a larger-than-life agenda of her own creation.

—Marion Goethals (Williams M.A. 1989), Interim Director, 2004–5

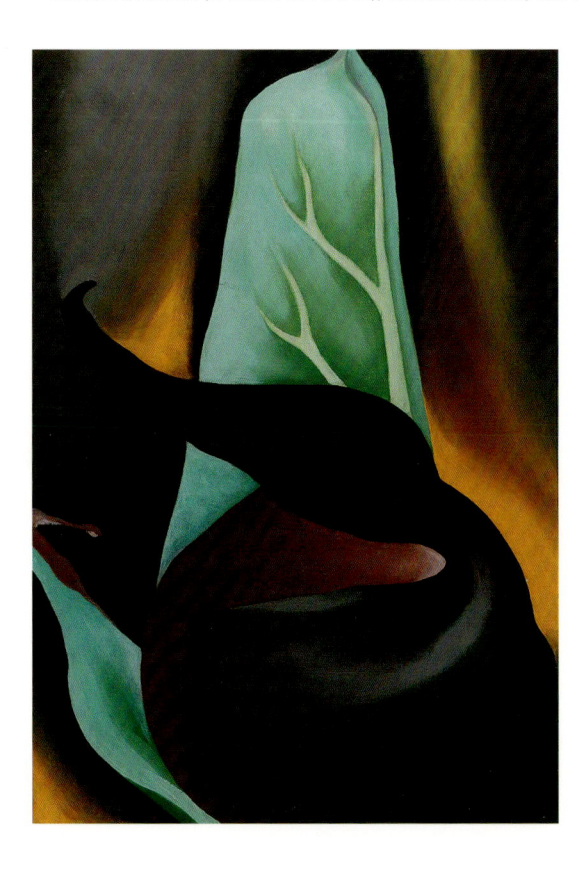

JAMES AUGUSTUS JOSEPH VAN DER ZEE
American, 1886–1983

The Last Good-bye
1923

Gelatin silver print
Image: 10 x 8 in.
Museum purchase, Karl E. Weston Memorial Fund (89.8)

James Van Der Zee liked to tell stories with his photographs. He would pack his studio with props that together suggested narratives that lay well beyond the lens. Here the flag identifies the soldier as American, with the helmet and field bag suggesting that he will soon be going off to battle. The superimposed print, clearly titled "The Last Goodbye—Overseas," adds to the anxiety about his future. We are to understand this as a farewell portrait, a typical theme for departing soldiers.

This type of narrative complexity made Van Der Zee one of the most sought-after portraitists in Harlem between the wars. Born in Lenox, Massachusetts, he had established a business in Harlem called Guarantee Photo Studio by 1918. Over the next few decades, his business soared, his subjects ranging from neighborhood friends to famous performers. After falling into obscurity after World War II, his work was resurrected during the early 1970s when curators around the country began to take interest in our long overlooked photographic heritage. Van Der Zee enjoyed a brief rejuvenation in his career during the final years of his long life as he worked to meet increasing demand both for his earlier work and for new portraits.

—John Stomberg, Associate Director

GASTON LACHAISE
American, 1882–1935

Portrait of John Marin
1928

Bronze
13 ¾ x 10 x 8 ½ in.
Bequest of Andrew S. Keck,
Class of 1924 (M.2004.5.1)

Torso
1912–27 (cast 1963)
Bronze
44 ¾ x 22 x 10 ¼ in.
Bequest of Lawrence H. Bloedel,
Class of 1923 (77.9.8)

In 1928 the magazine *Creative Art* asked the Parisian-born sculptor Gaston Lachaise to write "A Comment on My Sculpture." He chose four works to be illustrated, among which was his *Portrait of John Marin*. This portrait bust of the famous American watercolorist must have been one of Lachaise's favorite works. A realistic and specific rendering of a close friend, the sculpture could not be more different from the works for which Lachaise is best known: idealized, oversize, and stylized female nudes. Compare the portrait of Marin with the *Torso* in WCMA's collection: Marin's crooked nose and craggy, wrinkly face exude personality, uniqueness, and mortality while the clean lines of the nude seem to render her an eternal and ethereal goddess. The sculpture of Marin belongs to a group of works from the 1920s, when Lachaise experimented with the art of portraiture. Other portraits from this period include busts of the photographer Alfred Stieglitz and the poet e. e. cummings.

WCMA received this sculpture in 2004, as part of a larger bequest from Williams alumnus Andrew S. Keck (Williams 1924). Other casts of this work are found in major museum collections, including the Whitney Museum of American Art, New York; the Nelson-Atkins Museum of Art, Kansas City, Missouri; and the Milwaukee Art Museum, Wisconsin.

—Dana Pilson, The Edith and Herbert Lehman Foundation Publications Assistant

ERNST BARLACH

German, 1870–1938

The Singing Boy
1928

Bronze
20 x 12 x 24 in.
Bequest of Andrew S. Keck,
Class of 1924 (M.2004.5.5)

A sculptor, printmaker, and playwright, Ernst Barlach shuttled among various media in search of a means of communication that would best convey inner feeling through exterior form. Barlach began his artistic career as a student of sculpture at the Kunstgewerbeschule (School of Applied Arts) in Hamburg, Germany, and it is for his sculpture that he is best known. The artist's work in this medium was deeply influenced by a trip to Russia in 1906; the Russian peasants, in their simplicity and austerity, came to embody for Barlach his conception of humanity, in which individual lives are inevitably shaped by external circumstances.

Barlach's *The Singing Boy* of 1928 reflects the inspiration of his journey of more than twenty years before: rather than a particular individual, the figure is meant to represent the human condition. The artist simplified the body by using a robe, an article of clothing often found in his figural works, to create a solid form composed of interlocking pyramidal shapes. The focal points are the interlaced fingers, closed eyes, and open mouth, which emphasizes the act of singing, an activity to which the figure's entire being is committed. The work's solidity transforms a transient moment, perhaps the creation of a solitary note, into something permanent and timeless.

—Amelia Kahl Avdić (Williams M.A. 2004)

LOUIS ISIDORE KAHN
American, 1901–1974

Towers, San Gimignano
1929

Watercolor and red pencil on paper
12 1/8 x 9 1/4 in.
Museum purchase with funds provided by an Anonymous donor and with the J. W. Field Fund, John B. Turner '24 Memorial Fund, Joseph O. Eaton Fund, Karl E. Weston Memorial Fund, Bentley W. Warren Fund (94.14)

Louis Isidore Kahn was the greatest American architect of the post–World War II period. Born on an island in the Baltic Sea, he immigrated at a young age to Philadelphia. The family was desperately poor, but Kahn's talents were recognized: he was trained in painting in high school and then in architecture at the University of Pennsylvania, where he received a classical Beaux-Arts architectural education. He worked for years after graduating to earn enough money to support himself on a sketching trip to Europe, which lasted from April 1928 through April 1929. He spent five months in Italy, October to February, making his way slowly south down the peninsula.

Kahn made an important distinction between painting and architectural drawings. A painting is itself, he argued, while architectural drawings, like a musical score, represent something other than what one sees on the page. Accordingly, we should enjoy this watercolor of an architectural subject, the Torri dei Salvucci in the Tuscan town of San Gimignano, as a skillful use of the medium, with delicate washes laid over a scaffolding of red outlines that are allowed to show through. But it is also important to note the subject, which Kahn obviously chose because it appealed to him. The picture is dominated by two great vertical masonry shafts, family towers built in the twelfth or thirteenth century for defensive purposes. They are the largest objects in the picture, and the darker one is located almost dead center on the page. Clearly Kahn was fascinated by the power of the simple geometric shapes created by the undecorated planes of stone walls.

As Kahn moved through Italy, he began to concentrate on sketching medieval and vernacular structures. There is no evidence that Kahn ever drew any of the great Gothic buildings of northern Europe, although the path of his trip offered him ample opportunities to do so. It was not the skeletal, translucent, seemingly weightless Gothic of France and Germany to which he responded, but rather the planar, opaque, massive Gothic of Italy. Modernist architectural theory, nascent in the 1920s, celebrated French Gothic buildings for their structural "honesty" and daring but largely ignored their Italian counterparts, which held little interest for the propagandist of a movement devoted to the dissolution of walls into planes of apparently weightless glass or thin veils of masonry.

Beginning in the 1940s Kahn became increasingly dissatisfied with modernist architecture, which he felt had sacrificed one of architecture's most powerful tools, monumentality. In his mature architecture, Kahn found a way to reintroduce the monumentality he had found at San Gimignano into his buildings. The towers he drew in 1928 became a major source for important parts of the building that secured him international fame, the service towers of the Richards Medical Research Building at the University of Pennsylvania (1957–59). In that building he reconciled modernity of materials with the grandeur of past architectural forms he had discovered on his voyage through Italy.

—Eugene J. Johnson (Williams 1959), Class of 1955 Memorial Professor of Art

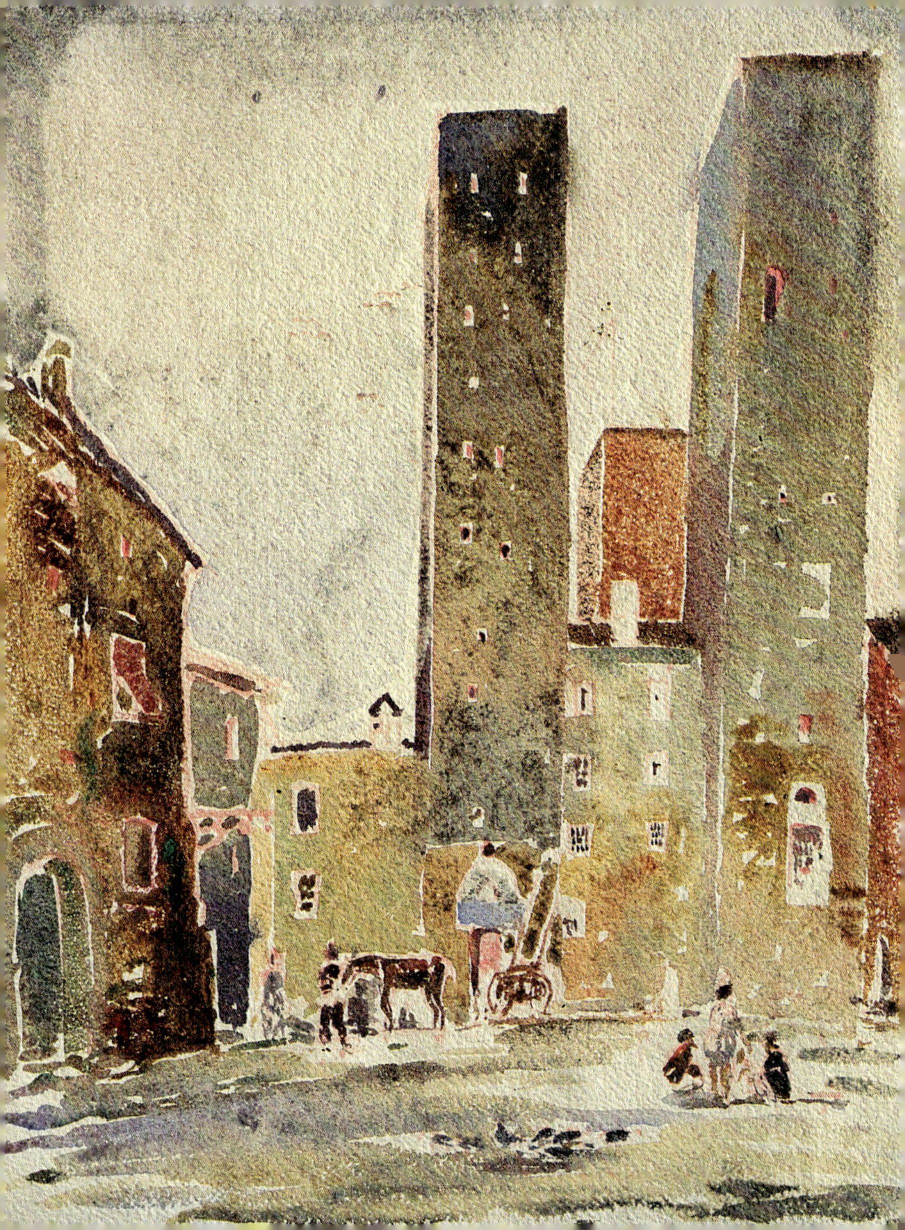

WALKER EVANS
American, 1903–1975

The Brooklyn Bridge (with a Poem by Hart Crane),
negatives 1929, prints 1994

Photogravures
Sheets: 17 x 14 in.
Gift of Jock Reynolds and the Eakins Press Foundation
(M2001.5a–i)

Walker Evans first met Hart Crane in New York City in 1928, just as the two men were becoming actively engaged in their nascent artistic careers, Evans in photography and Crane in poetry. Both artists lived in Brooklyn Heights in the shadow of the Brooklyn Bridge, which came to serve as their muse. In the late 1920s Evans and Crane each initiated individual rhapsodies on the mass of stone and steel—one in images and the other in words.

Though begun separately, these two projects would later come together in a serendipitous union. Crane's ode to the transfiguring nature of modern technology, entitled *The Bridge*, was originally intended to be published in book format with a painting by Joseph Stella as its frontispiece. Four months before publication, however, Crane asked Evans to illustrate the book's first edition with three selections from the photographer's *Brooklyn Bridge* portfolio. The photographs and poem join in an elegant symbiosis: the abstracted geometry of Evans's images serves as a striking counterpoint to the sweeping, lyrical quality of Crane's text. Both image and text encircle the bridge in a multitude of viewpoints that celebrate modern America's victory over space.

WCMA's *Brooklyn Bridge* series is a set of photogravures produced by Eakins Press from Evans's original negatives. To create a photogravure, the photographic negative is transferred to a copperplate, from which the image is printed on a heavy, finely fibered paper. Unlike the slickness of a silver gelatin print, photogravures have an organic texture and produce deep, rich tones, which account for the velvety quality of the images. These prints capture the lushness of the original photogravures published in the 1930 edition of *The Bridge*.

—Elizabeth Athens (Williams M.A. 2005), The Edith and Herbert Lehman Foundation Publications Assistant

102, 103

MAN RAY
American, 1890–1976

Électricité (from Électricité:
Dix Rayogrammes)
1931

Photogravures
Images: 10 1/4 x 8 1/16 in.
Museum purchase (92.18a–j)

This alluring image of a nude female, currents of electricity racing across her torso, debuted in a 1931 portfolio of photogravures created by Man Ray for an unlikely patron: a French electric company. The client, La Compagnie Parisienne de Distribution d'Électricité (CPDE), had just launched a campaign to promote the domestic use of electricity and hired the American avant-garde artist Man Ray to create a special gift for its shareholders and high-level customers. Man Ray produced for the CPDE *Électricité*, a suite of ten images that played with common electrical devices—such as a toaster, fan, iron, light bulb, and immersion heater—to create a dramatic visual expression of the company's marketing efforts. But with this daring image, simply titled *Électricité*, Man Ray made a broader commentary on the universality and omnipotence of electricity. Lee Miller, Man Ray's lover and photography assistant on this commission, recalled that the image was "a little tough for the officials because they were a public utility company." Today, in an era when companies routinely link sex and technology in their marketing strategies, this image still retains its potency, leaving us thankful to an unknown, forward-thinking electric company executive who was bold enough to publish it.

—Stefanie Spray Jandl (Williams M.A. 1993), Andrew W. Mellon Foundation Associate Curator for Academic Programs

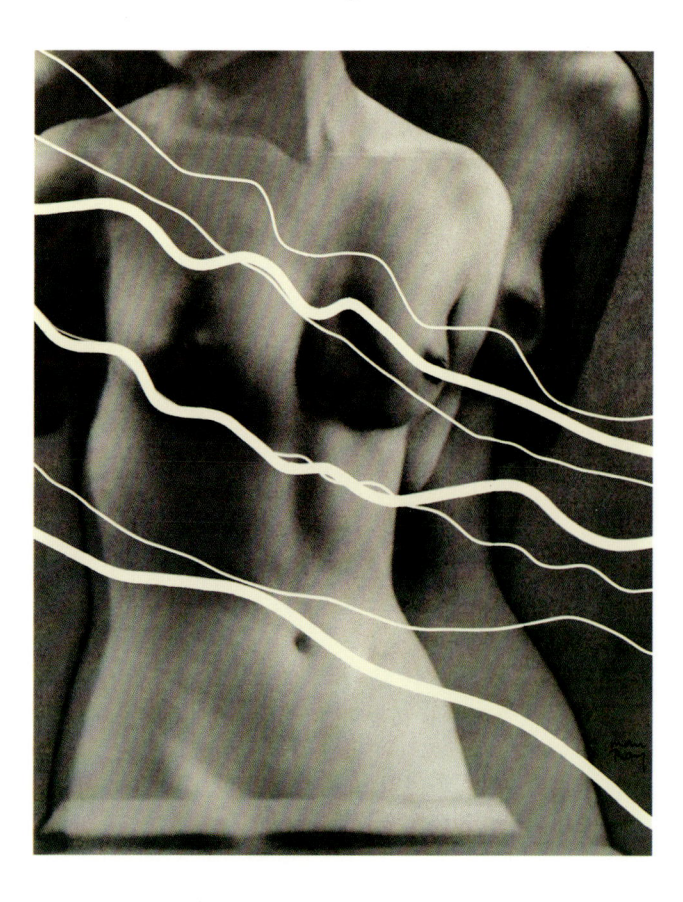

CHARLES DEMUTH
American, 1883–1935

Three Pears
1933

Watercolor over pencil on paper
10 x 14 in.
Bequest of Susan Watts Street
(57.11)

Charles Demuth's *Three Pears* is a quiet work: three humble pears lie on the merest suggestion of a table's edge. This is not the remains of a raucous party or a demonstration of wealth and bounty, as many Baroque still lifes were; it also diverges from the standards of the more contemporary Cubist experimentations with still life that often displayed the remains of a modern social encounter, suggesting a Parisian café scene with wine bottle, pipe, and musical instrument. Rather, Demuth's pears, like many of his other still lifes that feature humble American products like corn or peaches or squash, quietly present themselves to the viewer without giving any kind of social context. The fruits display a monumentality conveyed by their large scale, giving them an importance and gravity usually reserved for portraiture and reminiscent of the artist's poster portraits of the early 1920s. At the time the work was executed, Demuth's health was extremely poor, having struggled most of his adult life with diabetes, and he had retired to his mother's home in Lancaster, Pennsylvania; this isolation might explain a measure of the poetry of quiet calm present in this and in so many of Demuth's still lifes.

Three Pears also demonstrates the artist's virtuosity and absolute control of the watercolor medium. Demuth pared the composition to its purest state: three forms arranged on a plane. This ultimate reduction gives the artist free rein to play with the medium itself, creating mottled effects by blotting as well as using wax resist; Demuth probably either rubbed a candle on the paper before applying the pigment or may even have sprinkled salt on the pooled color. Demuth is devoutly representational, yet the work continues his flirtation with Cubism: his razor-thin graphite vectors crisscross the work vibrantly, and although the pears are shaded and many of the blotting effects create potentially representational lighting effects, he also plays with their planes of color. By reducing the composition to its purest point, Demuth amply demonstrates his inventiveness with his application of the ideas of Cubism as well as his virtuosity with watercolors.

—Ellery Foutch
(Williams M.A. 2003)

MARCEL DUCHAMP
French, 1887–1968

The Green Box
1934

Photographs, drawings, and handwritten notes in facsimile
13 1/8 x 11 x 7/8 in.
Gift of George Heard Hamilton and Polly W. Hamilton (91.25)

My early scholarship involved the Austrian-English philosopher of language Ludwig Wittgenstein (1889–1951) who, at times, clipped fragments from his typescripts and manuscripts and collected them in a box. These fragments were published by some of his students under the title *Zettel*. "Often fragments on the same topic were clipped together," his editors write, "but there were also a large number lying loose in the box."

The French-American artist and chess master Marcel Duchamp's masterpiece, the work that changed twentieth-century art and life (not to imply that there is a difference) is called, in English, *The Bride Stripped Bare by Her Bachelors, Even*. As part of this artistic project, Duchamp produced three hundred copies of what has become known as *The Green Box*: "a flat case," one of his editors writes, "containing ninety-four loose items; each handwritten note reproduced in exact facsimile including torn edges, blots, erasures and occasional illegibility." Duchamp's friend George Heard Hamilton, who donated *The Green Box* to WCMA, translated the notes.

When I discovered *The Green Box* at WCMA, it felt as if I were returning home (a slightly crazy, inverted home, but that happens in even the best of families).

Homework assignment: which passage below is found in Wittgenstein, and which in Duchamp?

Conditions of a language:
The search for "prime words" ("divisible, only by themselves and by unity").
I want to play chess, and a man gives the white king a paper crown, leaving the use of the pieces unaltered, but telling me the crown has a meaning to him in the game, which he can't express by rules.

—Steven Gerrard, Professor of Philosophy

GRANT WOOD
American, 1892–1942

Death on the Ridge Road
1935

Oil on masonite
32 1/8 x 39 in.
Gift of Cole Porter (47.1.3)

Grant Wood's *Death on the Ridge Road* is one of a number of his paintings that chronicle the rupture and shock that accompanied modernity's arrival in traditional and isolated communities. The main drama of the painting—an impending accident— plays out on a ribbon of paved road that curves its way over a hill and out of view. The artist's choice of three different motor vehicles—commercial truck, sophisticated sedan, and the ubiquitous, practical Ford of farmers and villagers—carried significant symbolic weight, particularly when sited on a ridge road.

Ridge roads serve as historical markers of the American Middle West. Carved out by settlers crossing the plains by wagon and by foot, these pioneer pathways traversed the higher ridges, avoiding the mud and slush of the lowlands. As territories developed, ridge roads often became major arteries between towns and were lined with fences to keep intruders from the fields and animals from the road. Having never been intended for the speed and density of cars, ridge roads were often narrow and winding, making the drama here exceptionally tense. What Wood renders is not simply an impending collision of automobiles, but a collision between opposing social and economic forces, as the faster-paced urban world meets head-on the simpler and slower traditions of agrarian living.

—Wanda Corn, Robert and Ruth Halperin Professor of Art History, Stanford University. Adapted from *American Dreams: American Art to 1950 in the Williams College Museum of Art*, 2001

WALKER EVANS
American, 1903–1975

Bud Fields and His Family, Hale County, Alabama
1936

Gelatin silver print
Image: 8 x 10 in.
Museum purchase, Karl E. Weston Memorial Fund
(77.23)

Walker Evans was splitting his time between *Fortune* magazine and the Farm Security Administration (FSA) in 1936 when he visited Bud Fields. His assignment was to cover sharecropping in the American South for the magazine, and the FSA was to keep the finished photographs. *Fortune* had already assigned one of its writers, James Agee, who had requested Evans as the photographer. They spent three weeks visiting a handful of families, determined to get to know their subjects before photographing them. Agee's agonized text, filled with self-recriminations for displaying the private lives of these families even if it could help their plight, grew to something far too long for the magazine to accept, and the story was killed. The photographs went to the FSA as agreed.

Agee continued to work on the text, and the finished collaborative piece—*Let Us Now Praise Famous Men*—was published in book form in 1941. Though it failed to garner much critical attention then, the second edition, published in 1960, has become a classic source for studies of Depression-era America. At that point, Evans's cool, somewhat detached approach to his subjects had become the norm for what was by then called Documentary photography.

Despite the obvious squalor in which the Fieldses live, Evans has allowed them to organize themselves and to choose how they wished to be presented to the camera. He captures a simple dignity with his eye-level point of view and soft lighting. The facts are there for the viewer to read, including the simple interior, the old furniture, and the unlaundered clothes, but Evans did not wish to overtly editorialize any further. This was an approach that had far less appeal in the 1930s than it would in the 1960s, when Evans's reputation finally soared.

—John Stomberg, Associate Director

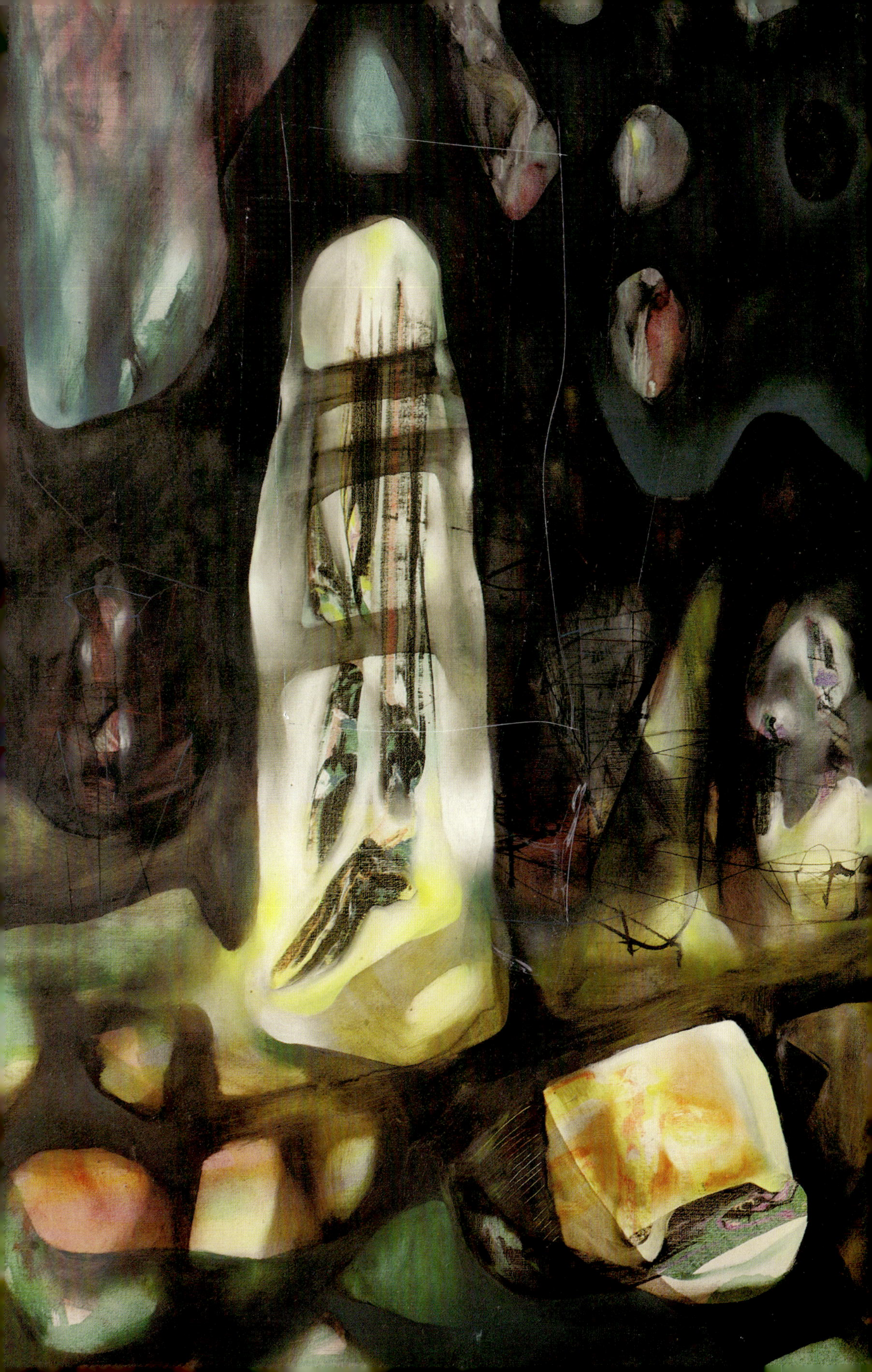

Drawings

FROM THE EARLIEST DAYS of the museum, drawings were valued for the teaching of art. The exquisite old master ink sketch *Via Crucis* by Cambiaso was one of the first drawings in the collection; now the museum holds more than 1,600 drawings from the Western tradition, as well as a significant number of works representing Asian and African cultures.

Students or visitors encountering these works can sample the many complex uses of drawing: to work out an idea, to prepare a subject for execution in another medium, to make a finished artwork as an end in itself. The museum uses the variety of drawings in its collection—from quick studies to densely complex compositions, all in a range of marking media—to help students of art and art history explore the many layers of the creative process.

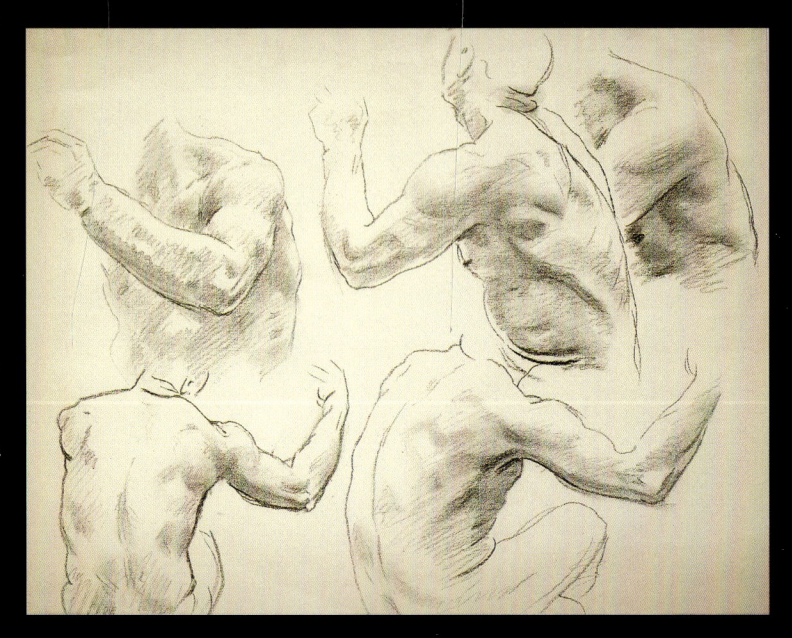

John Singer Sargent
American, 1856–1925
Studies of Male Nudes
ca. 1895–1916
Charcoal on paper
18 $1/2$ x 23 $1/4$ in.
Gift of Miss Emily Sargent and Mrs. Francis Ormond (30.4)

Joseph Stella
American, 1877–1946
Portrait of Joe Gould, ca. 1919
Silverpoint, pencil, and crayon on paper
13 $1/2$ x 10 $7/16$ in.
Gift of Richard T. York (86.24)

Luca Cambiaso
Italian, 1527–1585
Via Crucis, 16th century
Pen and ink on paper
8 $1/4$ x 12 $5/8$ in.
Gift of Karl E. Weston,
Class of 1896 (DI.1)

John Everett Millais
British, 1829–1896
Sketchbook, mid–19th century
Pencil on paper, bound in leather and cloth
6 x 9 in.
Gift of Mrs. Frank J. Mather, Jr. (55.25.1)

Paul Klee
Swiss, 1879–1940
Cat Accident (Unfall einer Katze), 1939
Crayon on paper
11 $7/8$ x 17 $3/4$ in.
Bequest of Jane T. Ritchie (85.24.14)

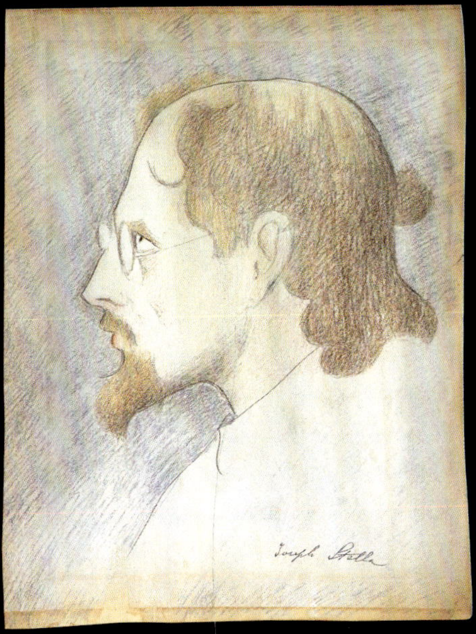
Joseph Stella

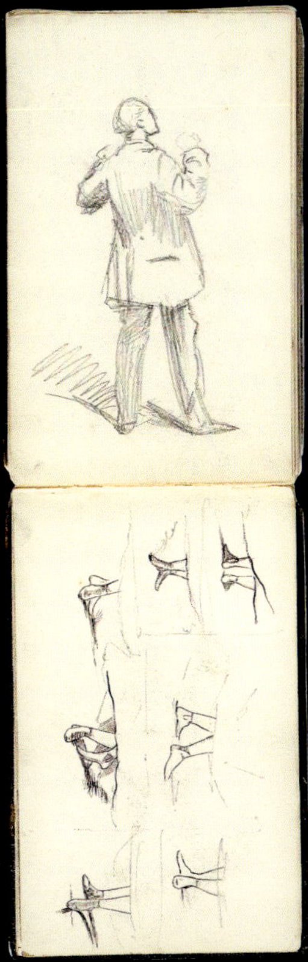

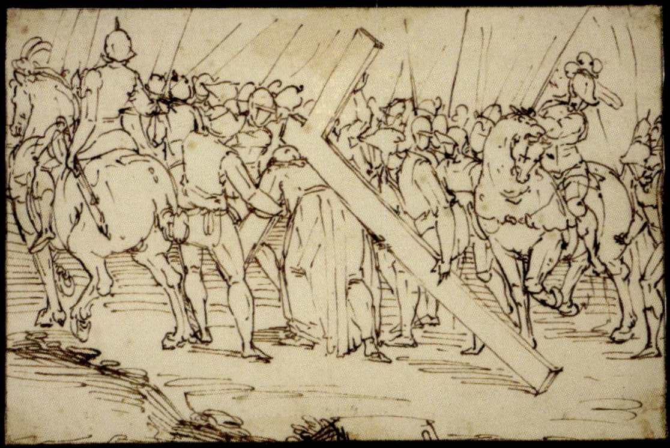

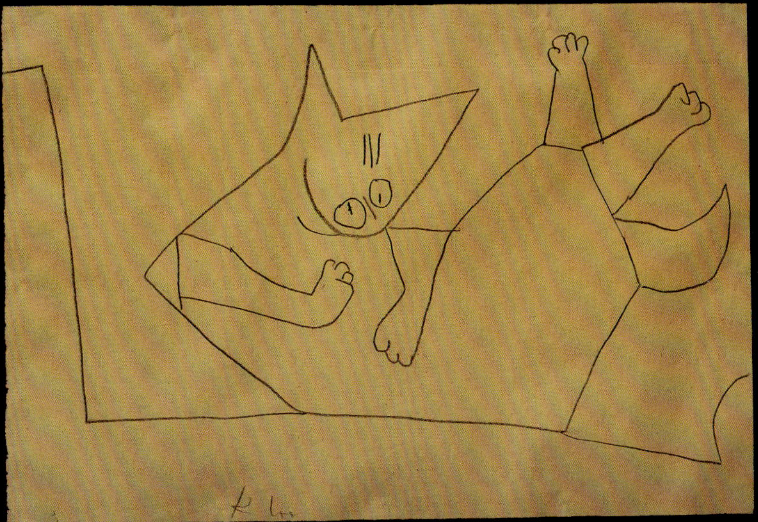

HENRY SPENCER MOORE
British, 1898–1986

Shelter Scene
1941

Pen and ink with wash on paper
Image: 10 7/16 x 8 1/4 in.
Gift of Lockwood Thompson, Class of 1923, Saluting the Classes of 1867, 1892, and 1923 (91.1.1)

Shelter Scene: Bunks and Sleepers
1942

Pen and ink with wash on paper
Image: 10 3/4 x 8 3/16 in.
Gift of Lockwood Thompson, Class of 1923, Saluting the Classes of 1867, 1892 and 1923 (91.1.3)

September 11, 1940: Air-raid sirens ring out as Henry Moore and his wife head home from dinner with friends. They leave their car and seek safety in the London Underground. The artist is struck by the sight of hordes of people taking refuge in the subway station, as opposed to the official air-raid shelters closer to the surface. During World War II Moore repeatedly went into the Underground and produced numerous sketches and eventually over seventy-five finished drawings, of which WCMA owns three. Figures defined by electric-bright wash emerge from the damp, chilly darkness: families cluster together to stay warm, children wrapped in blankets. A jerry-rigged platform overflows with sleepers, and the curved wall of the Underground gently cups the refugees. The straightforward, draped figural forms look forward to Moore's plaster sculptural works of the 1950s.

Moore described his experience: "I never made any sketches in the Underground. It just wasn't possible. It would have been like making sketches in the hold of a slave ship. One couldn't be as disinterested as that. Londoners had decided for themselves that the Underground was the safest place to be, and nothing was organized. There were no sanitary arrangements and no bunks. Some people brought their own mattresses, others simply lay on the concrete platform. Instead of drawing, I would wander casually past a group of people half a dozen times or so, pretending to be unaware of them. Sometimes I climbed the staircase so that I could write down a note on the back of an envelope without being seen. A note like 'two people sleeping under one blanket' would be enough of a reminder to enable me to make a sketch the next day."

—Dana Pilson, The Edith and Herbert Lehman Foundation Publications Assistant

114, 115

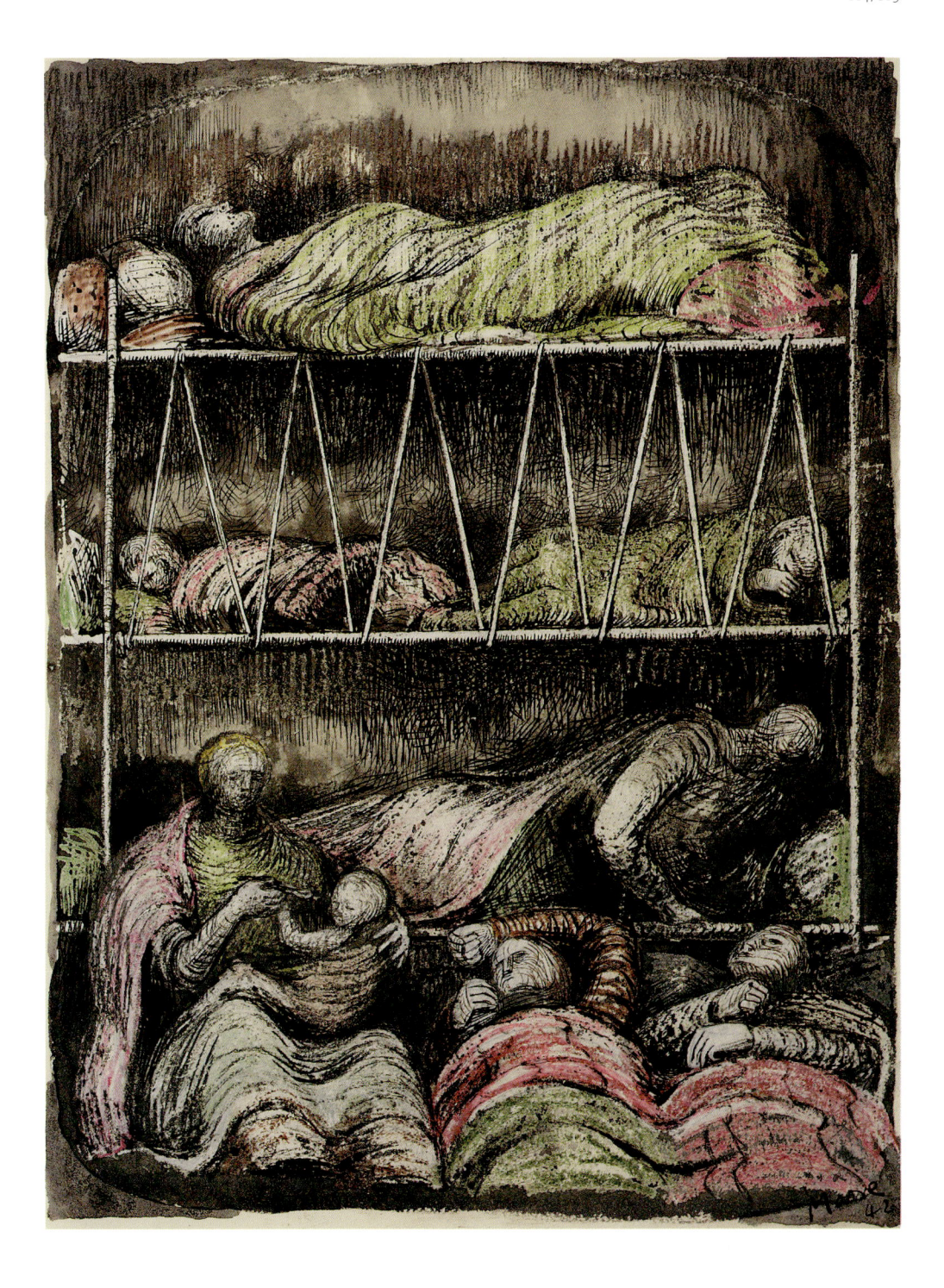

YVES TANGUY
French, 1900–1955

Equivocal Colors
1943

Oil on canvas
20 x 16 in.
Gift of the Lynes Family Collection (99.5)

What do such titles as *Mama, Papa Is Wounded!*; *The Mood of Now*; *Indefinite Divisibility*; *Slowly toward the North*; *The Hunted Sky*; *Multiplication of the Arcs*; *Genesis*; *Through Birds, through Fire, but Not through Glass*; and finally *Equivocal Colors*, reveal about the Surrealist painting of Yves Tanguy, who was born in Paris into a seafaring family of Breton origin in 1900 and who died in Woodbury, Connecticut, in 1955? Above all, that he was a painter of the equivocal, the enigmatic, the ambiguous, and the uncertain; that he was a visionary who saw the world as simultaneously abstract and concrete; an illusionist whose fantasies were modeled from a strange blend of rock-hardened lava, veined marble, and fossilized bone; a landscapist whose milky white dreamscapes were dominated by dense structural formations assembled from strangely polished forms and dark cast shadows; an architect who in the vast emptiness of an imaginary space and through the enigmatic conjoining of rectangles, ovals, triangles, trapezoids, circles, needles, and spirals created a geometry of dream; a colorist whose palette of soft and hard hues ran the gamut from hard and brilliant reds, yellows, greens, and blacks to softer, more pastel oranges, peaches, pinks, violets, blues, and grays; a collagist who joined in his sculptural, skeletal, and faintly anatomical still-life constructions a hallucinatory combination of biomorphic and lapidary forms (calcified bone, smoothed stones, heart-shaped rocks, egglike ovals, fossilized tree trunks with edges tasseled by rot); and, finally, an inventor who created, out of the bric-à-brac of dreams and with fragments taken from a quarry or an ossuary, an immense biomorphic machine, which inertly awaits the turning of a switch so that it may come alive in a new genesis of unimagined spatial and temporal realities: a world where, indeed, the imaginary does become *real*. This is a cosmos where we experience not only *Equivocal Colors* but, in the words of the title of another Tanguy painting, *The Certitude of the Never Seen*.

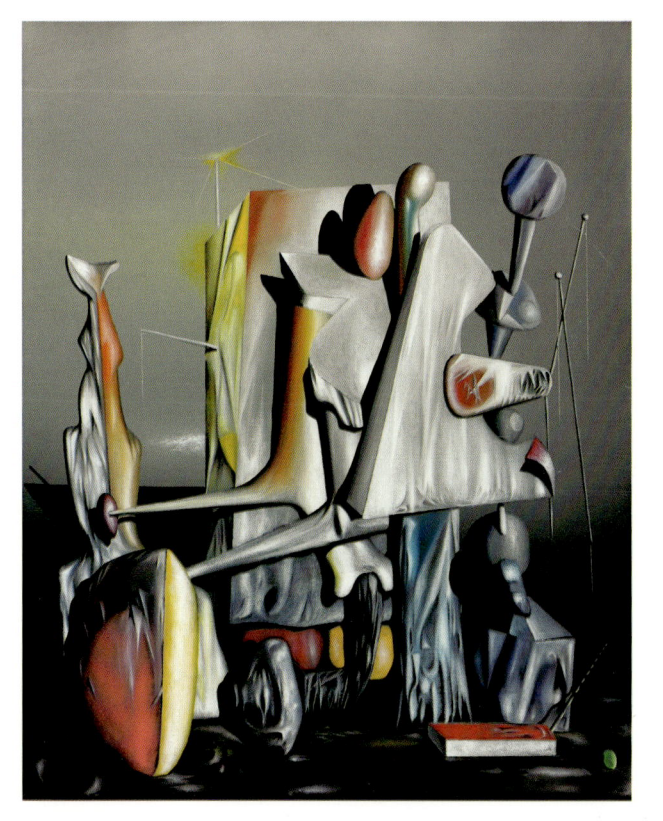

—Richard Stamelman, Professor of Comparative Literature

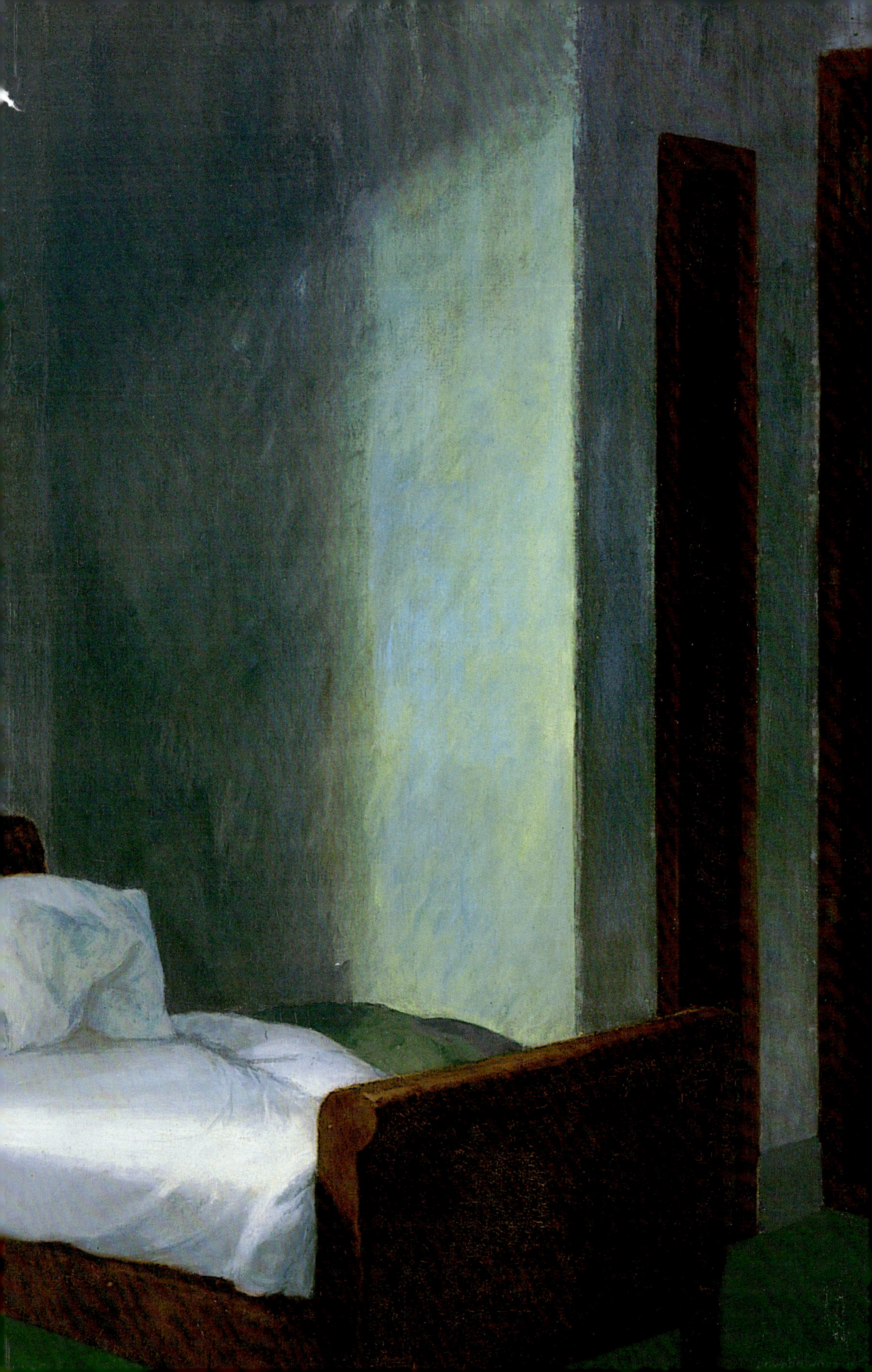

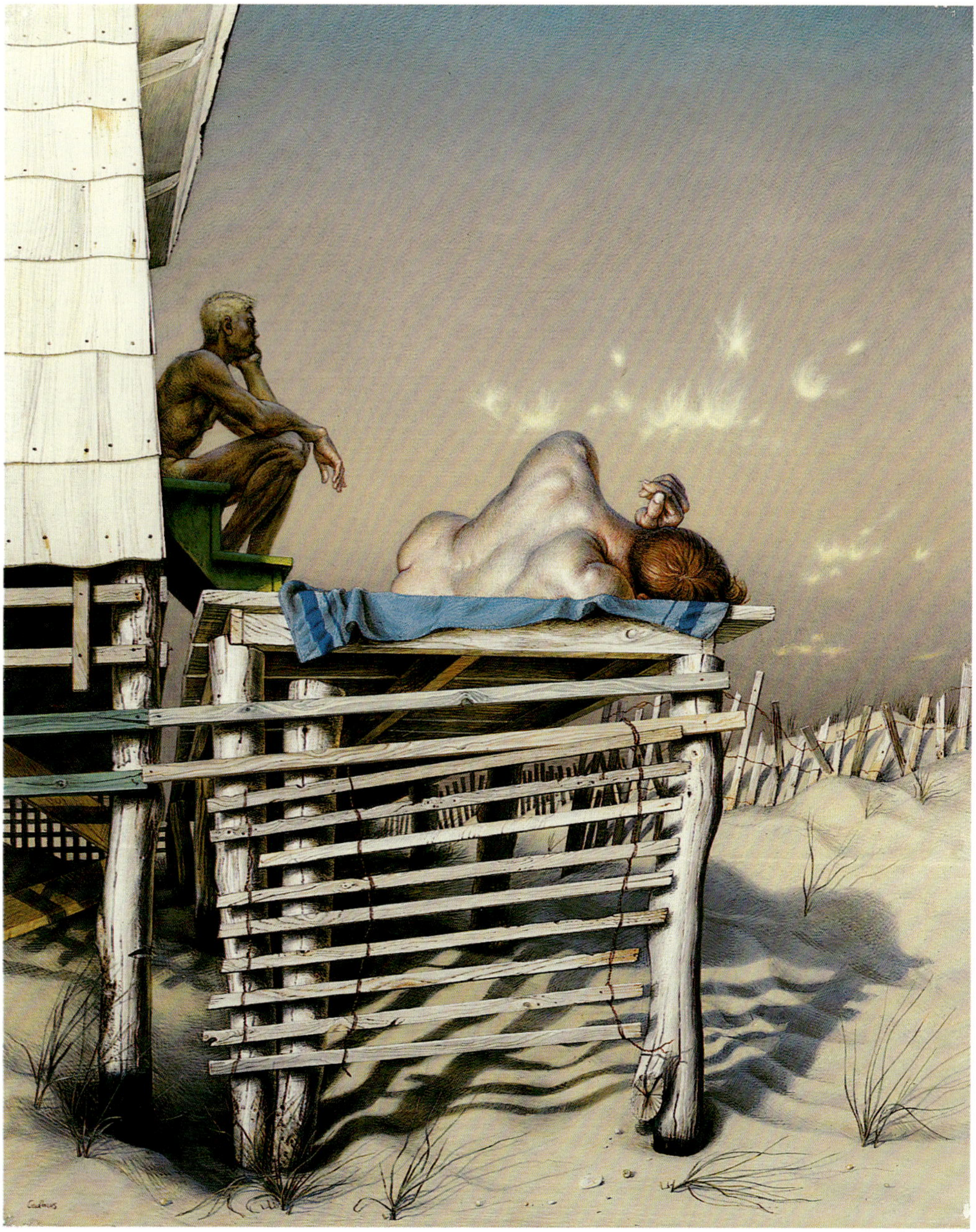

PAUL CADMUS
American, 1904–1999

Point O'View
1945

Egg tempera on panel
18 1/2 x 15 3/16 in.
Gift of Cole Porter (47.1.1)

Painted in the 1940s on Fire Island, New York, where Paul Cadmus summered with the painters Jared and Margaret French, *Point O'View* is dramatically different from the artist's earlier, densely packed satirical paintings. *The Fleet's In* (1943, The Naval Historical Center, Washington, D.C.), a potpourri of opposite- and same-sex pickups in body language leaving little to the imagination, won instant notoriety for the artist when Admiral Rodman and the secretary of the Navy had it pulled from an upcoming exhibition at the Corcoran Gallery of Art, Washington, D.C., for its supposed indecent rendition of sailors on shore leave. Cadmus's Fire Island pictures would appear to leave behind social critique for summer relaxation; both, however, share an interest in depicting desire that shifts in the 1940s toward a frank statement of homoeroticism.

The relationship between the two figures in *Point O'View*, whose peaceful self-absorption is somewhat deceptive, is a highly charged one. The figures' hands not only contribute to the lazy mood but also highlight the space between them, a space provocatively bridged by the sinuous contour of the foreground figure and the towel inching its way from one to the other. A similar counterpoint may be found in the deliberate opposition of the rectilinear grid of the house and deck and the animate curves of the figures. Rhythm is evoked too in the wavelike movement from left to right: beginning with the protruding roof down through the seated figure, onto his recumbent companion, then out to sea.

—Carol Ockman, Professor of Art. Adapted from *American Dreams: American Art to 1950 in the Williams College Museum of Art*, 2001

JACOB LAWRENCE
American, 1917–2000

Radio Repairs
1946

Gouache on paper
23 1/16 x 31 3/16 in.
Anonymous gift (M.2003.31)

In August Wilson's play *Seven Guitars*, the main characters sit close to a backyard radio to hear a fight between Joe Louis and Billy Conn on a spring evening in 1948 in the Hill District of Pittsburgh. As they intensely listen to the play-by-play, Hedley states, "The black man hit hard, you know." The announcer has just told the radio audience that Louis made a combination of a left and a hard right that brought his opponent to one knee. When Louis wins, several of the characters do the Joe Louis Victory Walk, with the radio continuing to speak Louis's praises in the background. The radio has allowed these men to celebrate with Louis in his moment of victory, making it their moment as well.

Radio Repairs is part of Jacob Lawrence's *Builders* series, which was begun in the late 1940s and completed in 1998. In *Radio Repairs*, and in other *Builders* series paintings such as *Cabinet Makers* (1946) and *The Seamstress* (1946), Lawrence focuses on African Americans in acts of contribution to the betterment of life in America. In the post–World War II era, many black men and women were apprenticed in newly (and forcefully) integrated trade unions and received new technology training. *Radio Repairs* documents the labor they generated, in small shops within an urban environment. The painting opens to the viewer a scene inside a repair shop, where two men are tinkering with the electronics, and one man is at the door bringing more to be fixed. Shapes on the walls and tables are those of wires at angles and crossings, coded messages to those in the know. Lawrence's focus on the work on radios marks it as skilled and important; it allows the world to be accessed by everyone.

—Annemarie Bean, Assistant Professor of Theatre and Co-Chair of Performance Studies Program

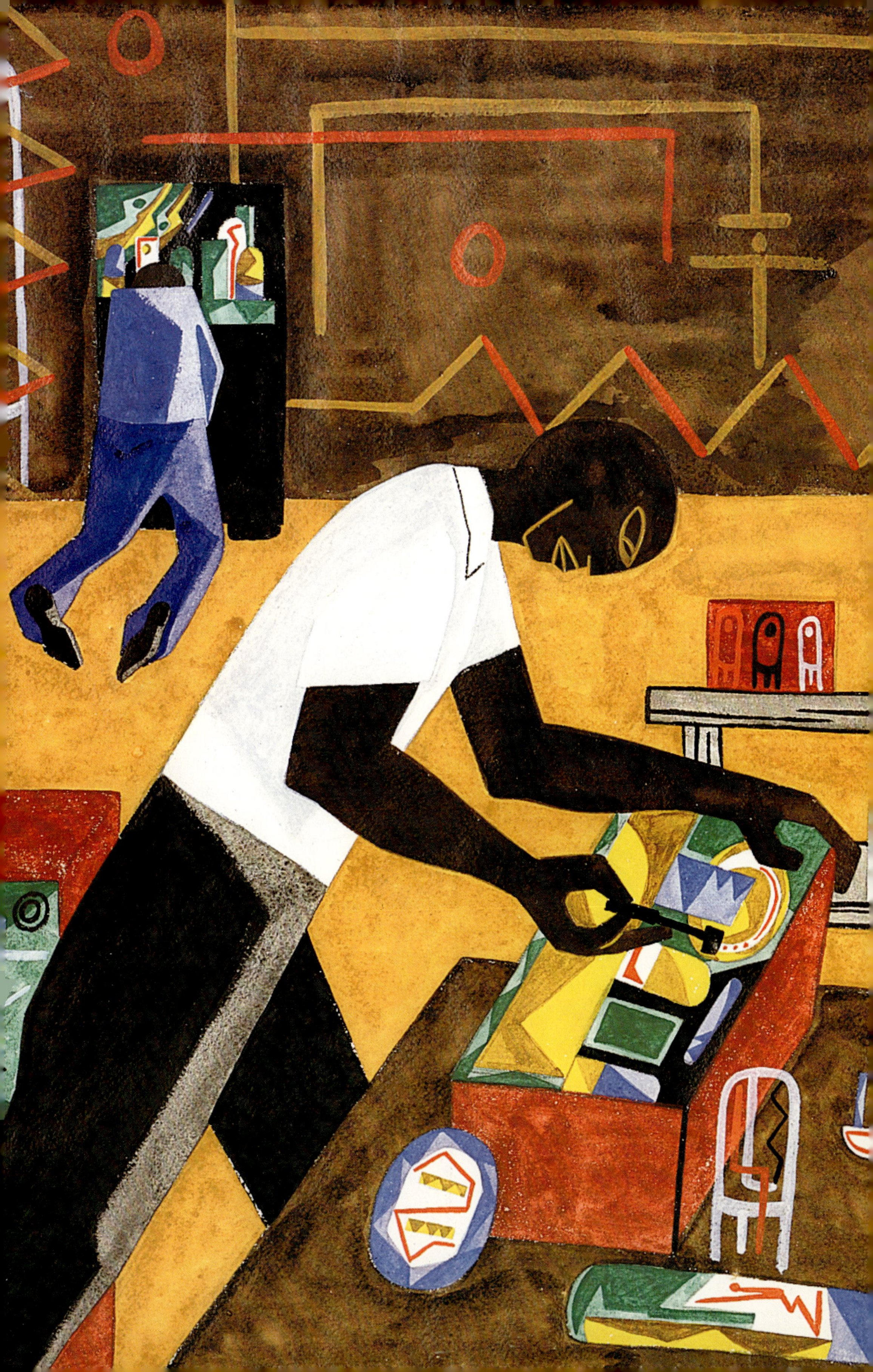

KURT SCHWITTERS
German, 1887–1948

PA-CO
1947

Collage and painting on paper
7 7/16 x 6 1/4 in.
Museum purchase, Joseph O. Eaton Fund (60.6)

Although Kurt Schwitters is typically associated with the Dadaists, his relationship with the Berlin branch of this artistic movement was deeply strained. In Berlin in particular, Dada's emphases on chaos, destruction, and revolution bled beyond artistic boundaries, making it as much a political ideology as an aesthetic one. Schwitters, who worked and lived primarily in Hannover, was regarded by the Berlin Dadaists as unapologetically bourgeois and unfit to join in their revolutionary art-making. For his part, Schwitters was largely disinterested in the political aims of the Berlin Dadaists and instead established his own strain of Dada, which he christened "Merz."

Schwitters's version of Dada was aimed primarily at the integration of art and life. Art had become so estranged from everyday life, he believed, that he needed a new approach to art-making to reunite them. Although his early paintings were typical of German Expressionism, Schwitters's working method shifted around 1918, when he began to experiment with collage. For Schwitters, collage was the ultimate merging of art and life: he would scour the streets of Hannover for everyday detritus—torn envelopes, candy wrappers, crumpled newspapers—and recombine them into works of art. He called these odds and ends "banalities," which would acquire new form, meaning, and life in his collaged and painted objects.

Although Schwitters generally avoided politics, he could not keep them from intruding on his life. In 1937 his work was included in the *Entartete Kunst* (Degenerate Art) exhibition organized by the Nazis, and as the Third Reich began increasingly to target avant-garde artists, Schwitters fled to Norway and finally to England. Despite being devastated by exile and weakened by illness, he continued to produce art during his final years. Shortly before his death in England, Schwitters created *PA-CO*, which partakes of his trademark collage technique. Like most of his collage elements, those in *PA-CO* include text purged of its original meaning, drawing attention to the visual form of the letters. To this he added daubs of paint, which juxtapose a traditional artistic medium with the quotidian, as represented by the work's scavenged elements.

—Elizabeth Athens (Williams M.A. 2005),
The Edith and Herbert Lehman Foundation
Publications Assistant

KAY SAGE
American, 1898–1963

Page 49
1950

Oil on canvas
18 1/8 x 15 1/8 in.
Bequest of Kay Sage Tanguy
(64.23)

Like Yves Tanguy's dreamscapes, Kay Sage's imaginary scenes are carefully rendered in a realistic style yet are distinguished by sharp, architectonic forms to which pieces of torn fabric are often attached. In *Page 49*, the sinuous quality of the drapery contrasts with the angularity of the architectural forms and suggests a human presence. There is a sense that these structures were once occupied, but are now abandoned.

Words such as "mystery" and "melancholy" are often used to describe Sage's paintings. The harsh light and cast shadows (a legacy of Giorgio de Chirico) contribute to these feelings, as does the subdued color scheme. Sage's titles, which often refer to time, place, or a literary theme, further augment the sense of mystery and ambiguity.

Sage discovered Surrealism in Paris in 1937 and within a year came to know members of the group personally and to work closely with them. Forced to return to the United States during the war, in 1940 she arranged a series of one-person exhibitions of Surrealist art in New York. The proceeds were used to assist French artists to flee Europe. Sage was responsible for bringing many artists to America, among them Tanguy, whom she married in 1941, and André Breton, the leader of the Surrealist group.

—Deborah Rothschild, Senior Curator of Modern and Contemporary Art

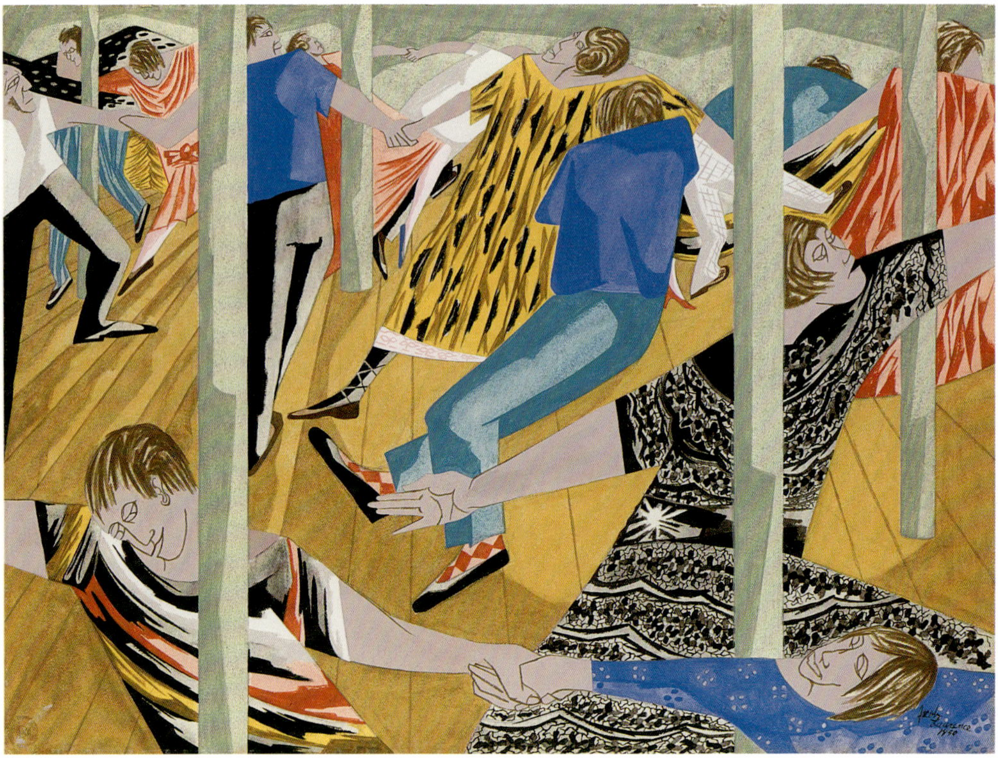

JACOB LAWRENCE
American, 1917–2000

Square Dance
1950

Casein on paper
21 5/8 x 29 5/8 in.
Bequest of Leonard B. Schlosser,
Class of 1946 (91.20)

Square dancing was experiencing a revival in the late 1940s. Developed in the nineteenth century in New England, square dancing was an immigrant amalgamation of French, English, Scottish, Irish, Mexican, and Spanish dance forms by the time it traveled down to the South and across the West. Primarily practiced in rural areas in the nineteenth century, in the twentieth century it was revived by Henry Ford, who believed that modernizing square dancing was a necessary part of his New England restoration project. Promoted primarily in urban centers, square dancing reached "fad" status about 1948. In Ed Gilmore's instructor manual printed in 1949, Gilmore claims that square dancing creates a community of active participants, in its "perfect demonstration of democracy. Here is one golden opportunity for a man or woman to let down their hair, to whoop and holler, let off steam and at the same time to be graceful and poetic through movement and rhythm, the latter being an instructive desire of man since the beginning of his history."

The releasing of an "instructive desire" could have been the reason Jacob Lawrence observed square dancing during his voluntary respites at a psychiatric institution in Queens in 1949 and 1950, the idea being that group dance is therapeutic. Lawrence was suffering from anxiety and depression, brought about by his recent successes and the mounting pressure to go beyond what he had already accomplished in his *Migration* (1940–41), *War* (1945), and *Builders* series (begun ca. 1946–48). According to his friends, Lawrence felt conflicted about being singled out from the group of African-American artists with whom he had worked. Lawrence's successes in the 1940s were monumental and overwhelming: he was the first African-American artist to be exhibited by a downtown New York gallery, and the first to be honored with an entire exhibition by the Museum of Modern Art.

Clearly, the room in which this dance was done was not intended for dancing, as the support poles interrupt the ability to move with pure abandon. The tilt of the bodies, the grasping of the hands almost to the wrists show a moment of high speed, where all the participants must hold on tightly to their fellow dancers or fall down. Yet, there is also an element of trust, because the person who leads you must make the right choice of direction to preserve the dance, satisfy the caller, and let the circle be unbroken. *Square Dance* may have offered Lawrence some assurance that if he were to lead in the art world, others could and would follow.

—Annemarie Bean, Assistant Professor of Theatre and Co-Chair of Performance Studies Program

FRANK LLOYD WRIGHT
American, 1867–1959

Revised Elevation—The Solomon R. Guggenheim Museum
1952

Graphite and colored pencil on white tracing paper
36 x 50 in.
Museum Purchase, John B. Turner '24 Memorial Fund, Vaccariello Fund, and Ruth Sabin Weston Fund
(83.23)

Dear Tom,

The section/elevation drawing by Frank Lloyd Wright for the Guggenheim Museum that you are considering for purchase would make a splendid addition indeed to the collection. I hope you get it. There is no question that Wright is the greatest American architect of this century, and it is arguable that his achievements surpass those of all his predecessors on these shores. In his very long career —roughly 70 years—he had three great bursts of creativity: the first decade of this century, the late 30's, and the period following World War II. Of this last, the Guggenheim is the preeminent building, in terms of international fame and in terms of its extraordinary formal and structural inventiveness, which foreshadowed works by other architects of a decade or more later. It also happens to be his only public building easily accessible to Williams students. They can study the drawing, which comes from one of the earlier phases of the design process and shows how Wright wanted the building to be. Then they can go to New York and see how the work turned out, after Solomon Guggenheim died and the New York building codes took their toll. To me, the unfinished nature of the drawing makes it more interesting for teaching purposes. One sees the artist at work and learns about the problems of architectural design that way. Moreover, there is a liveliness and immediacy in the sketches of the ramps that one rarely if ever finds in a finished Wright presentation drawing. The size of the piece, of course, gives it great presence.

Sincerely,

E. J. Johnson
Professor of Art

—Letter to Thomas Krens, Director of the Williams College Museum of Art, September 27, 1983

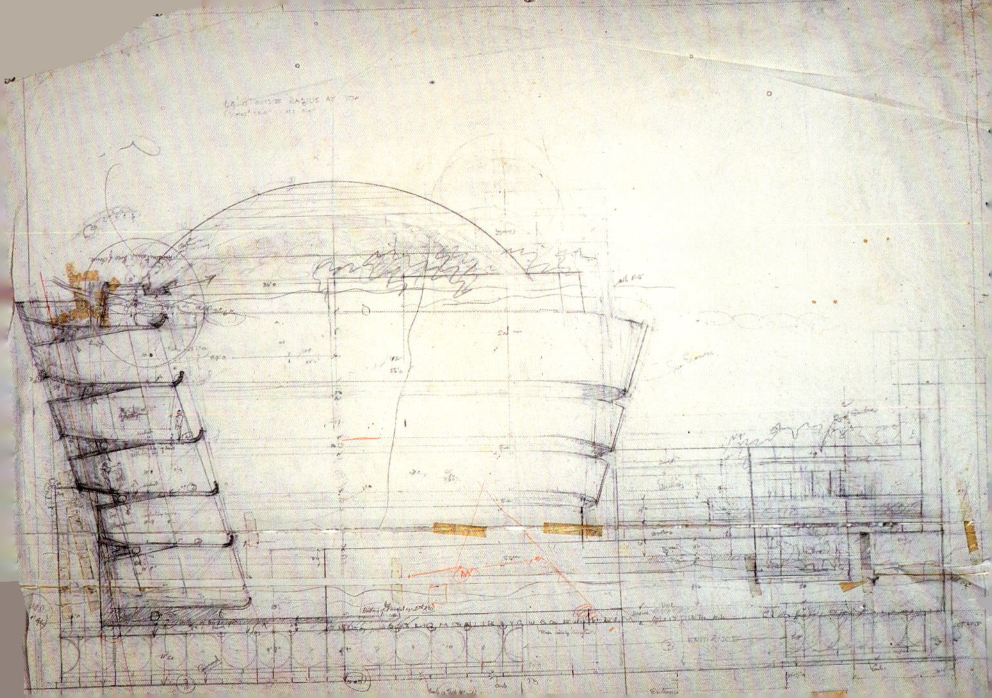
ENTRANCE

湖山清曉

甲午春日
賓虹年九十又一

HUANG BINHONG
(Huang Pin-Hung)
Chinese, 1864–1955

Clear Dawn on Lake and Mountains
1954

Ink and color on paper
15 1/4 x 31 1/2 in.
Gift of Tao Ho, Class of 1960
(M.2002.17.11)

Critics regard Huang Binhong as one of the two most important painters in twentieth-century China. Unlike his contemporary, the more popular Qi Baishi (Ch'i Pai-shih), Huang Binhong has been little studied and his artistic accomplishments little understood.

Huang Binhong lived through the major political and cultural crises of modern China and witnessed both the breakup of the old order and the clamor for a new society. Advocating a new art as part of the new order, many Chinese artists and intellectuals of the period espoused either a wholesale adoption of Western "realism" in Chinese art or an eclectic approach that borrowed from both Chinese and Western traditions. In contrast to this kind of innovation, Huang Binhong neither imitated nor borrowed from the West. Through his synthesis of the theories, techniques, and styles of the traditional painting of the Chinese literati, he was able to achieve innovation within tradition. His work therefore can be viewed as an attempt to reconcile the tension between China's simultaneous wish to modernize and desire to retain a traditional cultural identity.

Like other literati painters before him, Huang Binhong studied the work of the ancient masters and traveled widely in China to sketch different kinds of scenery. From his writings, however, it is clear that he developed his own theories of painting. According to Huang Binhong, there are three kinds of works: first, "those which completely resemble actual objects; they are mere gimmicks on which empty reputations are built"; second, "those which are completely devoid of any resemblance to actual objects; these, while pretentiously claiming to be the free improvisations of inspired minds, are actually fish eyes masquerading as pearls, and also belong to the gimmick category"; and third, "those which achieve both complete resemblance and complete non-resemblance; they alone are true paintings."

Stylistically, the paintings of Huang Binhong can be divided into four periods. In the last period, his style underwent a metamorphosis, and it was during this period that Huang Binhong achieved what he himself would ave called "true paintings."

son C. Kuo, Professor of Art History, University of Maryland. Adapted from
ation within Tradition: The Painting of Huang Pin-Hung, 1989

ANDY WARHOL
American, 1928–1987

25 Cats Name Sam and One Blue Pussy
New York, 1954

Bound artists' book with 36 pages and 18 plates (including cover), litho offset and hand-coloring
Written by Charles Lisanby and printed by Seymour Berlin
9 1/4 x 6 1/4 in.
Gift of Richard F. Holmes, Class of 1946 (95.18.4)

The drawings included in *25 Cats Name Sam*—one of Warhol's promotional books from his years as a commercial artist—reveal the telltale blotted line that would come to represent his early graphic work. Warhol used such a line to give his drawings a "printed" feel, many of which, like those in *25 Cats Name Sam*, were eventually serially reproduced via offset lithography. Each of the twenty-five sketches is accompanied by the name "Sam," written, not in the artist's hand, but in the distinctive, whimsical script of Warhol's mother. Originally from Slovakia, Warhol's mother, Julia, knew little English, so the artist would give her the text he wanted written and she would painstakingly copy it, occasionally dropping letters or making misspellings. "Name" in the book's title is an instance of this kind of accidental elision.

In addition to providing the handwriting for many of Warhol's works, Julia (along with many of the artist's friends) also helped color his line drawings with diluted dye, creating their signature patches of bold color. Warhol was deeply dependent on his mother throughout his life and lived with her and a brood of Siamese cats—which undoubtedly inspired the book *25 Cats Name Sam*—during his early years in New York City. Indeed, their lives were so closely entwined that Julia would occasionally assert that *she* was Andy Warhol.

—Elizabeth Athens (Williams M.A. 2005), The Edith and Herbert Lehman Foundation Publications Assistant

Mellon

THE WILLIAMS COLLEGE MUSEUM OF ART is a vital teaching resource whose collections, exhibitions, and programs are regularly incorporated into courses across the college curriculum. While the museum has a long history of working closely with the Art Department, in the early 1990s the scope of outreach was broadened to include non-art faculty as well. With the generous support of the Mellon Foundation, the museum now regularly works with numerous faculty from a range of departments including American Studies, Anthropology, Art, Chemistry, English, History, Music, Philosophy, Political Science, Religion, Romance Languages, Russian, and Theatre. Each year nearly 50 professors incorporate the museum's resources into their courses, roughly 1,250 college students visit the galleries with their classes, and an additional 2,500 students visit the Rose Study Gallery to study works of art not on display in the museum. In addition to this daily activity, Williams College faculty act as guest curators, recommend exhibition topics and art objects for acquisition, participate in and help develop exhibition-related programming, and contribute their expertise to the Labeltalk exhibition series, among other projects, making the museum not just a lively teaching resource but an important campus site for interdisciplinary collaboration as well.

Helen Frankenthaler
American, b. 1928
Savage Breeze, 1974
Woodcut on Nepalese handmade paper
31 1/2 x 27 in.
Gift of William H. McCulloch and Frank H. McCulloch, Class of 1968, in honor of Edith L. and Frank W. McCulloch, Class of 1926 (97.7)

ROBERT LOUIS FRANK
American, b. 1924

New Mexico
1955

Gelatin silver print
Image: 7 3/4 x 11 5/8 in.
Museum purchase, Karl E. Weston Memorial Fund (91.33.2)

A congregation of gas pumps attends the message, SAVE, and in the background there is only the never ending emptiness of the prairie. This is a quintessential image in Robert Frank's effort to picture America, here a land of traveling consumers and evangelical religion. Since its inception, the country has associated fiscal frugality with spiritual redemption, and Frank captures both the history and irony of this fact with incisive clarity.

The Swiss-born Frank came to New York in 1947 and made films as well as photographs. He was closely associated, and collaborated, with many of the Beats. His best-known work, the book *The Americans*, included images he made on a two-year Guggenheim grant in 1955–56. First published in France in 1958, when the book appeared in an American edition, in 1959, it included an introduction by Jack Kerouac in which he characterized Frank's images as capturing "that crazy feeling in America when the sun is hot on the streets and music comes out of the jukebox or from a nearby funeral. . . . "

—John Stomberg, Associate Director. Copyright Robert Frank, from "The Americans," courtesy Pace/MacGill Gallery, New York

DAVID SMITH
American, 1906–1965

Untitled
1956

Painted welded steel
25 3/8 x 27 15/16 x 9 13/16 in.
Gift of Susan W. and Stephen D. Paine, Class of 1954 (67.10)

Originally from Decatur, Indiana, David Smith moved at the age of twenty to New York City, where he began his study of art at the Art Students League. At first interested in painting, Smith studied with the Cubist painter Jan Matulka, making paintings with relief elements and some three-dimensional objects. Later, however, after seeing Pablo Picasso's metal sculptures, he switched to sculpture almost exclusively. Intrigued by Picasso's use of material, and already versed in welding techniques from working at a car factory, Smith swapped his paintbrushes for industrial metals, creating both large- and small-scale sculptures out of iron and steel.

Smith's sculptures, which range from the entirely abstract toward the representational, integrate a variety of geometricized forms that are alternately patinated or painted as a means of playing variations of color and texture against one another. As seen in this wholly abstract sculpture of 1956, the smooth swirls of black, maroon, gold, and vermilion paint serve as counterpoint to the jazzy glint of copper of the sculpture's circular component, most likely a found pipe-fitting the artist incorporated into the work. A contrast not only in color but also in shape, this round central piece serves as the locus from which the rectilinear elements radiate.

This untitled sculpture was one of three objects by David Smith in WCMA's collection before 2004, when alumnus Robert B. Meyersburg (Williams 1937) presented the museum with four drawings and one painting by the artist (illustrated on the following pages), dating from the last years of Smith's career.

—Elizabeth Athens (Williams M.A. 2005), The Edith and Herbert Lehman Foundation Publications Assistant

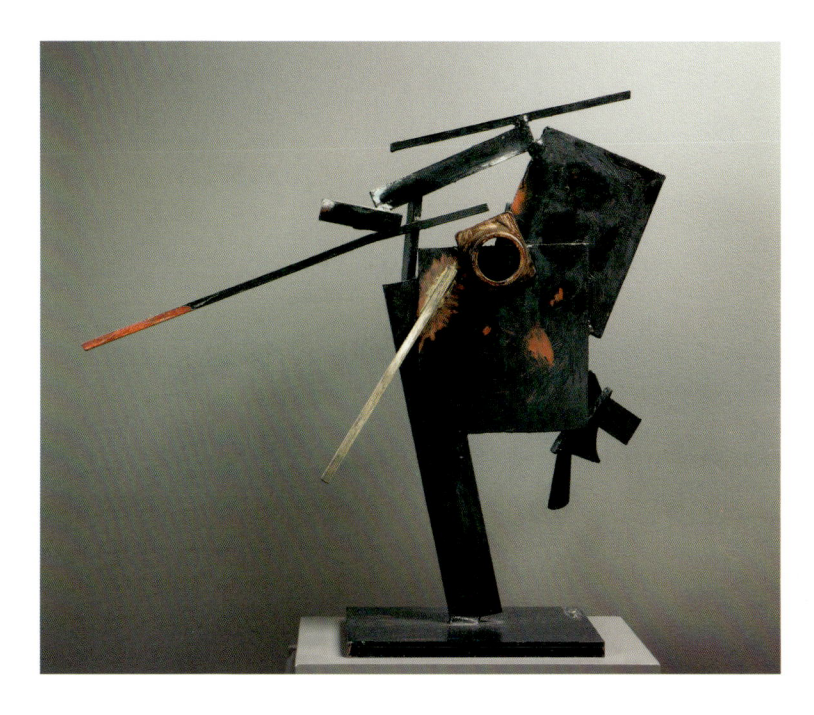

David Smith
American, 1906–1965

Antiwar Series
ca. 1940–41
Oil on panel
4 x 3 in.
Gift of Robert B. Meyersburg,
Class of 1937 (M.2004.17.5)

Untitled
ca. 1960
Spray paint on paper
9 ½ x 7 in.
Gift of Robert B. Meyersburg,
Class of 1937 (M.2004.17.1)

Untitled
1963
Spray paint on paper
10 x 8 in.
Gift of Robert B. Meyersburg,
Class of 1937 (M.2004.17.2)

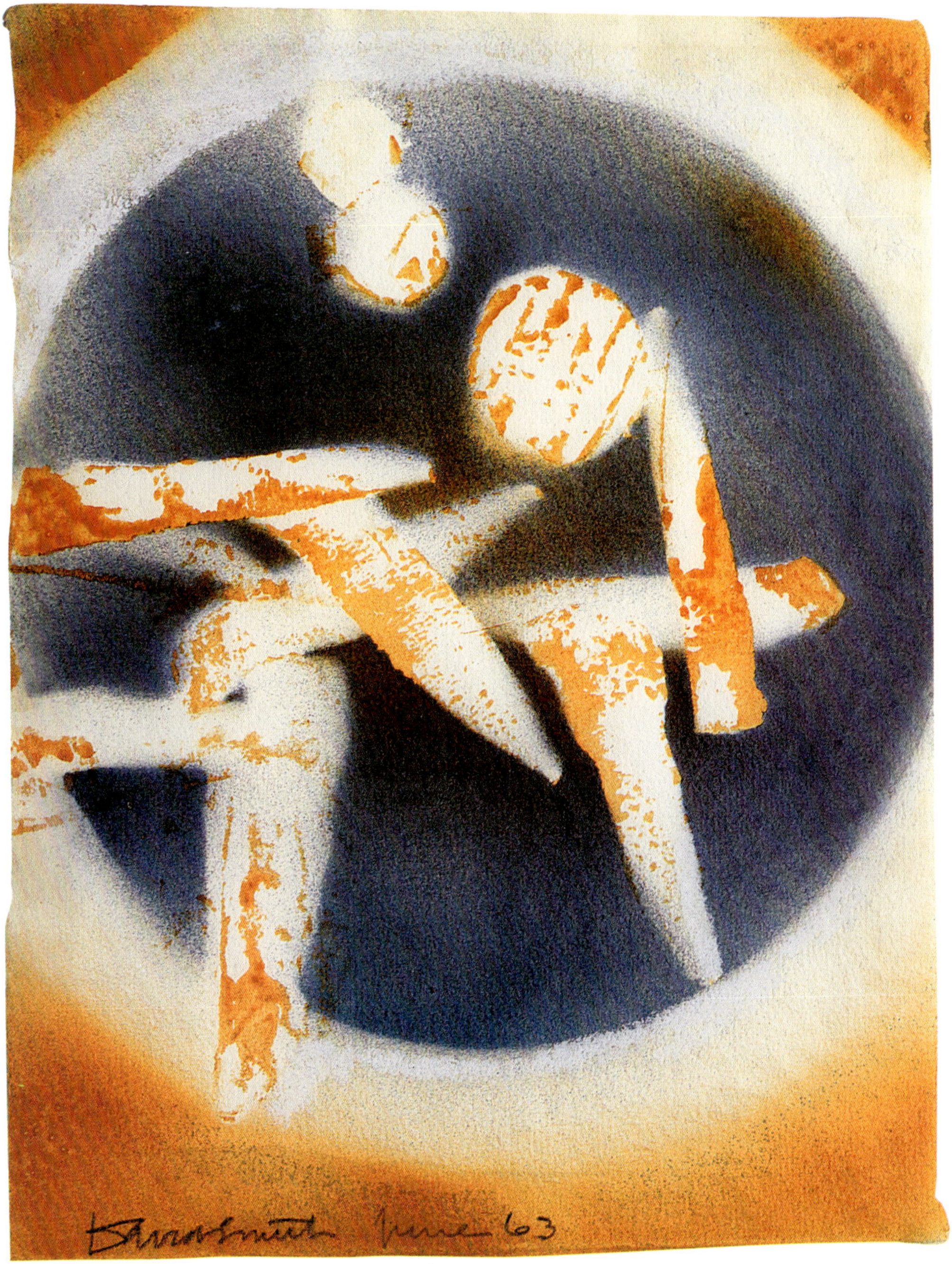
David Smith June 63

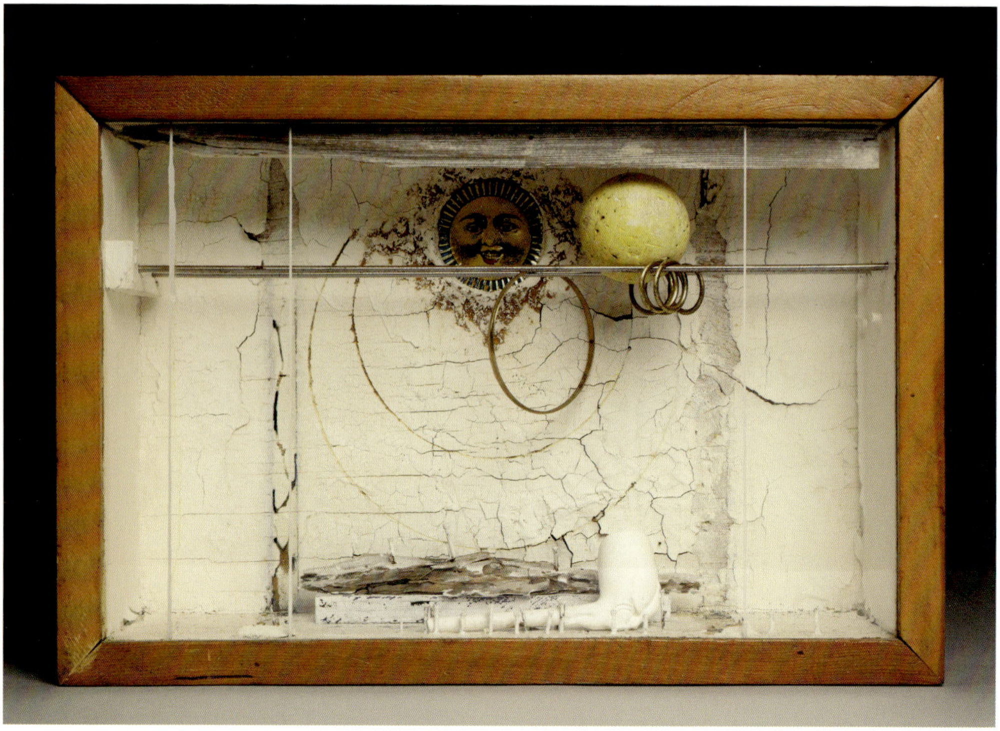

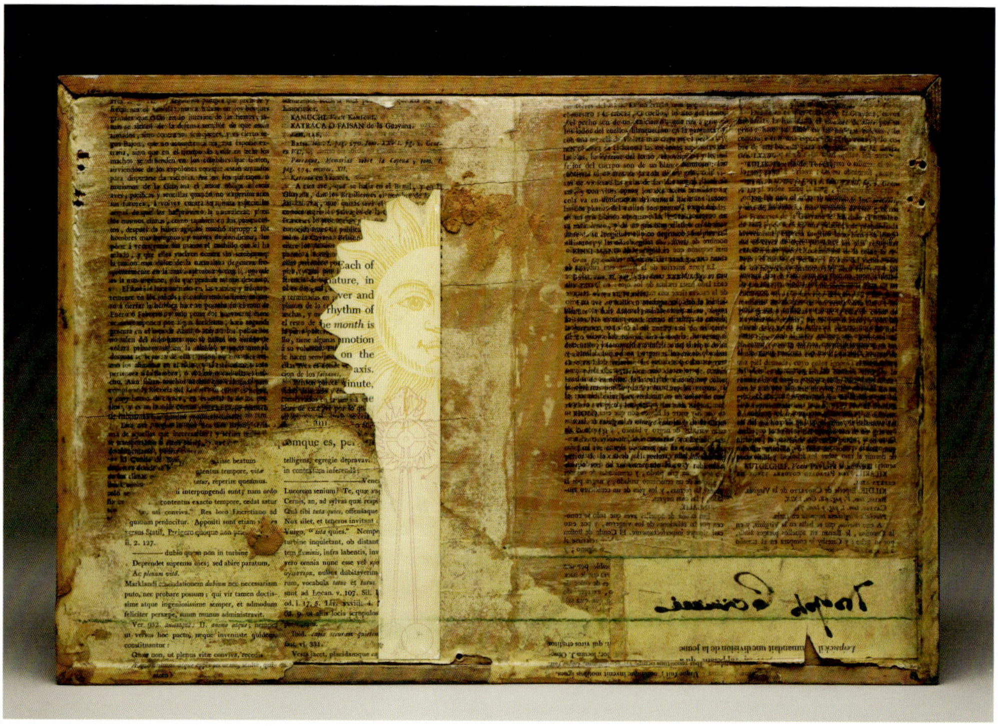

JOSEPH CORNELL
American, 1903–1972

Sun Box
ca. 1956

Wood, glass, metal, and paper
10 7/16 x 15 3/8 x 4 in.
Gift of Mrs. John A. Benton
(73.19)

The painted and papered boxes in which Joseph Cornell arranged his curious collections imbue the items they contain with a sense of preciousness. Carefully positioned, these quotidian objects acquire an air of mystery that leads us to ask: Why this pipe, or these rings, or this yellow ball? Bursting with unexplained meaning, Cornell's boxes mimic mazes in which myriad paths may be traced and retraced.

Throughout his life, Cornell worked primarily in a thematic fashion—he completed series of homages to famous actresses and dancers, aviary boxes, and celestial scenes. Although belonging to this last thematic grouping, *Sun Box* is somewhat atypical. While most of Cornell's celestial imagery centers on dark night skies, *Sun Box* unequivocally refers to the day. Rich golden hues, provided by the wood of the box and the aged newsprint that papers the back, give this work a warmer tone. Whereas the clusters of stars sprinkled in Cornell's other works suggest travel guided scattershot by the skies, the sun in *Sun Box* seems to refer to something more central and permanent than the wandering implied by the night scenes.

WCMA has thirteen Cornell objects in its collection, eleven of which were given by the artist's sister, Mrs. John A. (Betty) Benton.

—Elizabeth Athens (Williams M.A. 2005), The Edith and Herbert Lehman Foundation Publications Assistant

ANDY WARHOL
American, 1928–1987

SUZIE FRANKFURT
American, 1931–2005

Wild Raspberries
New York, 1959

Bound artists' book with 40 pages and 18 plates, litho offset and hand-coloring with tissue overlays
17 1/2 x 11 1/4 in.
Gift of Richard F. Holmes, Class of 1946 (95.18.8)

Like all good social art, *Wild Raspberries* is more than just a series of vivid images, and like all good cookbooks, it offers more than just recipes. This oversize book is impossible to understand apart from the culture that gave rise to it, the world of New York high society in the 1950s. A collaboration among Warhol, interior designer Suzie Frankfurt, and Warhol's mother, Julia, *Wild Raspberries* parodies the lifestyles of the rich and famous by means of outré recipes. "Continental dining" was all the rage in the 1950s, and any sophisticate worth her mink was expected to be conversant with European, especially French, food. Cookbooks of the era were often pretentious, and *Wild Raspberries* spoofs the genre in its call for such rarefied ingredients as plover's egg and cock's kidneys. At the same time, the book mocks the authors' own pretensions, especially Warhol's penchant for celebrity. Sprinkled throughout the text are references to Cecil Beaton, Princess Grace, Dorothy Killgallen, and Greta Garbo. The recipes themselves provide an A list of purveyors of foods to the social elite: for "piglet," Warhol and Frankfurt recommend sending the chauffeur in his Cadillac to pick up a forty-pound suckling pig at Trader Vic's.

Warhol illustrated Frankfurt's recipes, then invited some neighbor boys to hand-color the illustrations. The wonderfully ornate calligraphy was done by his mother, whose limited command of English led to frequent mistakes in spelling and grammar. Warhol and Frankfurt hoped to sell all thirty-four copies they produced but ended up giving most of them away as Christmas presents.

Wild Raspberries reflects Warhol's keen sense of his times. For its pure embodiment of the intersection of food and culture the book is perfect for my course in culinary history. *Wild Raspberries* reveals America's erstwhile love affair with the Continent and our attendant anxiety. It is at the same time a delightful work of graphic art, full of tongue-in-cheek humor.

—Darra Goldstein, Professor of Russian

Piglet

Contact Trader Vic's and order a 140 pound suckling pig to serve 15. Have Hanky take the Carey Cadillac to the side entrance and receive the pig at exactly 6:45. Rush home immediately and place on the open spit for 50 minutes. Remove and garnish with fresh crabapples.

Modern & Contemporary

Andy Warhol
American, 1928–1987
A Gold Book
(New York, 1957)
Designed by Miss Georgie Duffie, 1956
Bound artists' book in first-issue gold boards with 40 pages and 19 plates, litho offset and hand-coloring throughout
14 ½ x 11 ½ in.
Gift of Richard F. Holmes, Class of 1946 (95.18.7)

Laylah Ali
American, b. 1968
Untitled, 2004
Gouache on paper
19 ⅜ x 27 ¾ in.
Museum purchase, Kathryn Hurd Fund, in honor of Linda Shearer, Director 1989–2004
(M.2005.1)

IN EVERYDAY PARLANCE, the words "modern" and "contemporary" seem virtually synonymous, both referring to something that occurs in the present or has taken place in the very recent past. When applied to art, however, these terms take on separate identities: for WCMA's collection. "Modern art" typically refers to work made between the 1890s through the 1970s, whereas "contemporary art" indicates something more recent, from the 1980s, at the earliest, to the present.

Because these terms are never precisely defined—in particular, because the temporal boundaries that demarcate contemporary art shift with the passage of time—the two categories of modern and contemporary art are often considered together as a single specialization in a museum's permanent collection. So it is at WCMA, whose holdings of art of the most recent decades form one of the most developed areas of the museum's collection. This is, in part, owing to the personal interest of the institution's directors and curators, and to gifts of alumni and friends. Most noticeably, the museum's collections were transformed in 1977 through the extraordinary bequest of more than one hundred twentieth-century American artworks owned by Lawrence H. Bloedel (Williams 1923), who had assembled this group of objects with the advice of WCMA director S. Lane Faison, Jr. In 1982 a purchase fund was established by the Estate of Kathryn Hurd for the collection of artworks by living American artists, allowing the museum to continue to expand its modern and contemporary collection with such major purchases as Robert Morris's *Hearing*, Nancy Spero's *Codex Artaud XXV*, and Tony Oursler's *Keep Going*. The intensity and focus that WCMA's staff and donors have directed toward the collection of art of the recent decades have made its holdings of modern and contemporary art stand out among college museum collections.

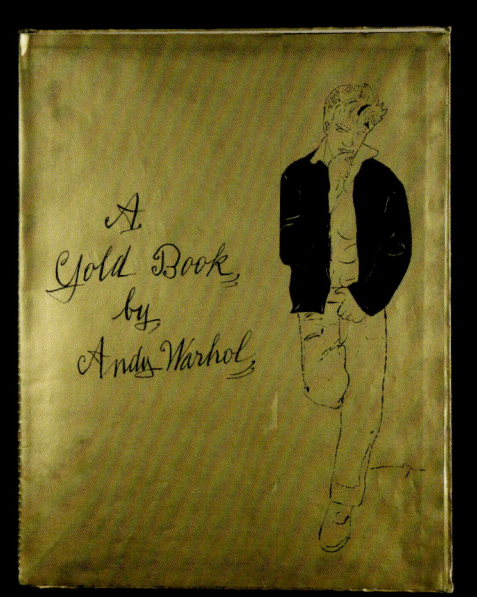

WCMA has continued the legacy established by these earlier bequests by inviting contemporary artists to the museum and providing facilities in which they can work. In effect, the museum has served as a laboratory in which artists can experiment and develop art in nontraditional media.

A number of works created under these circumstances have come into the collection, including Faith Ringgold's quilt *100 Years at Williams College, 1889–1989* and Carrie Mae Weems's *The Hampton Project*, a multimedia installation of hanging scrims, historical photographs, and audio recordings. WCMA's ongoing commitment to modern and contemporary art fosters the development of cutting-edge artwork and at the same time provides a venue for its exhibition and interpretation.

LARRY RIVERS
American, 1925–2002

Amel-Camel
1962

Carbonate, collage, and oil on canvas
39 3/8 x 39 9/16 in.
Gift of Mrs. Lawrence H. Bloedel
(83.4.4)

Camels, palm trees, sand, pyramids: what seems to be an advertisement for Egyptian tourism is actually a takeoff of the design for a package of Camel cigarettes. Larry Rivers was enamored by this imagery and produced an extensive series of paintings and drawings, at least fourteen, that feature the Camel cigarette package. Typical of the Pop art movement, *Amel-Camel* is based on a recognizable subject yet reworked to be more playful and imaginative than the commercialized original. Rivers included the left-facing camel that appears on the cigarette pack and added a second camel, striding toward the right. The large pyramid and palm trees are only sketchily rendered. He co-opts the "Camel" font but leaves off the "C" and includes only the ampersand from the phrase "Turkish & Domestic Blend Cigarettes" that appears at the bottom of the packaging. The design and layout of the cigarette pack were so well known that Rivers left it up to the viewer to complete the image. Indeed, the Camel design has remained essentially unchanged since RJ Reynolds introduced the brand in 1913. The company attempted to update the design in 1958 but met strong resistance from loyal Camel smokers. Rivers may be playfully alluding to this misguided revamping attempt through his alteration of the image.

Two years after this work was made, Surgeon General Luther L. Terry released the Surgeon General's Report on Smoking and Health, the first official recognition that smoking causes cancer and other serious diseases.

This painting was one of four works by Larry Rivers in Lawrence Bloedel's collection. Not part of the original 1977 Bloedel bequest of artwork, *Amel-Camel* came to WCMA in 1983 as a bequest from his widow.

—Dana Pilson, The Edith and Herbert Lehman Foundation Publications Assistant

EDWARD KIENHOLZ
American, 1927–1994

Bunny, Bunny, You're So Funny
1962

Mixed media
31 1/2 x 12 5/8 x 33 1/16 in.
Gift of Susan W. and Stephen D. Paine, Class of 1954 (85.44)

Bunny Bunny
You're so funny
You're so rainy
When it's sunny
Upside down and
Gender Bent
Iron twisted
Grim Intent
Oh my girl
stand on your legs
Frozen form
don't make me beg
You've come undone
You're two not one
Your darker half
now moons the sun
Bunny Bunny
You're my honey
so broke down split
so eggyolkrunny
You're a joke, dear
it's not funny
Upside down
you've lost your head
now your body's covered/read
Once upon a time you were so
young and strong
and real: secure
Now, my girl you're statuesque
Your body does an arabesque
you have no head
you have no eyes
after the fall
there's no disguise
a woman made
art into trade
constructed scraps
our nowhere maps
bunny bunny you're so funny
Hey, don't worry 'bout it honey
oh my heart is broke in two
when my eyes fall upon you.

for Marilyn Monroe who died in 1962, the year that this statue was made and Marilyn came undone.

—S. Paige Baty, Assistant Professor of Political Science (1990–94). Published in *Labeltalk*, 1995

Edward Kienholz was to Pop art's examination of popular culture what Joseph Cornell was to the assemblage spirit of modernism. Each artist was intrigued by societal refuse, yet Cornell's romanticism of his objects' histories became Kienholz's realism. Kienholz made little effort to distance the used, discarded, and sometimes brutal pasts from his finished objects.

This dismembered mannequin, with its pubic shield of steel wool, metal garters, and steel net stockings, represents a stylized pulp icon of a masculine fantasy. The artist offers the viewer a former Woolworth's window odalisque in repose. This unromantic sculptural use of the female figure becomes a less ambiguous play on Dell Comics' Superwoman: aerial in its gravity-free orientation yet made immobile by its lack of limbs, the absent head offers no argument. This American portrait is an unflattering social commentary.

—Edward A. Epping, Alexander Falck Class of 1899 Professor of Art. Adapted from *Labeltalk*, 1995

ROMARE HOWARD BEARDEN
American, 1914–1988

Prevalence of Ritual: Baptism
1964

Photograph on masonite

37 x 48 in.

Museum purchase (69.14)

*Wade in the water
Wade in the water, children,
Wade in the water
God's a-going to trouble
 the water*

*If you don't believe I've
 been redeemed
God's a-going to trouble
 the water
Just follow me down to the
 Jordan's stream
God's a-going to trouble
 the water*

Traditional spiritual

African masks, flowing water, a faraway church, hovering trees, hands, teeth, and hair collectively form a dizzying and energetic baptismal scene. The faithful line the shore of the river: members of the church, respected ministers and deacons, and anxious new initiates, anticipating their immersion. The congregation applauds and sings. Universal themes of freedom and renewal echo throughout, while the African water spirit mask reminds us that several traditional African religions also submerge members in water to cleanse the body and the soul. Bearden stated that he wanted to "paint the life of my people as I know it—passionately and dispassionately as Breughel painted the life of the Flemish people of his day."

In 1964 Bearden created a series of four collages of papers, foil, inks, paint, and graphite. All shared the title *Prevalence of Ritual*, and each had an individual subtitle: *Conjur Woman*, *Woman as Angel*, *Tidings*, and *Baptism*. Bearden photographed the collages and affixed the enlarged black-and-white images to Masonite. The starkness and size conveyed great power. The original *Baptism* collage is in the collection of the Hirshhorn Museum and Sculpture Garden in Washington, D.C., and WCMA owns a color photo lithograph/silkscreen of *Tidings* (79.74.5).

—Dana Pilson, The Edith and Herbert Lehman Foundation Publications Assistant

146, 147

ANDY WARHOL
American, 1928–1987

Jackie
1964

Synthetic polymer paint and silkscreen ink on canvas
blue: 20 x 16 in., gold: 20 x 17 in., white: 20 x 16 in., white: 20 x 16 in.
Partial gift of The Andy Warhol Foundation for the Visual Arts, Inc. and museum purchase from the John R. Turner '24 Memorial Fund and Karl E. Weston Memorial Fund
(95.11.1–2, 94.15.1–2)

These four *Jackies* were part of an exhibition organized by Assistant Professor of Art C. Ondine Chavoya, to accompany his course on Pop art. This entry was part of a group of wall texts written by students to accompany the exhibition.

Andy Warhol's investigation of Jacqueline Kennedy began in 1964, one year after the death of her husband, President John F. Kennedy. Jackie was a celebrity in her own right, ubiquitous in the media and beloved by the public. In *Jackie*, Warhol examines the relationship between public and private life, manipulating famous source images of the First Lady before and after the historic tragedy. This photographic juxtaposition of Jackie smiling and weeping highlights the public nature of this iconic figure's private struggle. America openly mourned while Jackie maintained dignity and composure through the postassassination period.

The source photographs are so famous that they are easily recognized even when the barest traces of the original images remain. Images of Jackie at the assassination, funeral, and Vice-President Lyndon Johnson's swearing-in were shown with such repetition in print and on television that the line between Jackie's mourning and the public's mourning became blurred. Thus, Warhol displays the public image of private grief, already omnipresent in the media, and the multiplication of Jackie's portraits mimics the media's repetitive use of such images.

—Meredith Sanger-Katz (Williams 2006)

ROBERT MOTHERWELL
American, 1915–1991

Open No. 1975
ca. 1970

Acrylic on canvas
72 x 36 in.
Gift of Sylvia and Joseph Slifka (M.2004.4.5)

It is perfectly possible in my work to see, say, windows, or to see a wave breaking in the sea, or to see a teddy bear, if you want, or the sky; but that's not the "real" subject matter. The real subject matter is an assumption that what painting is is the pressure of the brush with a colored liquid on a flat surface, that it involves placing what degree of spatial regression one wants; how much one wants to contract and shove in, or open up and expand, whether one wants to radiate a tender kind of feeling, or make an aggressive gesture, or whatever.

—Robert Motherwell, *On the Humanism of Abstraction*, February 6, 1970
© 2005 Dedalus Foundation, Inc.

Throughout his career, Motherwell worked in series. He commenced the *Open* series in 1967, exploring both the traditional notion of painting as a window onto the world as well as the influence of Spanish architecture with its deeply cut dark doorways and windows. The *Open* works are often sparse and uncomplicated, usually with crisply defined rectangular shapes. *Open No. 1975* seems a departure from the bare, geometric works of the series; a blue rectangle is instead almost entirely obscured by thick, black calligraphic lines that seem to create silhouetted limbs and wispy creatures. The saturated color and vertical orientation recall the color field paintings of Motherwell's friend Mark Rothko, who committed suicide in 1970. Perhaps the real subject here is a "tender kind of feeling" reflecting on friendship and loss.

A bequest from the estate of the New York collector Sylvia Slifka, this is the first painting by Motherwell to enter WCMA's collection. The museum also owns seven prints, one drawing, and one collage by the artist.

—Dana Pilson, The Edith and Herbert Lehman Foundation Publications Assistant

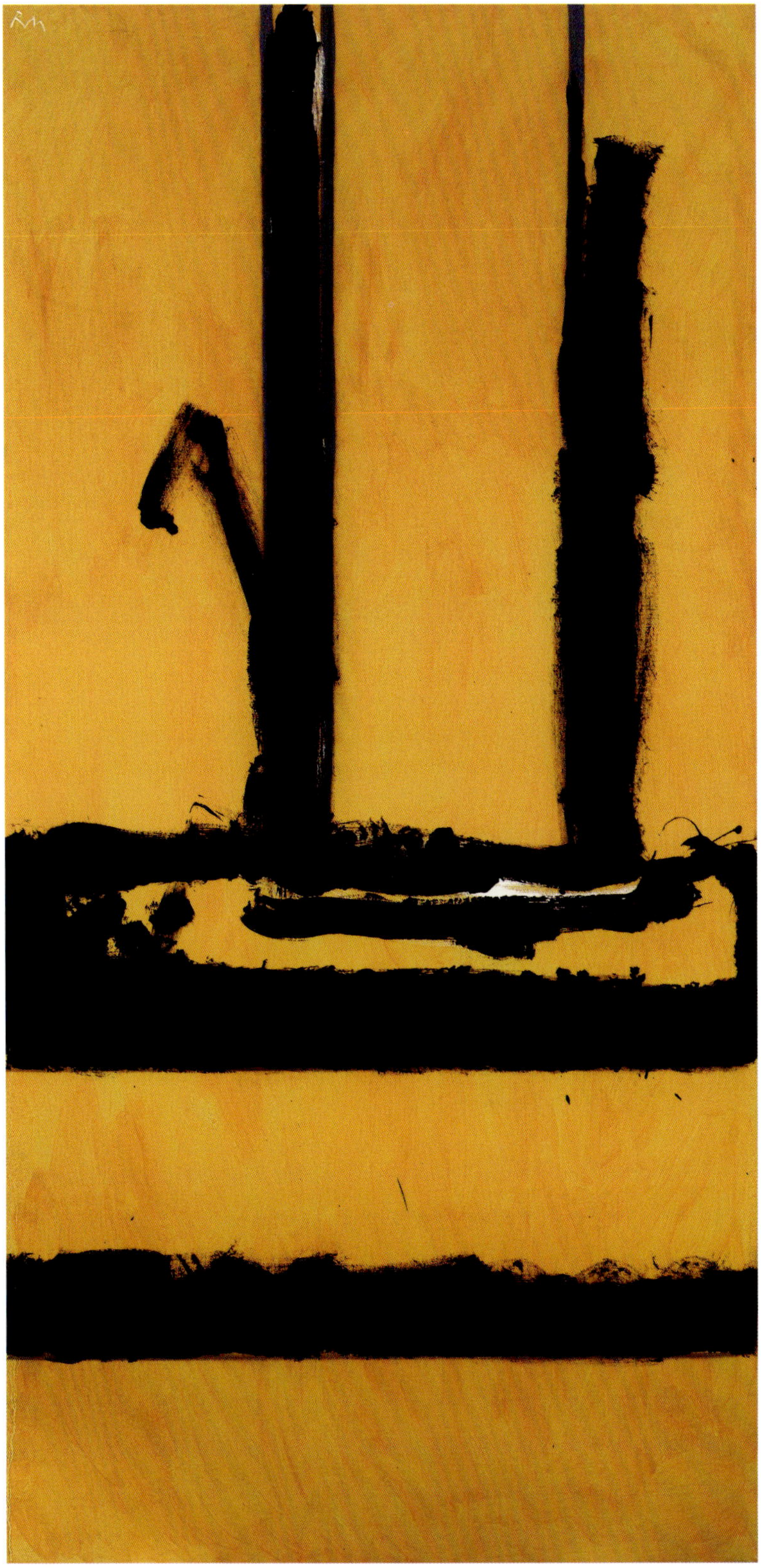

NANCY SPERO
American, b. 1926

Codex Artaud XXV
1971–72

Ink, paint, and collage on paper
24 x 192 in.
Museum purchase, Kathryn Hurd Fund (97.4)

Codex Artaud XXV is one of a series of thirty-three scroll drawings created by Nancy Spero between 1971 and 1972. Each scroll is composed of sheets of rice paper glued end to end, onto which the artist drew and collaged fantastical figures, juxtaposing them with text by the French poet Antonin Artaud (1896–1948). Best known for his *Theater of Cruelty*, Artaud wrote of pain and anger and an anxiety of abandonment, but also of a tenacious will to create. As a woman artist trained in a figurative tradition during the hyper-male art world obsessed with abstraction and Minimalism of the 1960s, Spero identified with the marginalized Artaud on both a professional and a personal level.

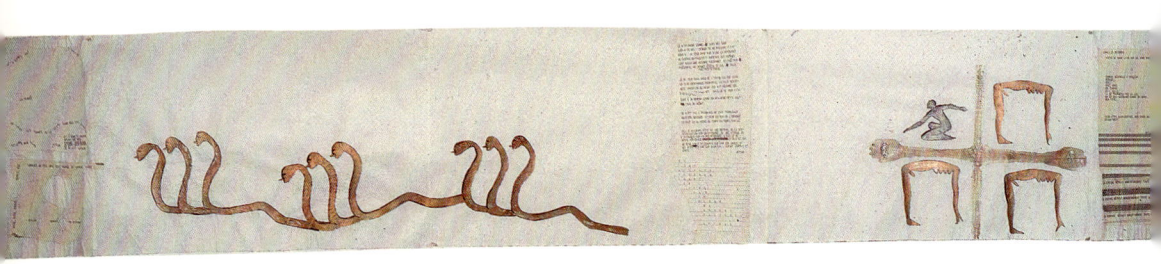

Measuring sixteen feet in length, the composition of *Codex Artaud XXV* consists of three distinct blocks of text in Artaud's original French. Spanning the scroll are drawings of bizarre hybrid beasts, such as interconnected three-headed snakes, their tongues protruding from human faces, and mutated hermaphroditic figures. These beings relate to Artaud's text, which discusses sexual ambiguity and lingual castration, both metaphoric and literal.

Spero's *Codex Artaud* series, with its angry tone and graphic depictions, garnered much-deserved critical attention. Artaud's writing served as both an inspiration and a foil, through which the artist expressed her frustration with the social, political, and artistic position of women. The *Codex* marks an important turning point in Spero's prolific career and provided an example for women artists of future generations to follow.

—Lisa B. Dorin (Williams M.A. 2000), Assistant Curator of Contemporary Art, The Art Institute of Chicago

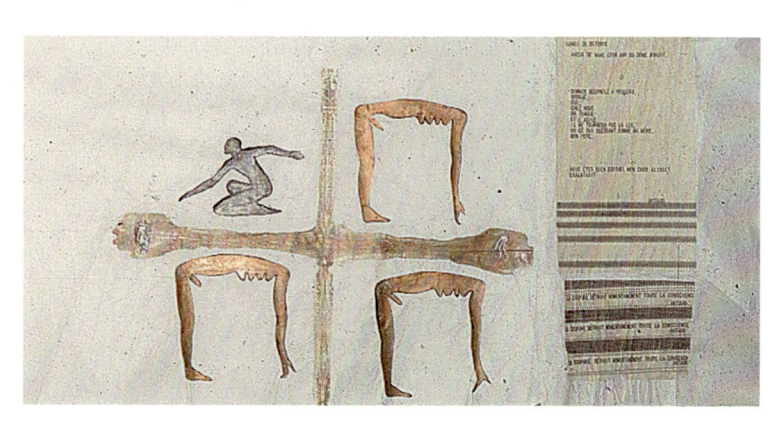

ROBERT MORRIS
American, b. 1931

Hearing
1972

Mixed media
Three-and-one-half-hour stereo tape, stereo tape recorder, amplifier, two speakers; copper chair with water and immersion heater, 48 x 24 x 30 in., zinc table, 36 x 78 x 36 in., lead-covered bed, 24 x 72 x 10 in., and wet-cell batteries buried in sand in a bronze trough; on wood platform 6 in. high, 12 ft. square, with 24 in. square sections cut from each corner.
Museum purchase, Kathryn Hurd Fund and Karl E. Weston Memorial Fund (86.5)

Robert Morris's work spans an eclectic mix of media: he is well known for his influential critical essays; for his work as a choreographer; and, equally important, for his Minimalist sculptures. An outgrowth of his involvement in dance, Morris's sculptures were originally intended as stage props but later were designed and exhibited as art objects in their own right.

In a sense, choreography—dictating people's movements—underpins Morris's sculptural installation *Hearing*. The work consists of three stylized pieces of furniture: a lead bed, a copper chair, and an aluminum table, which are placed on a brass base filled with dirt. A trench in the base connects the bed and table and is filled with transparent batteries. Facing this display sit rows of chairs as well as two speakers, which issue forth a three-and-a-half-hour mock courtroom inquisition. The dialogue is intended to keep visitors spellbound and seated until its abrupt conclusion, signaled by a strike of the gavel, releases them from their chairs. Free to roam about, they approach the collection of objects, where they finally are able to read the signs mounted on the floor near the installation's base: "Caution: Injurious heat and amperage. Do not touch objects or step on platform."

With their aural, visual, and tactile senses engaged, visitors are held in their seats by sound, drawn to the curious visual presentation of the three metallic furniture pieces, and, finally, pushed away by the signs' warning of injury. In dictating movements and responses, Morris's *Hearing* is a work of art that serves as choreographer to the gallery's visitors.

—Elizabeth Athens (Williams M.A. 2005), The Edith and Herbert Lehman Foundation Publications Assistant

Labeltalk

Roman
Sarcophagus Fragment of Hercules, Triumph of Dionysos
late 3rd century
Marble
33 11/16 x 25 3/16 x 8 15/16 in.
Museum purchase, John B. Turner '24 Memorial Fund
(86.19)

Max Beckmann
German, 1884–1950
Jahrmarkt, 1921
Drypoints on Japan paper
Sheets: variable 16 1/4 x 9 3/4 in. to 21 x 15 1/2 in.
Partial gift of David P. Tunick, Class of 1966, in memory of J. Kirk T. Varnedoe, Class of 1967, and Museum purchase, Karl E. Weston Memorial Fund
(M.2003.25a–j)

North Indian, Mughal
A Prince with Ladies on a Terrace, ca. 1735
Opaque watercolor on paper, heightened with gold
9 1/2 x 13 5/16 in.
Bequest of Mrs. Horace W. Frost (91.15.36)

Indian, Bihar or Bengal
Black Stone Stele of a Crowned Buddha, 9th–10th century (Pala Period)
Black chlorite
28 x 14 x 6 1/2 in.
Museum purchase, Anonymous Fund and Karl E. Weston Memorial Fund (96.14)

THE LABELTALK EXHIBITION SERIES, funded by the Andrew W. Mellon Foundation, is dedicated to an interdisciplinary exploration of art. Based on the premise that a work of art can have multiple meanings, depending on the perspective of the viewer, Labeltalk examines some of those meanings through the viewpoints of Williams College faculty members. Each exhibition shares a similar format: for each work of art, there are three or four interpretative texts, each written by faculty members from different departments. For example, an African mask included in the 1995 Labeltalk exhibition was explored by an art historian, a historian, a professor of English, and a professor of dance. Together, the different texts bring out diverse and often surprising dimensions of the work of art. Indeed, several Labeltalk texts will be encountered in this book.

To date there have been six Labeltalk exhibitions with more than 110 faculty members contributing texts, making the series a lively and effective way to integrate the museum's collections, exhibitions, and programs into the life of the campus.

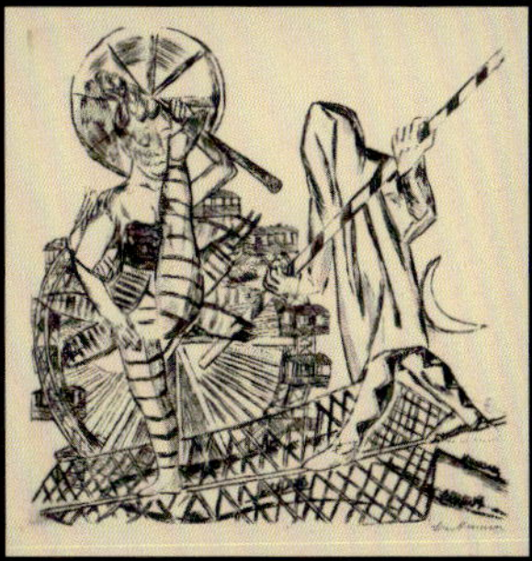

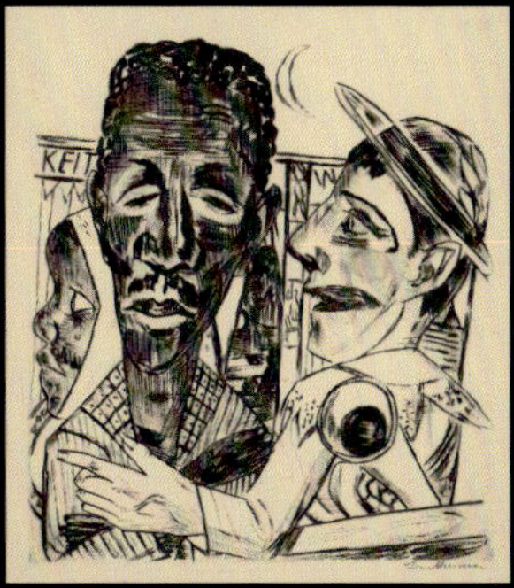

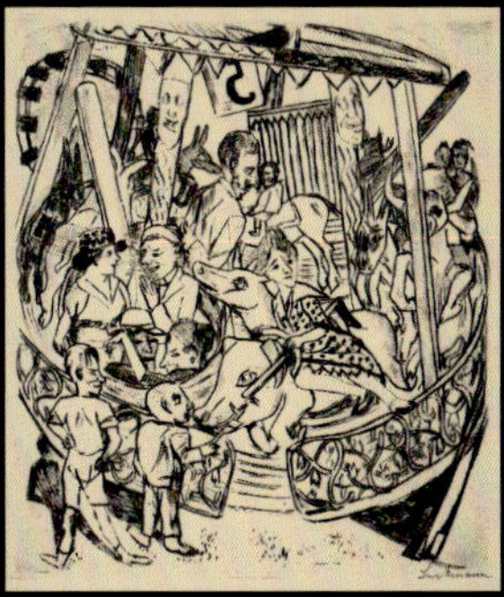

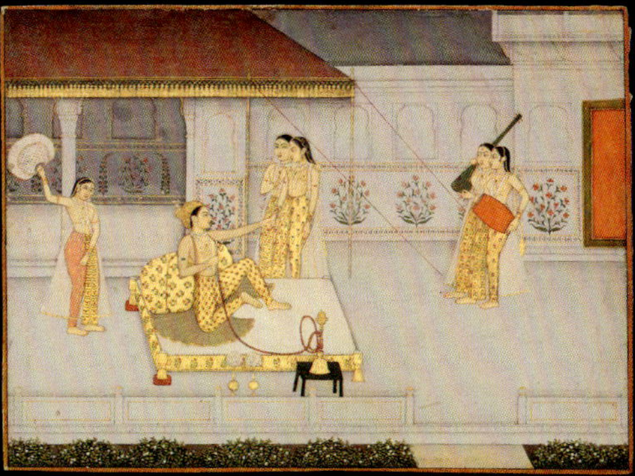

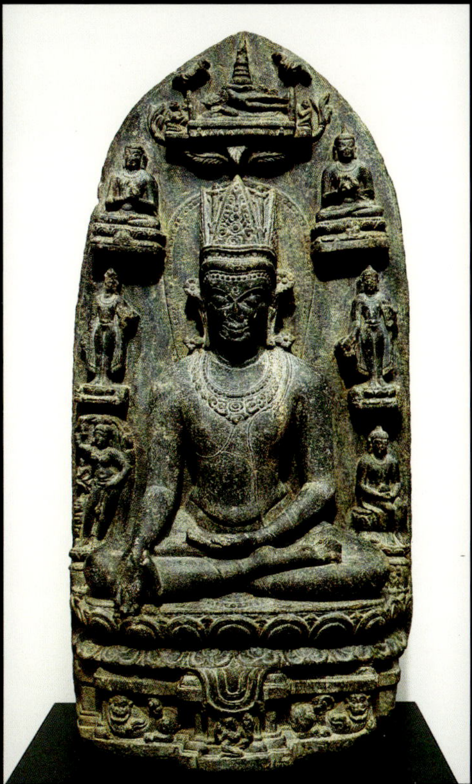

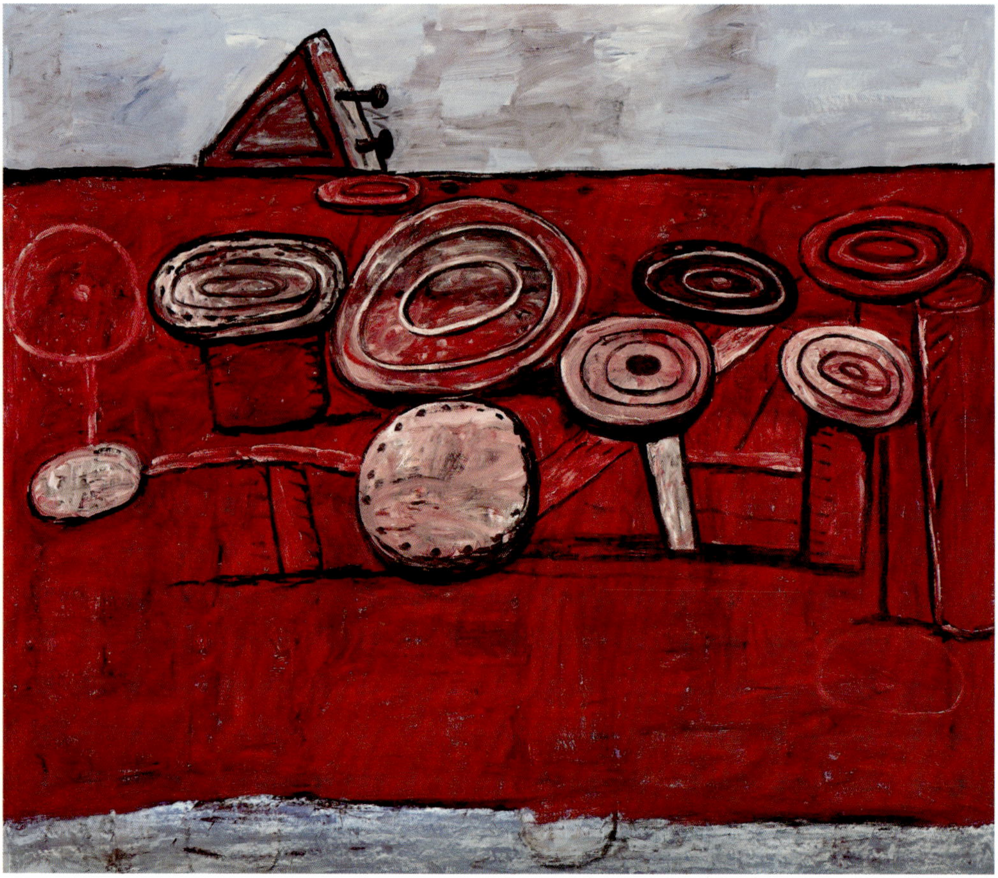

PHILIP GUSTON
American, 1913–1980

Game
1978

Oil on canvas
81 1/8 x 95 1/16 in.
Bequest of Musa Guston
(92.24)

Melancholy, tidal, enveloping, mnemonic, caustic, poignant—all words that come to me when I sit and look at the painting by Philip Guston so cryptically titled *Game*. It is a work heavy with experience, both in its sheer physicality and in its ability to speak to the cacophony of a lifetime of painting.

Game speaks to powerful artistic experiences and hints at the evolutionary nature of Guston's work. We are able to glimpse his role as inventor, locator, witness, and storyteller. And sifting through the maze of formal questions posed, we begin to understand the physicality of the painting. One senses that the viscous, cakelike paint quality not only holds complicated emotional tones but describes the simple acts of faith that painting sometimes requires. Similarly, he chose color not only for its obvious ability to describe form (black nails) but for its profound ability to evoke movement, sensations, mystery, and memory (so prominently found in the dark red veil form that is filling the pictorial space with tidal action, ebbing and flowing).

Game presents a narrative that is ambiguous in nature, using forms that are layered in our sense of recognition. They are forms that support the title *Game*. And if we speculate, are we in the presence of what's left of some nonsensical, rowdy, plate-spinning circus act? Witness to some desolate, sacred place? Or is it a landscape whose presence is being marred by an awkward, fatuous pyramid intent on scrubbing the horizon of all that constitutes memory?

Or are we simply in the presence of a kind of dimly lit, frozen essence of the painting experience itself? Is it a painting that speaks of finality, quiet with tremulous anger and resignation? What's left, in other words, after making, and scraping off, a multitude of Guston's late images? Gone are the light bulbs, hoods, shoes, knees, clocks, food, shields, figures, and almost the wit. Left behind are twelve orbs frozen in motion, celestial, and a brooding, red veil that is resting on a ghost ball. And poignantly located below, a swath of blue that inverts the sky above.

—Frank Jackson, Assistant Professor of Art

GILBERT AND GEORGE
British, est. 1967

Life without End
1982

Hand-dyed black-and-white photographs
13 ft. 10 in. x 36 ft. 2 in.
Museum purchase, Kathryn Hurd Fund (85.29)

In the 1980 film *The World of Gilbert and George*, the duo announced that they were "fascinated by the richness of the fabric of our world." Indeed, the images of trees, plants, and male figures that are dispersed across the thirty-six-foot image, *Life without End*, offer a slice-of-life frieze that one imagines could go on as an endless document of life's profuse multiplicity.

Gilbert and George met in art school and have lived and worked together since 1967. Always dressed in matching conservative suits, they make frequent appearances in their work; indeed, their own combined persona is the cornerstone of their art. Here they bracket the composition—kneeling in prayer on the left and standing together on the right, with Gilbert looking at George who, with his hand in a victory sign, performs a benediction-like gesture. In between, images of adolescent boys, part of a church, and trees evoke Spitalfields, the diverse, multicultural, working-class corner of London where they live. Gilbert and George "attack viewers with beauty so that they will take notice" and accept as beautiful what might otherwise be maligned. George noted in a 2001 interview, "There is nothing in the whole world that is not inside every person. We need to open ourselves up and accept more and more."

—Deborah Rothschild, Senior Curator of Modern and Contemporary Art

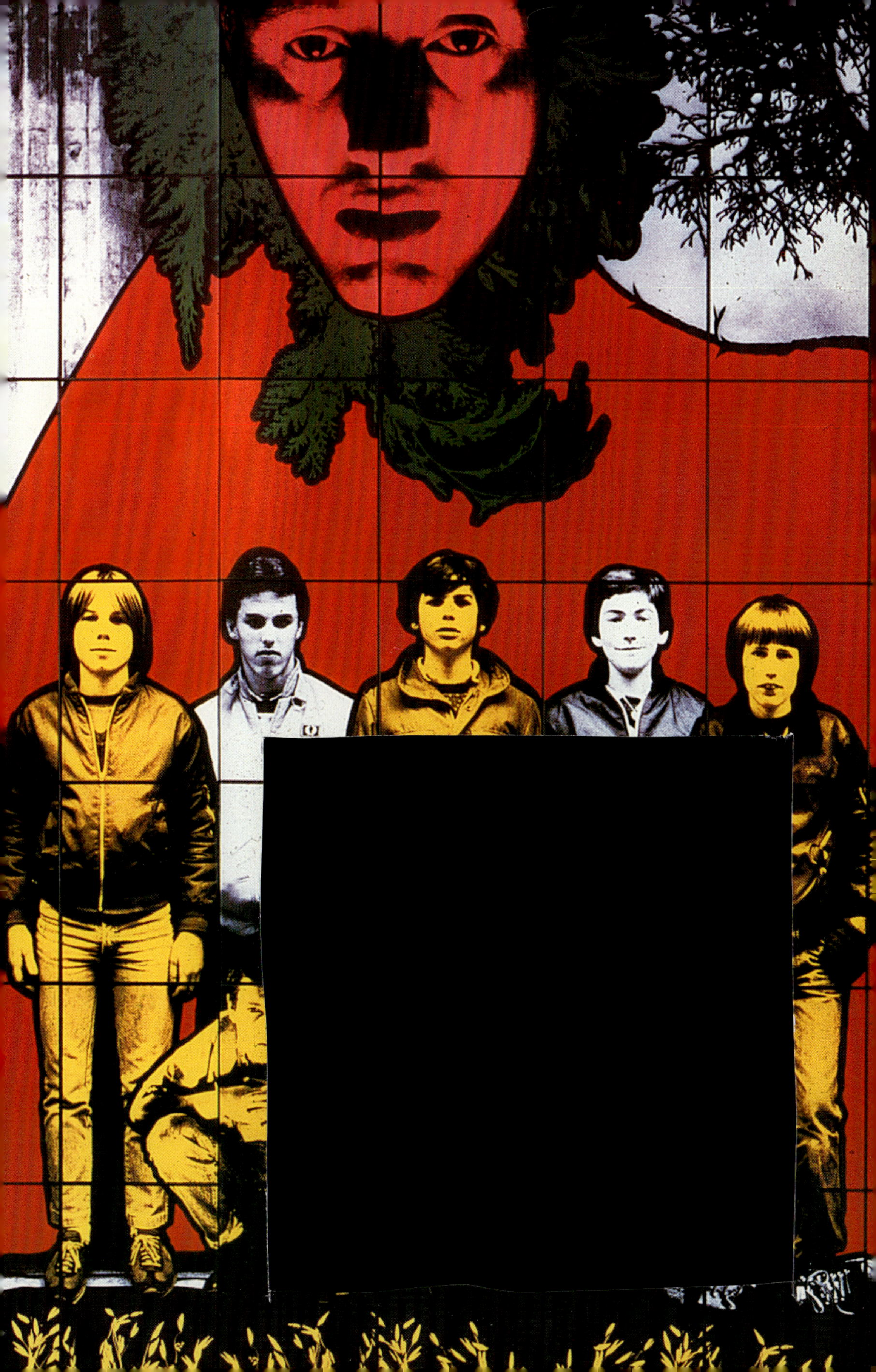

ANDY WARHOL
American, 1928–1987

Self-Portrait
1986

Synthetic polymer paint and silkscreen ink on canvas
106 1/2 x 106 1/2 in.
Museum purchase, Kathryn Hurd Fund (86.6)

*Andy Warhol looks a scream
Hang him on my wall
Andy Warhol, Silver Screen
Can't tell them apart at all*
—David Bowie, "Andy Warhol," 1971

Self-portraiture was a central theme in Andy Warhol's extensive body of work. The most recognizable image Warhol produced may have been his own. Warhol became a cultural symbol and his face is now as familiar as the celebrity and commercial icons he depicted and serialized: Marilyn Monroe, Elvis Presley, and Campbell's Soup.

Perhaps the most haunting and enigmatic of Warhol's self-portraits were his last. This portentous self-portrait is from a series commissioned in 1986 by the Anthony d'Offay Gallery for exhibition in London, only a few months before the artist's death on February 22, 1987. Enlarged to monumental proportions, these final self-portraits focus entirely on the artist's face, which emerges dramatically from a black background. The spiked strands of his signature silver fright wig animate the otherwise spectral, masklike portrait. Warhol stares directly ahead, as if mesmerized by his own reflection in the lens of the camera, and thus his gaze is ominously fixed on the viewer.

The vivid coloration intensifies the dramatic dissonance of the image as the bright yellow face radiates from the stark background. This phosphorescent glow generates the peculiar effect of a nimbus, and, from this perspective, the protruding spikes of his wig can be perceived as a halo or attributes of martyrology, such as the arrows that pierce the body of St. Sebastian. Warhol projects himself as a resplendent enigma bathed in the luminescence of a television screen or ghostly afterimage. At the very least, as the David Bowie pop song proposes, "Andy Warhol, Silver Screen/Can't tell them apart at all."

—C. Ondine Chavoya, Assistant Professor of Art

ALLEN GINSBERG
American, 1926–1997

William S. Burroughs, New York
1986

Gelatin silver print
14 x 11 in.
Museum purchase, John B. Turner '24 Memorial Fund and Wachenheim Family Fund
(M.2003.29.4)

The poet Allen Ginsberg had a secondary career as a photographer. Beginning in the late 1940s he carried a camera with him constantly. It was only later that he realized he had amassed a valuable visual record of the legendary poets, novelists, and artists of the Beat Generation. Ginsberg met Neal Cassady, Jack Kerouac, and William Burroughs while he was a student at Columbia University in the 1940s. Their freewheeling, antiestablishment actions paved the way for the revolutionary youth movements of the 1960s.

In this photograph, Ginsberg records his friend of forty years, the underworld novelist, drug addict, wife slayer, and media philosopher William Burroughs as he is about to leave the Soho loft of Obie Benz. Benz was the director and producer of the 1988 documentary film *Heavy Petting*, in which Burroughs appeared along with Sandra Bernhard, David Byrne, and others.

The epitome of laconic cool, the writer stands in front of a window. Who would think this austere figure direct from central casting for *The Puritan* was an outlaw and iconoclast for most of his eighty-three years? Ginsberg humorously rhymes Burroughs's dour rectangular face with the similar geometry of the window frame. The horizontal lines of the trenchcoat epaulets and hat brim are further echoed by the radiator and the industrial buildings glimpsed beyond. Ginsberg was friends with the photographer Berenice Abbott, and he picked up from her the practice of annotating his photographs.

—Deborah Rothschild, Senior Curator of Modern and Contemporary Art

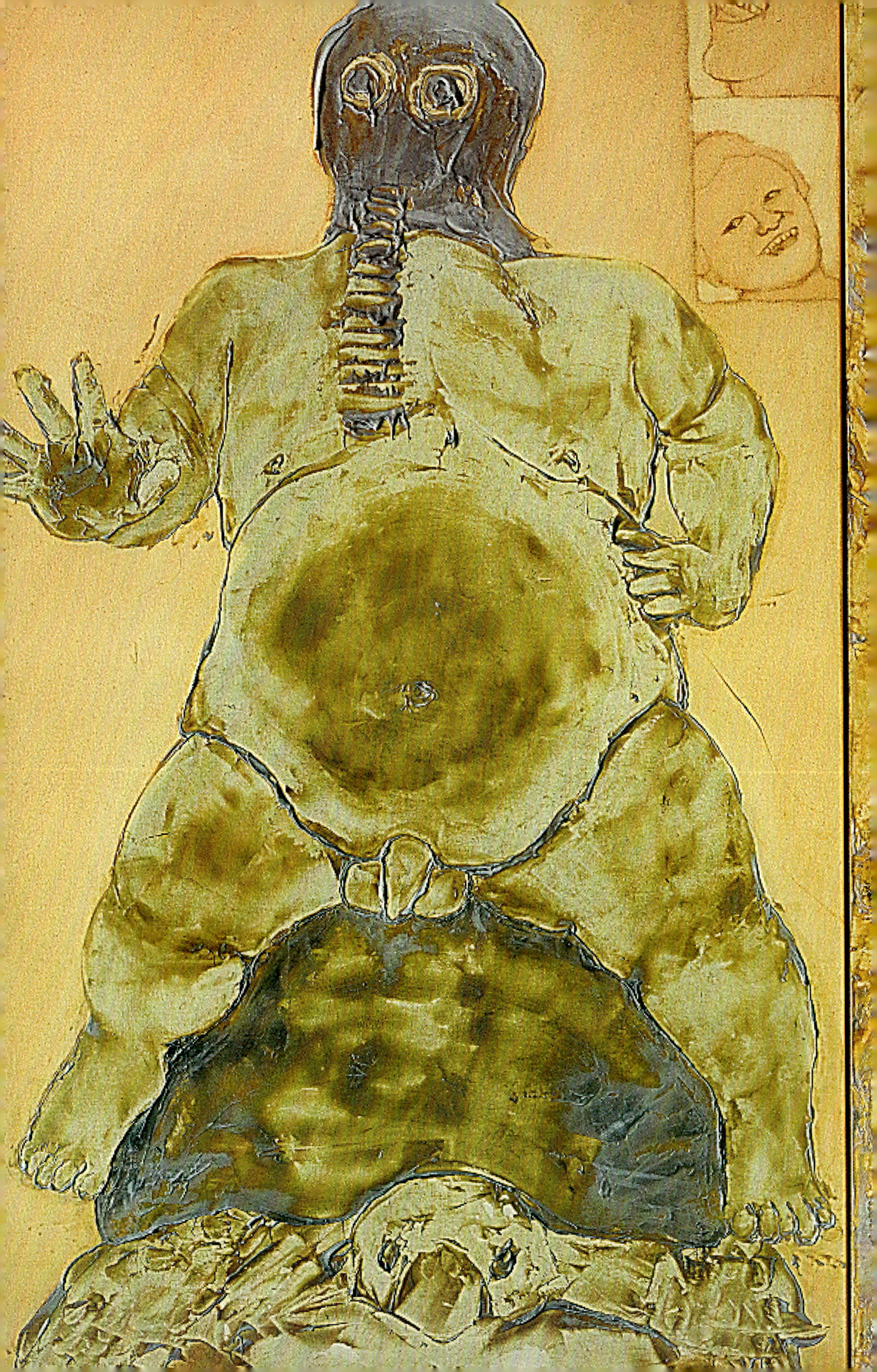

IDA H. APPLEBROOG
American, b. 1929

Boboli Gardens
1987

Oil and encaustic on 5 canvases
86 x 132 in.
Museum purchase, Joseph O. Eaton Fund, Kathryn Hurd Fund, and Karl E. Weston Memorial Fund (88.1)

*Known as The Fountain of Bacchus (the turtle peacefully spews water), the statue by Valerio Ciolo (1560) depicts Pietro Barbino, who was in the retinue of Cosimo de' Medici.

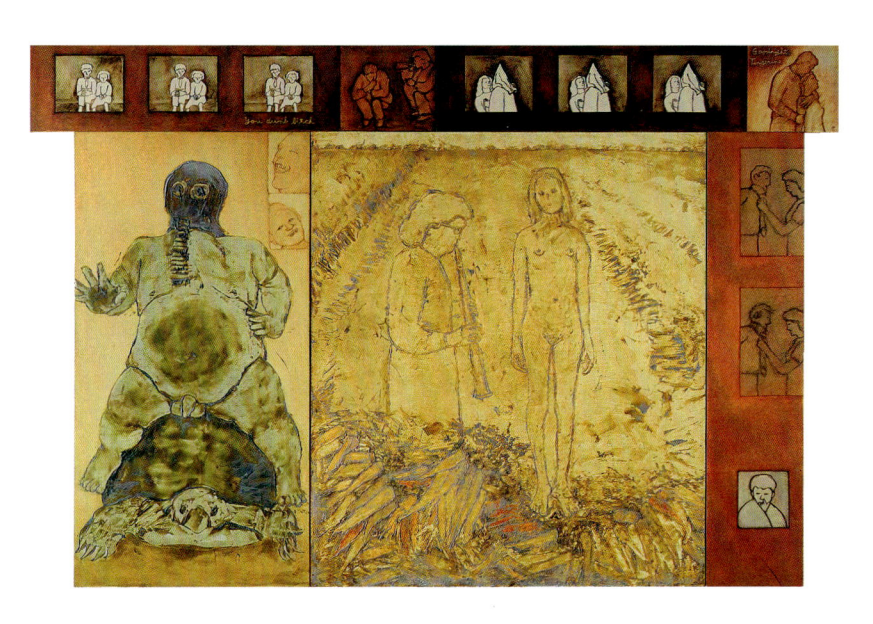

At the entrance to the Boboli Gardens in Florence, the statue of a fleshy, naked dwarf astride a turtle has been making people laugh for centuries.* In Ida Applebroog's large polyptych, this jester, his pudgy face covered by a gas mask, also welcomes the visitor. The artist sabotages the bountiful delights of the garden at every turn. If the picture's earthen hues of arid tan and warm sienna nostalgically recall the frescoes and landscape of Tuscany, the paint—in places applied in thick, waxen blobs flattened by a palette knife or spatula—produces intestinal queasiness rather than tactile pleasure.

An ode to nature zapped by culture, the central panel showcases a desolate field with a bumper crop of phallic carrots that will seemingly be left to rot. Marking the boundary between them, a knock-kneed, nubile, Botticellian Venus, strikingly devoid of any gestures of modesty, is transported, not by the gusts of Zephyr and Cloris, but by the tune of a schoolmistress-like Pan. That *Boboli Gardens* is an ode to vulnerability rather than innocence is reinforced by the smaller images arranged rhythmically across the surface above and to the right. Suggesting penmanship exercises, carefully written phrases —"You dumb bitch" under repeated images of well-behaved children, "Goodnight, Tangerine" below an embrace that borders on stranglehold— underscore the violence of hierarchical relationships in which women and children are subservient, helpless, and mute.

The multiple panels, whose smaller images recall predellas (as well as film strips, freeze-frames, and comics), constitute an altarpiece for the modern world. *Boboli Gardens* simultaneously intones warnings and invokes supplication about sins committed and suffered. And, for those who are listening, the sermon addresses both the disenfranchised and the powerful.

—Carol Ockman, Professor of Art

ADRIAN PIPER
American, b. 1948

Vanilla Nightmares #18
1987

Charcoal on newspaper
22 3/16 x 13 11/16 in.
Gift of the American Academy and Institute of Arts and Letters, New York; Hassam, Speicher, Betts and Symons Funds (91.5)

Vanilla Nightmares is a series of drawings on pages of the *The New York Times*, where according to Adrian Piper, "blacks intrude on the luxurious and elaborate life-style fantasies of white Americans that have been created and perpetuated by Madison Avenue." The series, begun in 1986, alerts us to the hidden messages prevalent in advertising and so-called factual reportage that feed prejudice in barely noticeable and therefore especially dangerous ways. In *Vanilla Nightmares #18*, for example, the advertising copy, "Membership has its privileges," is addressed to the average *New York Times* reader—affluent, educated, and white. Piper draws on the ad the countless multitude excluded from this group, those who by implication are devalued by not being "members." The sea of black faces, who do not qualify for credit cards and concomitant entry into the American Dream but who also are denied basic human rights, press against an invisible barrier. They frighten and threaten the viewer; they are shut out now, but, judging from their numbers and unstoppable "Night of the Living Dead" advance, they will not be shut out for long. Piper said, "In *Vanilla Nightmares* I am pushing beyond the benign stereotype of blacks, such as Uncle Tom and Aunt Jemima, to the deep fears that express the 'fear of the other.' These stereotypes result from white people's need to simplify and reduce 'the other' in order to manage the overwhelming specter of black people as potent, sexy, strong, virile, and endowed with supernatural qualities."

—Deborah Rothschild, Senior Curator of Modern and Contemporary Art

In the spring of 2003 Mark Reinhardt, Professor of Political Science, taught a seminar examining American representations of slavery, emphasizing accounts of the journey from slavery to freedom. Students examined artwork by Winslow Homer, Glenn Ligon, Thomas Nast, Adrian Piper, and Kara Walker, and wrote essays examining issues of slavery, cultural production, and political power. A jury of faculty and WCMA staff selected thirteen essays, of which this is one, for the catalogue *Representing Slavery*.

Hundreds of black faces are crowded inside the boundaries of a newspaper advertisement, and they certainly were not invited by American Express. In the image *Vanilla Nightmares #18*, Adrian Piper takes her revenge on the creators of the ironic 1980s slogan "Membership has its privileges." Membership implies choice and desirability, but these people did not choose the color of their skin; nonetheless, society will not let them forget it. Hemmed in by the construction of race, these protesters demonstrate that in their case, racial membership brings hardship and isolation rather than privilege. The sheer number of heads on the page is powerful, but is their force enough to break down the invisible barrier that they confront? Their hands push against the surface of the work, but their efforts appear futile. Futile, that is, unless one takes into account their psychological power as figures capable of haunting others' consciences in a "vanilla nightmare."

—Betsy J. Thomas (Williams 2003). Adapted from *Representing Slavery*, 2003

MEMBERSHIP HAS ITS PRIVILEGES

JENNY HOLZER
American, b. 1950

"I go to schools . . ."
from *Laments*
1989

Nubian black granite sarcophagus with electronic LED sign
24 3/8 in. x 6 ft. 10 in. x 30 in. Museum purchase, acquired with matching funds from Michael and Leslie Engl, Allan and Judith Fulkerson, Frederick and Dorothy Rudolph, Linda Janovic, Elaine Kend, Frederieke Taylor, Micheline Engel, and an anonymous donor; and the National Endowment for the Arts and the Kathryn Hurd Fund (91.4)

Jenny Holzer has created an ironic juxtaposition between two methods of transmitting language: the incised words recall ancient funeral steles and the hush of antiquity, while the ephemeral words on the LED screen bespeak modern news tickers and the hubbub of New York's Times Square. "I go to schools . . ." is part of a much larger exhibition piece titled *Laments*, shown at the Dia Foundation, New York City, in 1989. *Laments* featured thirteen pairs of sarcophagi and screens, yet WCMA's piece functions on its own as a microcosm of the whole. Thirteen such pairs could be overwhelming—the viewer might not have the time to read all of the texts. Here, we can relax, read the texts more than once, savor the words, and contemplate the artist's intentions. "I go to schools . . ." was installed in the WCMA rotunda soon after its purchase in 1991. It was the sole work of art in the gallery, and the large, cool, columned room took on an eerie, tomblike feel. One could almost imagine that left out of Holzer's text is the line, "I go to funerals . . ."

—Dana Pilson, The Edith and Herbert Lehman Foundation Publications Assistant

Incised into the Nubian black granite sarcophagus are the following words:

I go to schools
To see children
Run hard.
I observe people
When they stand
To have sex.
I photograph Presidents.
I look at
Animals in fires.
I am not worried
Which is what
Every human being
Has wanted from
The Beginning.
I was not
Born live.
This body grew
But I did not
Feel cells split.
How I act
Does not matter.
I am waiting for
Everyone to die
Because that
Is the point.

164, 165

Diane Arbus
American, 1923–1971
Child with a Toy Hand Grenade in Central Park, NYC
1962
Gelatin silver print
14 3/4 x 14 5/8 in.
Museum purchase, Karl E. Weston Memorial Fund (93.4)

Lewis Wickes Hine
American, 1874–1940
Tenement Child, 1909
Gelatin silver print
Sheet: 5 3/8 x 7 3/8 in.
Museum purchase, Karl E. Weston Memorial Fund (77.43.10)

Keith Cottingham
American, b. 1965
Single (from Fictitious Portraits), 1992
Color coupler print
45 1/2 x 38 in.
Gift of Anne R. Avis, Class of 1981 and Gregory Avis, Class of 1980 (M.2001.9.a)

THE PHOTOGRAPHY COLLECTION at the museum is best defined along the same lines as the college's educational philosophy, for creativity distinguishes both the collection and the liberal arts (*artes liberales* as opposed to *artes illiberales* or vocational training). Whether it is the scientific inquiries of Eadweard Muybridge's motion studies and Harold Edgerton's stroboscopy or the overt artistry of Julia Margaret Cameron's tableaux vivants and John O'Reilly's montages, the museum collects photography that mirrors the college's focus on the liberal arts and, by extension, creativity.

The earliest period for which the museum has significant holdings is the later nineteenth century. By that time, photography had split into two camps, the objective and scientific on the one hand, and the subjective and artistic on the other. Although this linkage of approach to application has become increasingly loose ever since, the distinction between approaches—between straight and altered—continues to have currency today. In this collection, we can look to nineteenth-century views by Samuel Bourne, the Alinari Brothers, Francis Frith, and Carlo Naya for the stylistic ancestry of later straight photography by artists from Ansel Adams to Robert Adams. Likewise, we can witness early altered photography and its legacy with work by artists ranging from Cameron and James Van Der Zee to James Casebere, Robert Heinecken, and Joel Peter Witkin.

The museum holds important collections of photographs created since the 1930s. From the American documentary tradition, both social and subjective, it includes examples of early-twentieth-century images by Lewis Hine, work from the 1930s by Walker Evans and others commissioned by the Farm Security Administration—including a magnificent suite of color photographs—and numerous examples of those who followed, such as Diane Arbus, Robert Frank, and Kristin Capp. The collection is also particularly rich in photography created since the 1950s, starting with the generation of Aaron Siskind and Harry Callahan, through that of Gary Winogrand and Lee Friedlander and on to that of Nan Goldin and Cindy Sherman. Today, though, much of the recent work collected falls under the rubric of contemporary art. Perhaps the second greatest story about twentieth-century art—after the rise of modernism—

is the steadily increasing importance of art created with photographically based media. Photography has won not just acceptance but in many ways dominance in current art practices.

Likewise, the study of photography has grown exponentially. Rather than a simple polarity between objective and subjective or straight and altered (or staged), photography today is mapped within a more complex, nuanced matrix whose axes are defined by these terms. There is also greater curiosity about the role that photographs play as objects originating from specific coordinates of time and space and images that continue to flow through society, simultaneously influencing and reflecting culture and knowledge in infinitely complex ways. As photography studies become the natural habitat of an expanding array of academic specialties—from political science to social anthropology to philosophy—the collections that the museum has amassed become ever more central to achieving the college's mandate for a true liberal arts learning environment, one defined at heart by its focus on creativity.

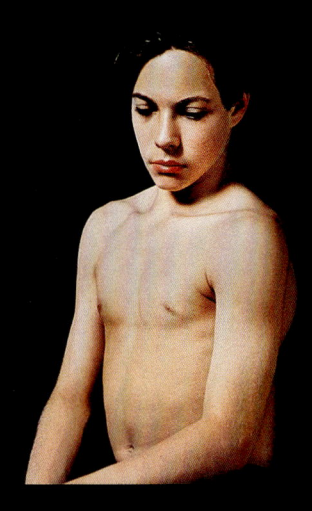

CINDY SHERMAN
American, b. 1954

Untitled
1989

Cibachrome print
33 1/4 x 24 in.
Museum purchase, Kathryn Hurd Fund (91.17)

Cindy Sherman's photography forged new territory for contemporary art in the 1980s and 1990s. In this self-portrait, the artist so convincingly assumes the guise of a Tuscan lady, in pose and dress, that the casual viewer might not notice the ruse. But Sherman has done nothing to hide the ridiculous prosthetic nose she wears. By revealing—if not reveling in—the artificial nature of the image, her art confronts and celebrates photography's fictive possibilities. She also asserts her role as author of the work by continually foregrounding her own image. In this way, she denies any lingering notion that photography is based in objectivity and provokes a reconsideration of our basic expectations for its use as an art medium.

For these reasons, among others, Sherman established a new vanguard for photography and encouraged numerous theories regarding the role of individual agency in the art of the later twentieth century—and this worries her. "Maybe the work doesn't mean anything," she suggests. "When [the art critics are] writing about it, they're just finding whatever to attach their theories to. I just happen to illustrate some theories." Ultimately, it is exactly the malleability of her images (in terms of meaning) that encourages convoluted, even conflicting, interpretations of her work. We find endless fascination in the honesty of her deceptions, the simplicity of her complexities, and the reality of her theatricality.

—John Stomberg, Associate Director

MATT MULLICAN
American, b. 1951

Mid-19th-Century Railroad Roundhouse with Steam Engines
1989

Oil on 5 canvases
10 x 20 ft.
Gift of Mr. and Mrs. Michael S. Engl, Class of 1966
(M.2003.26.1a–e)

Leo Marx's 1964 groundbreaking study, *The Machine in the Garden: Technology and the Pastoral Ideal in America*, examines the role of technology and industrialism and the changes they brought to a pastoral nation. The railroad is the nefarious machine that enters the pristine garden, transforming towns and bringing with it the onset of America's industrial age. George Inness's painting *The Lackawanna Valley* (ca. 1856, National Gallery of Art, Washington, D.C.) advertises the achievements of the Delaware, Lackawanna, and Western Railroad and ambiguously illustrates the degradation of the landscape necessitated by the railroad's success. A large roundhouse in the middle distance further announces the railroad's prominence, and while the structure echoes the round forms of the mountains behind, it spews steam and lords over a landscape pockmarked with tree stumps. Mullican's painting, composed of five canvases placed side by side, shows the interior of a nineteenth-century railroad roundhouse and finds beauty in the filigreed iron supports, glass windows, and gently rounded forms that create dizzying concentric circles. Deceptively delicate, the sturdy roundhouse is the locus for the storage and turning around of the enormous and powerful locomotives. The image is soaked in blood red paint, perhaps a reference to the toil of the many laborers who built the nation's networks of railroad. Within this scene from the nation's past, Mullican inserts a contemporary-looking banner displaying an image from his repertoire of symbols relating to humankind's place in the universe.

—Dana Pilson, The Edith and Herbert Lehman Foundation Publications Assistant

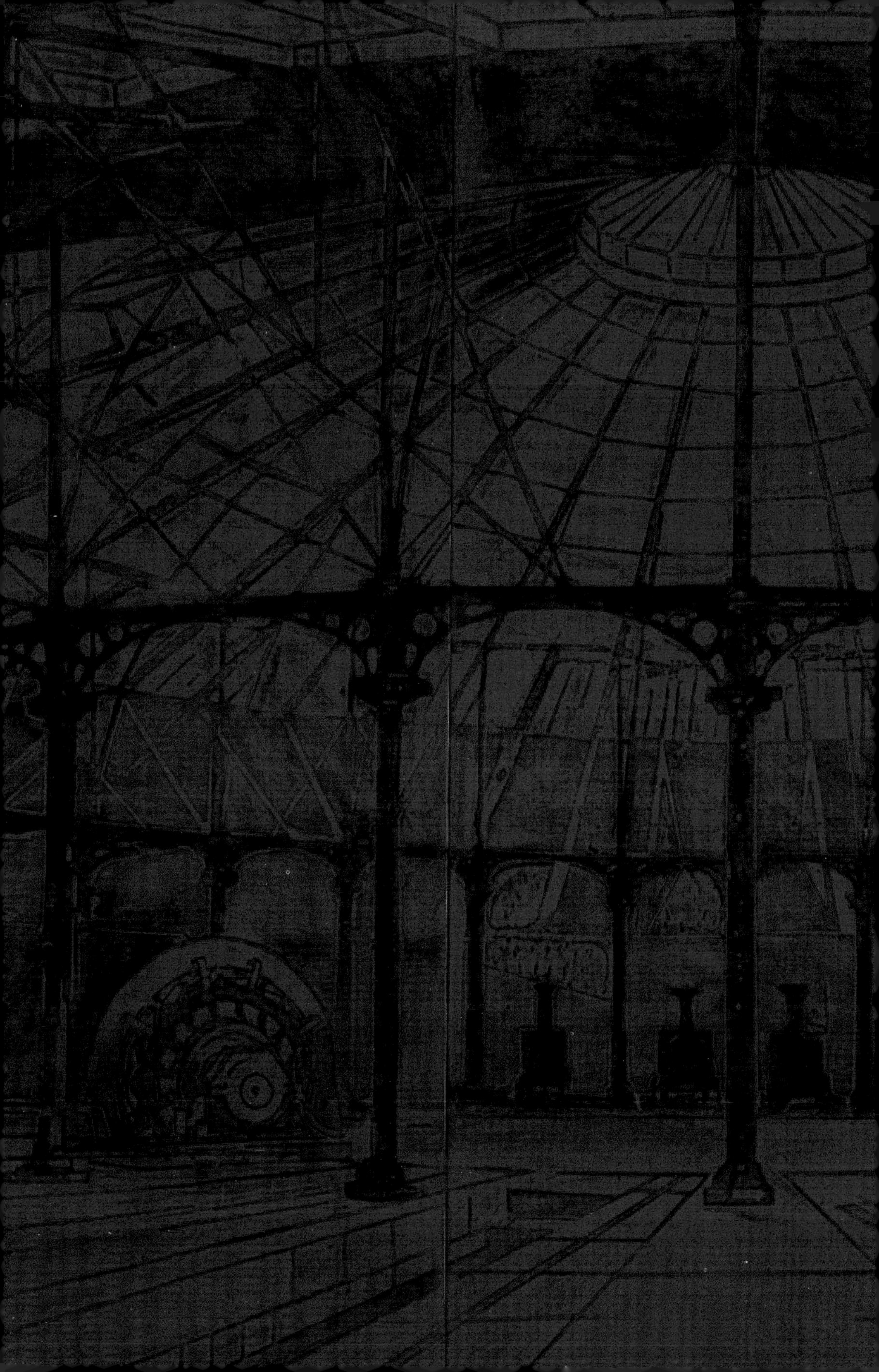

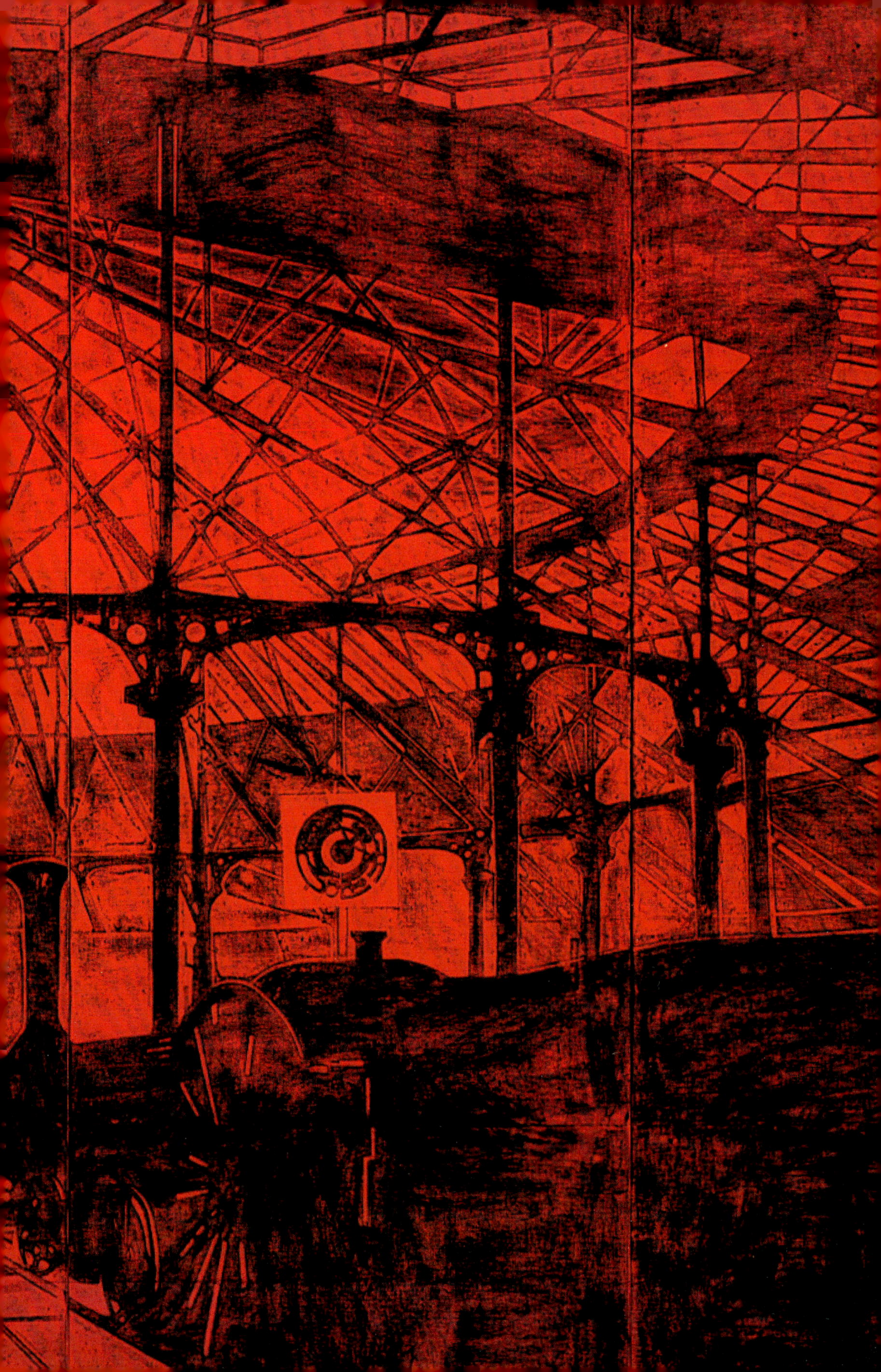

FAITH RINGGOLD
American, b. 1930

100 Years at Williams College, 1889–1989
1989

Acrylic paint on canvas with printed and pieced fabric
86 3/4 x 120 in.
Museum purchase, John B. Turner '24 Memorial Fund, Kathryn Hurd Fund, and Karl E. Weston Memorial Fund (89.7)

I have never forgotten that I am a Williams man, and if there is one thing in the world of which I am proud, almost to foolishness, it is that fact. . . .
—Gaius Charles Bolin
(Williams 1889)

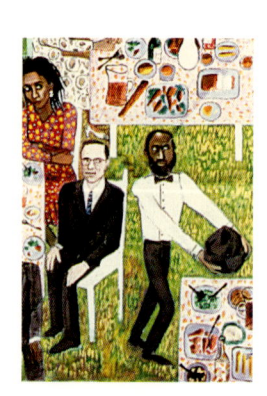

Since 1982 the noted artist Faith Ringgold has been producing her own untraditional brand of story quilts that combine fabric, paint, and written text. The quilts reflect a social and political awareness particularly attuned to issues of race, gender, and black history. On the occasion of the 1989 Bolin Centennial, which commemorated the one-hundredth-year anniversary of the enrollment of blacks at Williams, the Williams College Museum of Art commissioned Ringgold, an African American herself, to create this quilt about the history of blacks at the college.

Except for the carefully wrought portraits of twenty important black alumni that frame the central picture, the painting is rendered in the folk art style the artist generally prefers. Space is flat. Tables are uptilted. Lively colors and patterns dance across the surface. The scene is a happy occasion, an imaginary picnic that gathers together people from Williams College and the town from 1889 to 1989.

At this picnic there is a students' table and an alumni table. There's a table reserved for the presidents of Williams, spanning that century. There is also a table for those faculty and administrators intimately involved in guiding this quilt project. In addition, at a table on the right, the artist has included the museum staff that buttressed this commission. And, on the left, a witty and personal moment where Ringgold herself sets up the artist's table. Pictured are Ringgold's boisterous dealer, Berenice Steinbaum, with mouth thrown open; Steinbaum's daughter; Ringgold's assistant, Gail Liebig; and Faith Ringgold herself. The artist, who had recently shed more than one hundred pounds, displays herself in all her hard-earned svelteness.

Other figures also need to be introduced. Standing in cap and gown is Gaius Charles Bolin. Near him in a waiter's uniform is Abe "the Bunter" Parsons, a black townsperson who, in Bolin's day, was a kind of buffoon around the college, a source of amusement to many Williams students and a source of some embarrassment to Bolin. Abe "the Bunter" had a hard knob on his forehead with which he would split wood. In this picture he carries a huge rock "which he threatened to break with the legendary knot on his head."

Also present on this quilt are two fictional characters: standing behind the presidents, they are Aunt Haddie, a maid at Williams in the nineteenth century; and the attractive Francie, an affluent Williams alumna who works as a corporate lawyer. All Ringgold's story quilts are narrated by women, and Francie is the narrator here. The vehicle for her story is a letter she is writing to her fiancé Josh, also a Williams grad. In it she describes a dream she has about Williams, in which all these people gather in the purple-glowing perfection of this valley.

—Eva U. Grudin, Senior Lecturer in Art. Adapted from *Stitching Memories: African-American Story Quilts*, 1989

172, 173

JUDY PFAFF
American, b. 1946

**Del Flusso e Riflusso
(from Half a Dozen of the
Other series)**
1992

Soft-ground, sugar-lift aquatint, hard-ground, spit-bite aquatint, aquatint, and relief printed dots on paper
Image: 36 x 45 in.
Museum purchase, Kathryn Hurd Fund (M.2000.1)

Del Flusso e Riflusso seems a reflection of process and movement. Its ovoid shapes and soft color washes evoke a "primordial soup" in which forms shift and develop. The title, translated as "of ebb and tide," stems from Judy Pfaff's interest in Leonardo da Vinci's writings and drawings on the flow of water. The print's delicate lines, swirling forms, and geometric spheres suggest both the flux of natural life and an ordered, scientific understanding of it.

Pfaff created *Del Flusso e Riflusso* using a similarly complex mix of printing techniques. A departure from her well-known, large-scale installations, the print is part of a series of six entitled *Half a Dozen of the Other*. Pfaff's processes range from drypoint, which the artist creates by scratching the surface of the printing plate directly, to relief-printed dots, made by placing cutout inked pieces of paper on the plate. In this print, however, Pfaff primarily explored etching and aquatint techniques that use acid to bite grooves and textures into the printing plate. After the plate has been prepared, it is spread with ink and then wiped clean, leaving pigment only in the recessed areas. When the plate is run through the printing press, the ink caught in these grooves and pits is transferred to the paper.

To create an etching, the artist covers the plate with a (hard or soft) resin-based, acid-resistant ground. She then draws over the ground with a pointed metal tool to expose areas of the plate before dipping it in an acid bath. For aquatint, the artist sprinkles a fine, even layer of small resin particles on the plate around which the acid bites, creating tiny pits. When printed, the visual effect is similar to a watercolor wash—smooth where the particles are small, grainy where the particles are larger. The spit-bite aquatint process is similar to regular aquatint, except that the artist paints the plate with acid, rather than dipping it into a bath, to create a more uneven surface. Sugar-lift aquatint allows the artist to draw the aquatint areas directly. For *Del Flusso e Riflusso*, Pfaff used a combination of drypoint, relief, etching, spit-bite, sugar-lift, and aquatint on three separate plates, each of which provided a different layer of the final image.

—Amelia Kahl Avdić (Williams M.A. 2004)

TONY OURSLER
American, b. 1957

Keep Going
1995

Cloth, stand, LCD video projector, VCR, tripod, and videotape
78 x 20 x 35 in.
Museum purchase, Kathryn Hurd Fund (99.4)

In the life-size effigy *Keep Going*, a mismatched plaid suit hanging limply from a tripod provides the armature for a pillow head onto which is projected an unscripted videotaped performance by the composer-filmmaker Tony Conrad. Using exaggerated facial expression and lens distortion to great effect, Conrad takes on the role of a megalomaniacal Hollywood-style movie director who constantly changes his mind while barking out impossible commands. In the space of twenty minutes he calls for an erupting volcano, a wheat field on fire, electronic hail, an alien landing, a crash between a train and a bus, alpine horn music emanating from trees, and the script line "rhubarb, rhubarb, rhubarb." In quick succession our brains conjure this series of incongruous and ridiculous scenarios. For example, Conrad—his eyebrows shooting upward in perpetual alarm or consternation—orders the romantic leads to kiss. As we begin to visualize this, he screams, "No, not each other! Kiss the thing!" What are we to visualize now?

Conrad is brilliant at lampooning American filmmakers' addiction to pyrotechnic special effects; after he decides the volcanic eruption is not sufficiently stupendous, he tries a collision of a train and a bus and an alien landing. Nothing seems to meet his grandiose expectations, and he maniacally alternates between poking and stroking his crew—"We have to get some energy going today, people! There's nothing happening here . . . You incompetent boobs, I'm going to fire you all . . . No, I take it back. You people are good. You stick with me, and I know I change my mind. I love you. . . ."

With *Keep Going*, Tony Oursler attains his goal of suspended disbelief as audiences become actively involved with the video projection. Perhaps the character seems real because he is so loopy and so aggressive. Viewers tend to re-create in their minds the elaborate scenarios Conrad describes. At times viewers have been seen attempting to carry out his directives. Children in particular have responded to his commands to "Be quiet!" "Don't look at me," and "You, yes, I'm talking to you, move to the left." Humor, a constant in Oursler's work, dominates this piece, which holds audiences captive through its playful hilarity.

—Deborah Rothschild, Senior Curator of Modern and Contemporary Art

DAVID HAMMONS
American, b. 1943

Rock Fan
1997

Fabric mounted on paper and stone
12 x 18 x 17 in.
Museum purchase, Kathryn Hurd Fund (M.2004.10)

In October 1993 David Hammons created controversy on campus with his installation *Rock Fan*, an outdoor work sited in front of venerable Chapin Hall that was part of a larger exhibition at WCMA entitled *Yardbird Suite*. *Rock Fan* consisted of a twelve-ton boulder topped with an ungainly assortment of about twenty-five rotary fans. The students were not pleased. They covered the piece with computer printouts and Post-it Notes with such messages as, "Ban the fan, it's a scam," "I don't want my college tuition paying for this," and "Nothing this ugly could be art."

At an impromptu question-and-answer session in front of the piece, Hammons told angry students, "Why do you have to judge it, it's just a baby, four days old, give it a chance. It doesn't matter if you like it or dislike it, what I'm primarily interested in is confronting and challenging people with images that they aren't used to seeing or which seem out of place, that are outside normal reality. This is something new on the planet, and anything new is rejected. It takes time for your eyes to get used to it." He was right. In the course of five months the piece went from pariah to mascot. Within the first week it was doused with purple paint and surrounded by an old vacuum cleaner, parts of a turkey, and other detritus. Later on it became the chief subject of winter carnival sculptures and the site for a "Rock Fan" Concert.

Early on a student placed around the sculpture an arrangement of twelve small rocks to which were glued fans made of folded newspaper. This was a response in keeping with Hammons's brand of mocking irony. A few years later he created his own version of the student's *Rock Fan*. As in his early sculptures such as *Spade in Chains* (1973), it combines common, everyday materials—newspaper has been replaced with wallpaper—with wordplay and the elegant simplicity of modern abstraction.

When pressed about the meaning of the *Fan* Hammons said at that outdoor session with students, "It's just a rock fan. It's no deeper than that. This is a rock and roll show. It's related to most of you, hopefully." But there was more going on in the piece. *Rock Fan* referred to New Englanders' penchant for using boulders as markers and monuments but filtered that observation through an African-American sensibility. The encrustation of irregular elements refers to what Hammons calls "negritude." He said, "I just love to watch the way Black people make things, houses or magazine stands in Harlem, for instance. Just the way we use carpentry. Nothing fits, but everything works. The door closes, it keeps things from coming through. But it doesn't have the neatness about it, the way white people put things together." The original *Rock Fan* was one such irregular structure made of cast-off objects. Hammons had deliberately positioned a black aesthetic in the center of white WASPdom. He said it was "like picking a fight." The piece also fit into an abiding theme in Hammons's work—that of yearning for flight and freedom.

—Deborah Rothschild, Senior Curator of Modern and Contemporary Art

178, 179

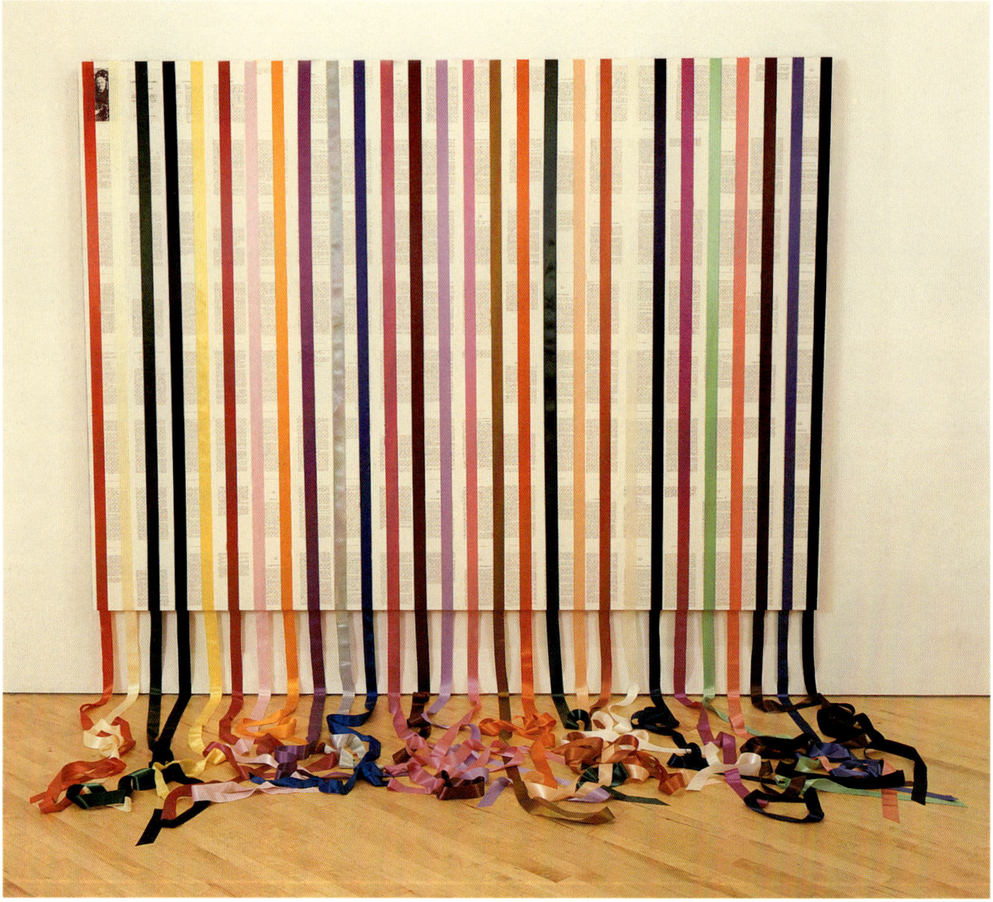

TIM ROLLINS AND KIDS OF SURVIVAL
American, b. 1955

Diary of a Slave Girl
(After Harriet Jacobs)
1998

Satin ribbons; book pages on linen

70 x 98 in.

Museum purchase, Kathryn Hurd Fund, Miscellaneous Gifts Fund (98.9)

WCMA's education department, working with college students, grade-school kids, teachers, families, and the general public, wants people not just to look and listen but to have personal and meaningful experience with art. The emphasis is on learning to *really* look at art, to trust one's own observations, and to make connections among artworks from all over the world, from contemporary to ancient, made of anything from bronze to bottle caps.

Tim Rollins and K.O.S.'s *Diary of a Slave Girl* is a piece that crosses lines, both physically and figuratively. Colorful ribbons form the lines that cut the text of Harriet Jacobs's autobiography, *Incidents in the Life of a Slave Girl* (1861), into pieces. But instead of obscuring its meaning, the ribbons draw the viewer in by making one look beneath the surface to untangle a message. WCMA's Museum Associates, undergraduate education volunteers, had many opportunities to work with Rollins at WCMA as a part of their weekly training sessions.

In his foot-stamping, charismatic presentations, Rollins explained that the colors of the ribbons represent the colors of joy for the members of K.O.S. These kids from the South Bronx had experienced the death of their youngest member, and the despair they felt had left them unable to make art or anything else. With Rollins they read *Incidents in the Life of a Slave Girl* and then worked together to rebuild joy, to create happiness in and through their work. When Museum Associates and WCMA visitors look at the work now, they are able to find not only that joy but also their own. In the ribbons they see jail bars, but they also see the colors of the rainbow. In the pages of Jacobs's text they find the impoverished life of a slave but also the liberation of words and art. And, they make connections from this work to pieces in the museum as varied as the Sol LeWitt wall drawing or a Cindy Sherman photograph.

—Barbara Robertson, Director of Education (1989–2004)

The work of Tim Rollins and K.O.S. vitiates the criticism often leveled at postmodern art: that it traffics in shallow signifiers, valuing pastiche over history. In fact, Rollins and his collective present a rereading of Jacobs's narrative that is as critically engaged and, yes, deeper than most traditional studies of the book. At first glance, this piece focuses on a slight episode sandwiched between two momentous chapters. (I myself had hardly noticed the description of Johnkannaus,* intent as I was on Jacobs's harrowing description of her seven years in the attic prison.) But K.O.S.'s work asks the viewer to take a step closer, to read between the lines (that are themselves multiply valent), and to meditate on the uses of literacy and the literary for the writer and for her readers. In these artists' hands Jacobs's struggle to survive, to witness, and to thrive by her art is made newly relevant. My reading and teaching of Jacobs's narrative retains the residue of Rollins's and his kids' viscerally personal, political, and aesthetic re-presentation of the text.

—Cassandra J. Cleghorn, Senior Lecturer in English and American Studies

*The term "Johnkannaus" referred to companies of slaves who entertained and begged for contributions at Christmastime.

CARRIE MAE WEEMS
American, b. 1953

The Hampton Project
2000

28 digitally reproduced photographs printed with ink on transparent muslin cloth and canvas; audio tape. Museum purchase, Kathryn Hurd Fund (M.2005: a–z, aa, kk)

Jim, If You . . .
(from the "Kitchen Table Series")
1988
Gelatin silver print
Image: 14 13/16 x 14 15/16 in.
Museum purchase, Bentley W. Warren Fund (89.9)

For twenty-five years, the American visual artist and folklorist Carrie Mae Weems has made powerful artwork—often with a fiercely ironic sensibility—rooted in sophisticated social observations. She knits her abiding concerns into photographic essays and installations that force the viewer to reassess his or her own moral compass, ethical boundaries, and the political and socioeconomic realities of contemporary America.

In 1990 Weems debuted what is arguably one of her finest group of photographs—*Untitled (Kitchen Table Series)*—an introspective and poetically evocative work laced with the visual richness of an expert theater set. Images coupled with text result in portraits of a young African-American woman in the company of female friends, children, and the occasional male visitor, a series of contemporary and very poignant vignettes. Beneath the stark glare of a single, hanging light, the cast takes its place at the far end of a kitchen table; the viewer's seat is at the near end. As Weems raises the curtain on her drama of an African-American household, we witness what is universal—everyman and everywoman involved in everyday associations and emotional experiences.

In 1996 WCMA commissioned Weems to work on an exhibition project dedicated to the history and legacy of the Hampton Normal and Agricultural Institute (now Hampton University), using the *Hampton Album* of 1900 by the photographer Francis Benjamin Johnston as her point of departure. Located on Chesapeake Bay in Hampton, Virginia, the Institute was founded by Williams College alumnus Samuel Chapman Armstrong in 1868 as a school for "select Negro youth" and, ten years later, for dispossessed Native Americans. Weems's *Hampton Project* bears witness to the language of photography as deftly applied to Johnston's largely documentary vision of Hampton and to Weems's evocation of the Institute as a site of recollection, reflection, and hopeful redemption.

This most recent commission was shaped in part as a response to the philosophy of Hampton's visionary founder, as well as to historical photographs of the Institute and period images of African Americans and Native Americans. Yet Weems looks even further into the past and to more recent events as well, referencing the initial contacts of Europeans and Native Americans, the Civil War, and the civil rights conflicts of the twentieth century to create a multilayered work of elegiac significance. Using vintage images as her starting point, the artist questions Hampton University's role in mainstreaming Native Americans and freed slaves yet also addresses the larger issue of maintaining one's own heritage while becoming a member of a diverse culture through force or free will.

—Vivian Patterson (Williams 1977, M.A. 1980), Curator of Collections

FROM A GREAT HEIGHT I SAW YOU FALLING
BLACK AND INDIAN ALIKE
AND FOR YOU I PLAYED
A SORROW SONG

LOUISE BOURGEOIS
American, b. 1911

Eyes
2001

Granite, bronze, and electric light
Commissioned on the occasion of the 75th anniversary of the museum with funds from the Museum Fellows, friends, and museum endowments. Wachenheim Family Courtyard given by Edgar Wachenheim III, Class of 1959, and Chris Wachenheim, Class of 1994 (M.2001.14.1–10)

Louise Bourgeois's *Eyes* is a permanent outdoor installation consisting of four pairs of disembodied eyes and one gargantuan eight-eye cluster. The eyes might appear inviting one minute, confrontational the next. They can be comical, even silly, but also elegant and sophisticated. For Bourgeois, the eyes are the locus of communication, so the viewer's interaction with the sculptures becomes a conversation of glances; the viewer looks and is looked at.

Bourgeois was among the first artists of her generation to think about sculpture as it relates both to its surroundings and to the viewer by bringing her sculptures down from the pedestal and by allowing the viewer a more intimate experience. With *Eyes*, she expands the idea further, by creating a site in which people physically interact with the sculptures. Their surfaces respond to environmental changes; shifts in daylight and seasons dramatically affect their appearance. They in turn affect their environment, for at night, blue lights project from the pupils of the eyes, uniting the entire quad in colorful splendor.

Appropriately, these representations of eyes are placed outside the art museum, a site where the primary activity is looking. The eyes foretell, without words, the treasures that await the visitor inside the walls of the museum.

—Lisa B. Dorin (Williams M.A. 2000), Assistant Curator of Contemporary Art, The Art Institute of Chicago

Dear Williams College, President Schapiro, faculty, students, and friends. It is with regrets that I am not with you in person today, but I want you to know that you are in my thoughts. . . . You have my work around you which is more me than my physical presence. It is a big honor to receive this commission to create this sculpture to mark the 75th anniversary of the Williams College Museum of Art. I am deeply touched, particularly since your school is known both for its museum and its art history department.

The theme of the eyes has preoccupied me for many decades. I have always said that with words you can say whatever you want, but the eyes never lie. The eyes are a metaphor for the truth, which is what I am after. Whether it is an eye that sees the reality of things or whether it is an eye that sees a world of fantasy, it is the quality of your eyes and the strength of your eyes that I express in this commission.

. . . My eyes are everything. The eyes relate to seduction, flirtation, and voyeurism. They are all subjects related to the theme of eroticism which is of great interest to me. The eye also relates to the subject of fear—when confronted with fear you have to be able to stare right back at it and deal with it. It is a confrontation with no escape.

—Louise Bourgeois. Text of videotaped artist statement presented at the Louise Bourgeois Symposium, Saturday, October 6, 2001

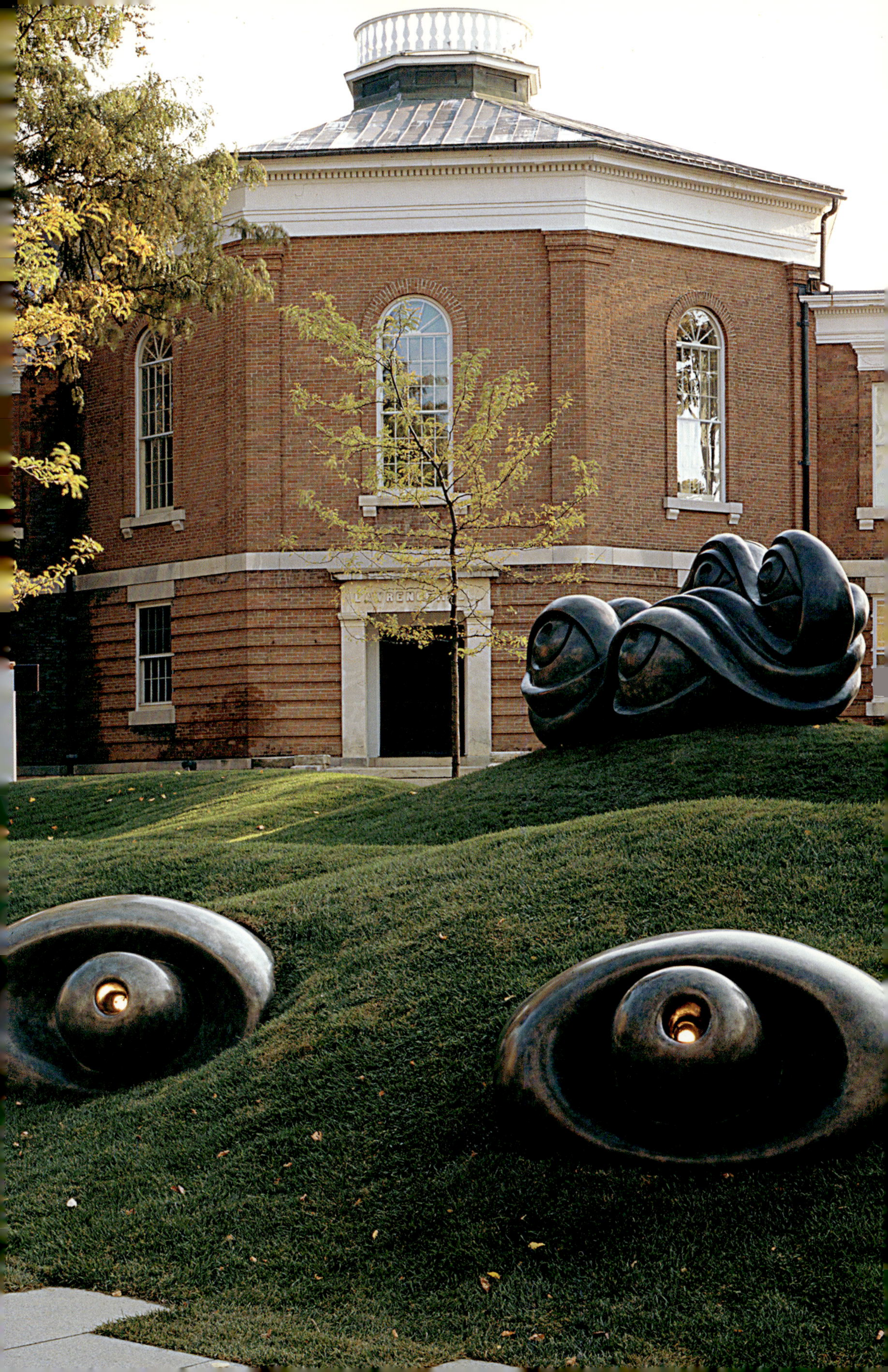

KARA WALKER
American, b. 1969

**Negress Notes
(Slavery Reparations Act)**
2003

Watercolors on paper
7 x 10 1/4 in. each
Museum purchase, Kathryn
Hurd Fund (M.2003.1a–m)

After a lecture at the Des Moines Art Center in 2000, a member of the audience asked Kara Walker how long she thought she could sustain the anger, passion, and energy with which she infused her work. Walker's response was, "As long as I am black and as long as I am a woman."

Non-negotiables run rampant in Walker's work—not surprisingly, as she takes on the heady issues of identity, racism, and social injustice. Her art is fierce and often belies the delicacy of her preferred medium, the cutout silhouette. She sets a stage for great dramas that resonate with each viewer's experience. Walker subtly combines episodes from history—the antebellum South—with wild visions drawn from her imagination to script the uncomfortable ways racist and sexist stereotypes intrude on and influence our daily lives.

Walker charms and engages us by using established aesthetic forms that make traditional art beautiful. She then insinuates her message into these alluring works, and that message, while always intellectual, can be aggressive. Her inventiveness merges the two to produce works that, though they exist initially as objects of contemplation and seduction, prevail as objects of provocation. Walker offers us pieces that seem to fit comfortably within the status quo, but prove to be irritants and catalysts, challenging viewers to confront their own beliefs, prejudices, and values. Hers is enticement with intent to confound and often disturb.

—Vivian Patterson (Williams 1977, M.A. 1980), Curator of Collections

Kara Walker responds in unsettling ways to the perplexities and paradoxes of our peculiar American moment, one in which "race" has become an intellectually suspect term even as it remains at the core of social experience. To be sure, she is hardly a producer of agitprop. Even when it seems utterly direct, her manner of addressing viewers proves to be elliptical, allusive, elusive. Walker makes art that is singular and in some ways deeply personal, perhaps even scandalously so. Yet she traffics in images that are so common as to be stereotypical, thereby engaging a problem that is as social in organization and historical in etiology as it is intimate and emotional at the point of individual contact—the problem of racial perception: how race, and in particular the perversely intertwined images of black and white, is seen, dreamed, fantasized, imagined, projected, internalized. Walker draws viewers into the symbolic work through which these interpretative operations proceed. She often conjures images from the American past, but always as part of a complex engagement with the culture and politics of the present.

Walker's art, then, is an intervention into certain ways of seeing. The works remind us at every turn that the visual perception of race is not in any way innocent of thought and feeling. Repeatedly, her images lure us into a kind of emotionally fraught intellectual play, connecting how we see and think about race to the most elemental structures of affect. The implicit premise of the enterprise is that the primal scenes in the lurid, sexually charged psychodrama of American racism still play out in nearly everyone's imagination, a persistence many of us deny to others and even to ourselves: we hide our affective investments behind a facade of propriety, struggling mightily to keep it in place. By restaging these scenes in shocking detail, Walker pries open the cracks in the facade and sketches what lies beneath. For many viewers, the result is both aesthetic pleasure and a profoundly uncomfortable sense of complicity. What does it mean to create such images? What does it mean to look at them? The pictures press the question but provide ambiguous answers. All we really know is that to witness Walker's spectacles is to enter into a transaction that is at least a little twisted, perhaps disreputable. Hence, much of the outrage the work has generated and hence, for me at least, her power as an artist.

—Mark Reinhardt, Professor of Political Science and Director of the Oakley Center for Humanities and Social Sciences. Adapted from *Kara Walker, Narratives of a Negress*, 2003

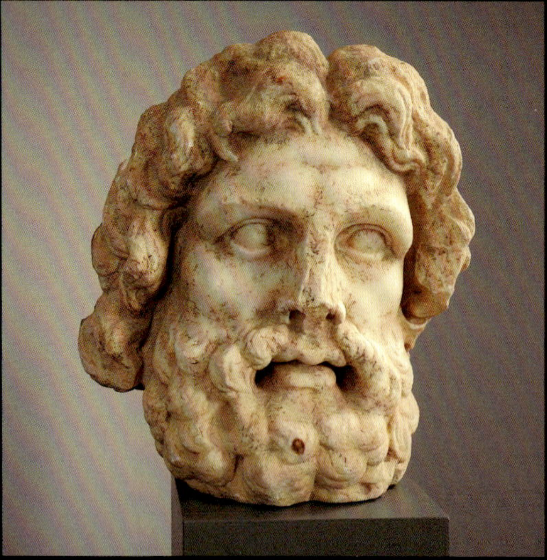
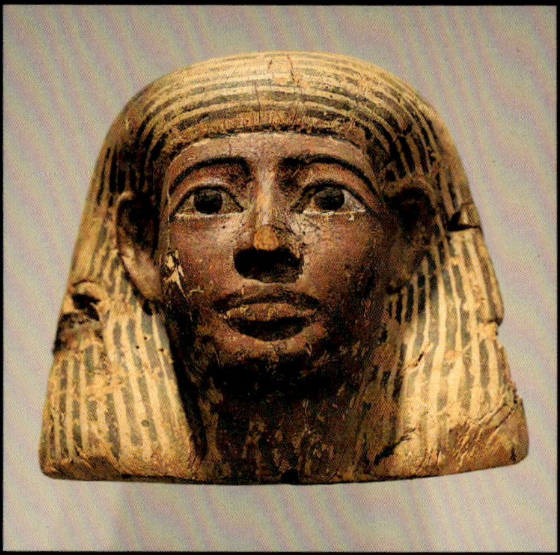
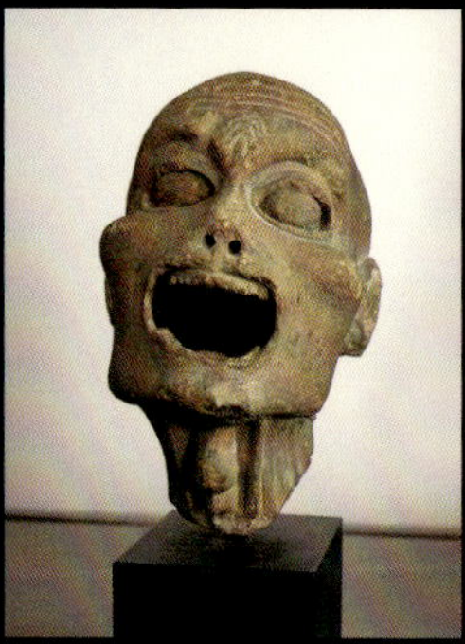
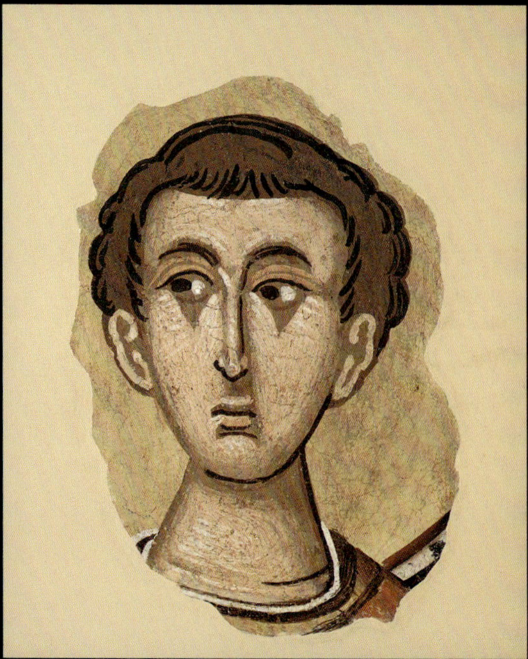

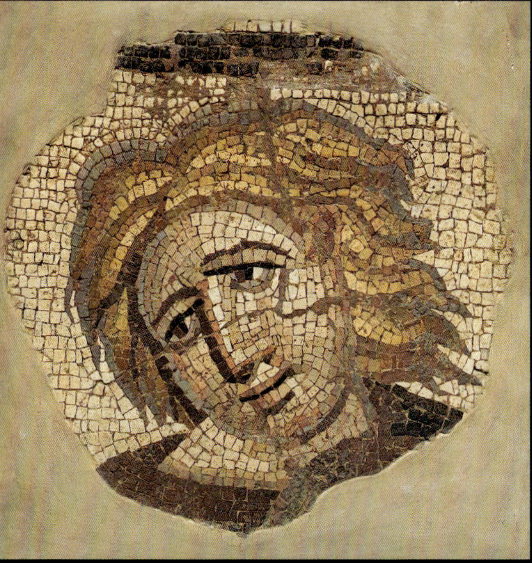
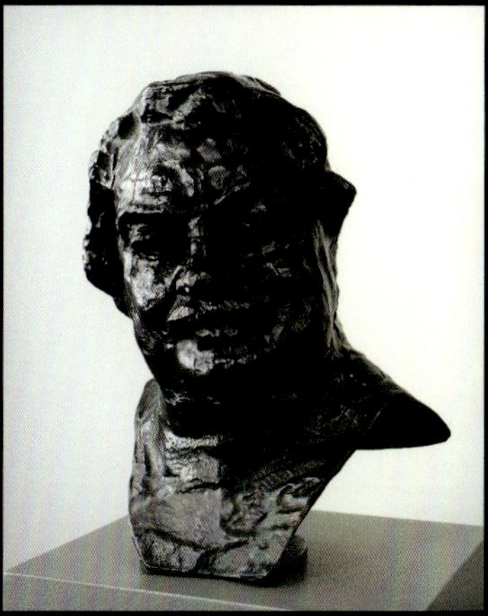
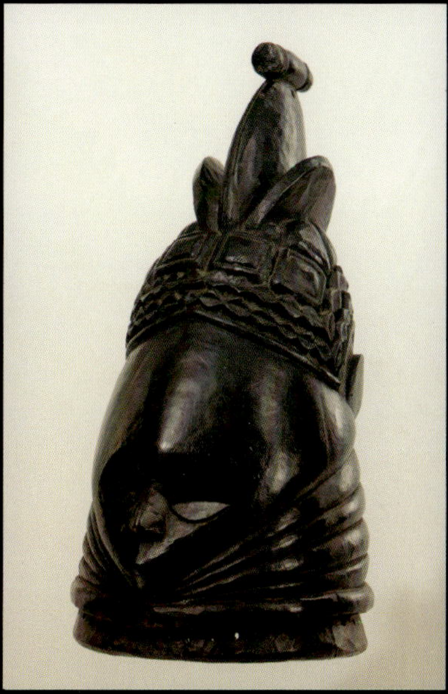
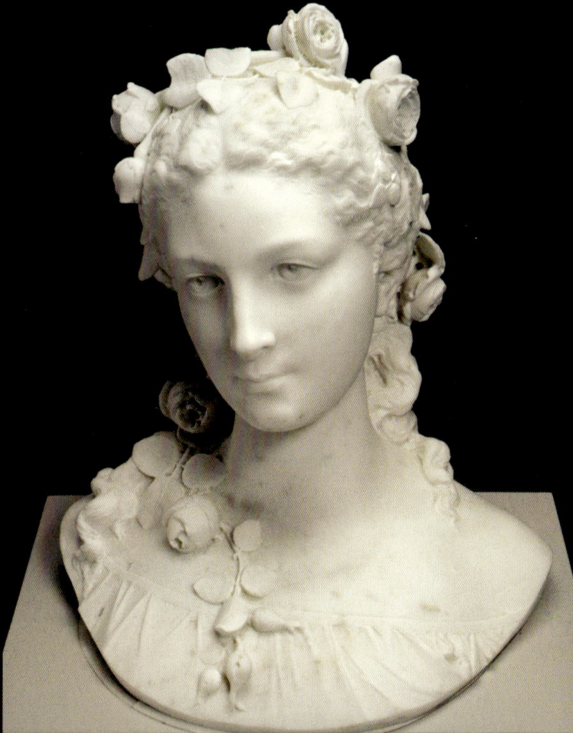

Photo captions from previous pages, left to right:

Greek
Head of Zeus(?), ca. 50 B.C.
Parian marble
11 7/8 x 11 1/8 x 7 1/4 in.
Museum purchase, Greylock Foundation and Karl E. Weston Memorial Fund (63.34)

Egyptian
Head, ca. 945–525 B.C.
Painted wood
8 7/16 x 10 x 7 11/16 in.
Museum purchase (61.4)

Roman
Head of a Warrior, ca. 300 A.D.
Mosaic
14 13/16 x 14 15/16 in.
Gift of Sir Henry Rawlinson through Dwight W. Marsh, Class of 1842, by exchange (41.5.4)

Auguste Rodin
French, 1840–1917
Head of Balzac, ca. 1893
Bronze
10 x 8 x 7 in.
Museum purchase, Karl E. Weston Memorial Fund (57.6)

Indian, Rajasthan
Head of Andhaka/Bhṛṅgi
ca. 11th century
Beige sandstone
6 1/2 x 4 13/16 x 6 5/16 in.
Museum purchase, Karl E. Weston Memorial Fund (77.30)

Byzantine
Head of a Male Saint
ca. 11th–17th century
Fresco
20 5/8 x 16 7/8 in.
Museum purchase (52.3)

African
Sierra Leone, Mende
Bundu Helmet Mask
20th century
Wood
14 x 8 1/2 x 9 in.
Gift of Oliver E. Cobb, Class of 1952 (M.2005.16.4)

Albert-Ernest Carrier-Belleuse
French, 1824–1887
Flora, ca. 1860–68
Marble
17 x 13 x 10 in.
Museum purchase, Karl E. Weston Memorial Fund (96.16)

Authors

Elizabeth Athens: 34, 37, 39, 88, 102, 124, 132, 135, 139, 151
Amelia Kahl Avdić: 99, 174
Suzanne Bach: 74
S. Paige Baty: 145
Milo C. Beach: 55
Annemarie Bean: 61, 122, 127
Robert H. Bell: 52
Magnus T. Bernhardsson: 17
Louise Bourgeois: 184
C. Ondine Chavoya: 147, 158
Cassandra J. Cleghorn: 181
Margaret C. Conrads: 62
Wanda Corn: 107
Lisa B. Dorin: 150, 184
Georges B. Dreyfus: 22
Samuel Y. Edgerton: 21
Edward A. Epping: 145
S. Lane Faison, Jr.: 83
Zirka Z. Filipczak: 42
Ellery Foutch: 105
Jamie Franklin: 54, 71
Steven Gerrard: 106
Marion Goethals: 96
Darra Goldstein: 140
Elyse Gonzales: 15
Eva U. Grudin: 172
Charles W. Haxthausen: 93
Barbara Howes: 19
Frank Jackson: 155
Stefanie Spray Jandl: 51, 81, 104
Ju-Yu Scarlett Jang: 26
Eugene J. Johnson: 46-47, 100, 128
Peter Just: 24
Thomas A. Kohut: 93
Ivar Kronick: 21
Jason C. Kuo: 131
Steven P. Levin: 65
Michael J. Lewis: 64, 78
Peter D. Low: 29
Nancy Mowll Mathews: 31, 66, 68
Elizabeth McGowan: 20
Carol Ockman: 121, 161
Vivian Patterson: 90, 182, 186

Dana Pilson: 80, 98, 110, 114, 144, 146, 148, 164, 169
Michael Quick: 58
Lawrence E. Raab: 117
Mark Reinhardt: 162, 186–187
Barbara Robertson: 181
Nancy A. Roseman: 42
Deborah Rothschild: 45, 75, 125, 156, 159, 162, 177, 178
Richard H. Sabot: 22
Meredith Sanger-Katz: 147
Karen L. Shepard: 117
W. Anthony Sheppard: 50
Oliver Sloman: 27
Stefanie Solum: 32–33
Richard Stamelman: 116
Whitney Snow Stoddard: 38
John Stomberg: 76, 77, 85, 86, 97, 108, 134, 168
Mark C. Taylor: 28
Betsy J. Thomas: 162
Jonathan Weinberg: 87

Index

Abbott, Berenice, 76, 159
Adams, Ansel, 166
Adams, Robert, 166
African, Benin, *Figure*, 95
African, Ivory Coast, *Portrait Mask*, 95
African, Mali, Bamana, *Kono Cult Animal Mask*, 95
African, Nigeria, Igbo: *Helmet Mask*, 74; *Helmet Mask*, 95
African, Sierra Leone, Mende, *Bundu Helmet Mask*, 189
Agee, James, *Let Us Now Praise Famous Men*, 108
Ali, Laylah, *Untitled*, 143
Alinari Brothers, 166
American, Southern New England, *Bonnet-top High Chest of Drawers*, 54
Applebroog, Ida, *Boboli Gardens*, 160–61
Arbus, Diane, *Child with a Toy Hand Grenade in Central Park, NYC*, 167
Armstrong, Samuel Chapman, 182
Art, Henry W., *Skunk Cabbage*, 96
Artaud, Antonin, 150
Assyrian: *Guardian Spirit*, 5, 14–17; *Winged Guardian Spirit*, 5, 14–17
Atget, Eugène, *Cabaret de l'Enfer [et du ciel], Boulevard de Clichy 53*, 76

Barbino, Pietro, 161
Barlach, Ernst, *The Singing Boy*, 99
Barye, Antoine-Louis, 56; *Horse Attacked by a Lion*, 57
Bearden, Romare Howard, *Prevalence of Ritual: Baptism*, 146
Beckmann, Max, *Jahrmarkt*, 92–93, 153
Bellocq, E. J., *Storyville Portrait*, 77
Binswanger, Karen, 61
Blashfield, Edwin Howland, 7
Bloedel, Lawrence H., 9, 142, 144
Bloedel, Mrs. Lawrence H., 144
Bourgeois, Louise, *Eyes*, cover, flaps, 11, 184–85
Bourne, Samuel, 166
Burroughs, William S.: Allen Ginsberg, *William S. Burroughs, New York*, 159
Byzantine, *Head of a Male Saint*, 188, 190

Cadmus, Paul, *Point O'View*, 7, 120–21
Callahan, Harry, 166
Cambiaso, Luca, *Via Crucis*, 113
Cambodian, Khmer, Koh Ker, *Female Divinity*, 24–25
Cameron, Julia Margaret, 166
Capp, Kristin, 166
Carrier-Belleuse, Albert-Ernest, *Flora*, 189
Casebere, James, 166
Cassatt, Mary, *Reflection*, 68–69, 81
Chagall, Marc, *The Flying Cow*, 80
Chinese, Ming Dynasty, *Ancestral Portrait*, 30–31
Chinese, Yüan Dynasty, *Seated Vairocana*, 26–27
Ciolo, Valerio, 161

Cluett, George Alfred, 8
Conrad, Tony: Tony Oursler, *Keep Going*, 176–77
Corrin, Lisa, 11
Cornell, Joseph, *Sun Box*, 138–39
Cottingham, Keith, *Single* (from *Fictitious Portraits*), 167
Crane, Hart, *The Bridge*, 102

Delacroix, Eugène, 56; *Lion*, 57; *Lion de l'Atlas*, 57; *Lion Devouring a Horse*, 56; *Sheet of Studies*, 57
Demuth, Charles, *Three Pears*, 105; *Trees and Barns: Bermuda*, 87
Duchamp, Marcel, *The Green Box*, 106
Dürer, Albrecht, *The Small Horse*, 41

Edgerton, Harold, 166
Egyptian, *Head*, 188
Evans, Walker, 166; *The Brooklyn Bridge (with a Poem by Hart Crane)*, 102–3; *Bud Fields and His Family, Hale County, Alabama*, 108–9

Faison, S. Lane, Jr., 8–9, 110
Field, Eliza Peters, 6
Field, John W., 6
Fields, Bud: Walker Evans, *Bud Fields and His Family*, 108–9
Franco-Flemish, *St. John the Evangelist*, 29
Frank, Robert Louis, 166; *New Mexico*, 134
Frankenthaler, Helen, 133
Frankfurt, Suzie, *Wild Raspberries*, 140–41
Friedlander, Lee, 77, 166
Frith, Francis, 166
Frost, Mildred K., 10

Gilbert and George, *Life Without End*, iv, 156–57
Ginsberg, Allen, *William S. Burroughs, New York*, 159
Giovanni da Milano, *St. Anthony Abbot*, 28
Goldberg, Rube, *How to keep bewhiskered uncle from kissing baby*, 88–89; *Now you know how to tie a full-dress tie*, 88–89
Goltzius, Hendrik, *Urania*, 41
Greek, *Head of Zeus(?)*, 188
Gumani, Chateri, *The Lion Hunt of Maharao Umed Singh of Kota*, 55
Guston, Philip, *Game*, 154–55

Hamen y León, Juan van der, 8
Hammons, David, *Rock Fan*, 178–79
Harnett, William Michael, *Deutsche Presse*, 65
Heinecken, Robert, 166
Hine, Lewis Wickes, 166; *Tenement Child*, 167
Hogarth, William, *Credulity, Superstition, and Fanaticism: A Medley*, 52–53; *Strolling Actresses Dressing in a Barn*, 51
Holzer, Jenny, *"I go to schools . . ."* from *Laments*, 164–65
Homer, Winslow, *Children on a Fence*, 62–63

Hopkins, Rev. Mark, 15
Hopper, Edward, *Morning in a City,* 9, 117–19
Huang Binhong (Huang Pin-Hung), *Clear Dawn on Lake and Mountains,* 130–31
Hunt, William Morris, *Niagara Falls,* 64

Indian, *Chauri Bearer,* xiv
Indian, Bihar or Bengal, *Black Stone Stele of a Crowned Buddha,* 22–23, 153
Indian, Rajasthan, *Head of Andhaka/Bhṛṅgi,* 188
Indian, North, Mughal, *A Prince with Ladies on a Terrace,* 50, 153
Inness, George, *Twilight,* 58–59

Jacobs, Harriet, 181: Tim Rollins and Kids of Survival, *Diary of a Slave Girl (After Harriet Jacobs),* 180–81
Johnston, Francis Benjamin, *Hampton Album,* 182

Kahn, Louis Isidore, *Towers, San Gimignano,* 100–101
Keats, John, "Ode on a Grecian Urn," 19
Kennedy, Jacqueline: Andy Warhol, *Jackie,* 147
Kensett, John Frederick, *Lake George,* 6
Kids of Survival, and Tim Rollins, *Diary of a Slave Girl (After Harriet Jacobs),* 180–81
Kienholz, Edward, *Bunny, Bunny, You're So Funny,* 145
Kirchner, Ernst Ludwig, *Gewecke und Erna,* 81
Klee, Paul, *Cat Accident (Unfall einer Katze),* 113
Krens, Thomas, 9, 128

Lachaise, Gaston, *Portrait of John Marin,* 98; *Torso,* 98
La Farge, John, *Magnolia Grandiflora,* 6
Lawrence, Amos, 4
Lawrence, Jacob, *Radio Repairs,* 122–23; *Square Dance,* 126–27
Layard, Sir Austen Henry, 16–17
Louis, Joe, 122

Madison, Ella: Marguerite Zorach, *Ella Madison and Dahlov,* 90–91
Man Ray, 76; *Électricité,* 104; *Électricité: Dix Rayogrammes,* 104
Mantegna, Andrea, *Entombment,* 40
Marin, John, *Black River Valley, Castorland, New York,* 82–83; *Harbor Scene,* 82–83; *Stonington, Maine,* 82–83
Marsh, Dwight W., 15–16
Matisse, Henri, 78, 110
Matta (Roberto Sebastian Antonio Matta Echaurren), *Rain: Mexico,* 110–11
Mayan, Mexico, Campeche, *Gadrooned Bowl with Hieroglyph Rim Text,* 21
Medici, Cosimo de', 161
Mellon, Andrew W., 152; Andrew W. Mellon Foundation, 133, 152
Millais, John Everett, *Sketchbook,* 113
Moore, Charles Willard, 9; *Untitled Sketch,* xvii
Moore, Henry Spencer, *Shelter Scene,* 114; *Shelter Scene: Bunks and Sleepers,* 114–15
Moreno, José, attrib., *Annunciation,* 39
Morris, Robert, *Hearing,* 142, 151
Motherwell, Robert, *Open No. 1975,* 148–49
Mullican, Matt, *Mid-19th-Century Railroad Roundhouse with Steam Engines,* 169–71
Muybridge, Eadweard, 66, 166; *"Lizzie M." trotting, harnessed to sulky, Animal Locomotion, plate 609,* 66–67

Nast, Thomas, *Drawings for "Uncle Tom's Cabin,"* 60–61
Naya, Carlo, 166

O'Keeffe, Georgia, *Skunk Cabbage (Cos Cob),* 10, 96
O'Reilly, John, 166
Oursler, Tony, *Keep Going,* 142, 176–77

Pannini, Giovanni Paolo, *Composition of Roman Ruins,* 46–49
Parsons, Abe: Faith Ringgold, *100 Years at Williams College,* 172–73
Peris, Gonçal, *St. Lucy* (formerly *St. Cecilia*), 34–35
Pfaff, Judy, *Del Flusso e Riflusso* (from *Half a Dozen of the Others* series), 174–75
Picasso, Pablo, *Dance of Salome,* 75
Piper, Adrian, *Vanilla Nightmares #18,* 162–63
Porter, Cole, 7
Pourbus, Frans the Younger, *Portrait of Infanta Isabella Clara Eugenia,* 36–37
Prendergast, Charles, 9, 72; catalogue raisonné, 9–10, 72; *Circus,* 73; *Man Dancing,* 73
Prendergast, Mrs. Charles (née Eugénie Van Kemmel), 9, 72
Prendergast, Maurice, 9, 72; catalogue raisonné, 9–10, 72; *Festa del Redentore,* 12–13, 73; *Rocky Shore, Natasket,* 73

Reider, Fanette: Morton Livingston Schamberg, *Study of a Girl (Fanette Reider),* 78–79
Remington, Frederic, *The Bronco Buster,* 70–71
Ribera, Jusepe de, *The Executioner,* 8, 38
van Rijn, Rembrandt Harmensz., 81; *Death of the Virgin,* 41
Ringgold, Faith, *100 Years at Williams College, 1889–1989,* 143, 172–73
Rivers, Larry, *Amel-Camel,* 144
Rodin, Auguste, *Head of Balzac,* 189
Rollins, Tim, and Kids of Survival, *Diary of a Slave Girl (After Harriet Jacobs),* 180–81
Roman: *Head of a Warrior,* 189; *Sarcophagus Fragment of Hercules, Triumph of Dionysos,* 20, 152

Sage, Kay, *Page 49,* 125
Sargent, John Singer, *Studies of Male Nudes,* 112
Schamberg, Morton Livingston, *Study of a Girl (Fanette Reider),* 78–79
Schiavo, Paolo, attrib., *Birth Platter: The Story of Diana and Actaeon,* 32–33
Schwitters, Kurt, *PA-CO,* 124
Shearer, Linda, 10
Sherman, Cindy, 166, *Untitled,* 168
Siskind, Aaron, 166
Smith, David, *Untitled,* 135, *Antiwar Series,* 136; *Untitled,* 136; *Untitled,* 137
Soby, James Thrall, 110
Solimena, Francesco, *The Miracle of St. John of God,* 42–43
Spero, Nancy, *Codex Artaud XXV,* 142, 150
Stella, Joseph, *Portrait of Joe Gould,* 112–13
Steinbaum, Berenice: Faith Ringgold, *100 Years at Williams College,* 172–73
Stieglitz, Alfred, 86, 98; *View from Rear Window, Gallery*

291, at Night, 84–85; *View from Rear Window, Gallery 291, Daytime,* 85
Stowe, Harriet Beecher, *Uncle Tom's Cabin,* 61; Thomas Nast, *Drawings for "Uncle Tom's Cabin,"* 61
Strand, Paul, *Blind Woman, New York,* 86

Tanguy, Yves, *Equivocal Colors,* 116
Tefft, Thomas A., 4
Troilos Painter, *Red-figured Stamnos Vase,* 18–19
Troy, Jean François de, *La Conversation galante,* 44–45; *La Déclaration d'amour,* 44–45
Van Der Zee, James Augustus Joseph, 166; *The Last Good-bye,* 97

Walker, Kara, *Negress Notes (Slavery Reparations Act),* 186–87
Warhol, Andy, *A Gold Book,* 142; *Jackie,* 147; *Self-Portrait,* iv, 158; *25 Cats Name Sam and One Blue Pussy,* 132; *Wild Raspberries,* 140–41
Warhola, Julia, 132; *Wild Raspberries,* 140–41
Weems, Carrie Mae, *The Hampton Project,* 143, 182–83; *Jim, If You . . .* (from the "Kitchen Table Series"), 182
Weston, Karl E., 7–8
Weston, Ruth Sabin, 8
Williams Art Association, 5–6
Williams College, Williamstown: founding of, 4; Hopkins Hall, Art Room, 5; Jackson Hall, 4; Lawrence Hall, 4–5, 7
Williams College Museum of Art, 8–12; Bolin Centennial, 172; drawings collection, 112–13; Labeltalk exhibition series, 133, 152–53; as Lawrence Art Museum, 7–8; modern and contemporary collection, 142–43; photography collection, 166–67; Prendergast Archive and Study Center, 72; print collection, 40; Rose Study Gallery, 11, 81, 133
Winogrand, Gary, 166
Witkin, Joel Peter, 166
Wood, Grant, *Death on the Ridge Road,* 7, 107
Wright, Frank Lloyd, *Revised Elevation—The Solomon R. Guggenheim Museum,* 128–29

Zorach, Dahlov: Marguerite Zorach, *Ella Madison and Dahlov,* 90–91
Zorach, Marguerite Thompson, *Ella Madison and Dahlov,* 90–91

Credits

All photographs taken by Arthur Evans except those below:

Michael Agee: pages 6 (figs. 9, 10), 7 (figs. 13, 16), 9 (fig. 24), 10 (fig. 32), 50, 55, 58–59, 64, 91, 96, 101, 107, 117, 118–19, 120, 145

Courtesy Laylah Ali and 303 Gallery, New York: page 143

Estate of Diane Arbus, LLC: page 166

© 2006 Artists Rights Society (ARS), New York/ADAGP, Paris: pages 77, 80, 110–11

© 2006 Artists Rights Society (ARS), New York/ADAGP, Paris/Succession Marcel Duchamp: page 106

© 2006 Artists Rights Society (ARS), New York/VG Bild-Kunst, Bonn: pages 92–93, 113, 124, 153

© Ernst Barlach Lizenzverwaltung Ratzeburg: page 99

Art © Romare Bearden Foundation/Licensed by VAGA, New York, NY: page 146

Art © Louise Bourgeois/Licensed by VAGA, New York, NY: cover, flaps, pages 11, 185

Courtesy Brown University Library: page 4 (fig. 3a) (photo by Arthur Evans)

Art © The Joseph and Robert Cornell Memorial Foundation/Licensed by VAGA, New York, NY: page 138

Courtesy DC Moore Gallery, NYC: page 120

Courtesy Demuth Museum, Lancaster, PA: pages 87, 105

© Walker Evans Archive, The Metropolitan Museum of Art: pages 102–3, 109

Courtesy Ronald Feldman Fine Arts, New York: pages 160–61, 167

Copyright Robert Frank, from "The Americans," courtesy Pace/MacGill Gallery, New York: page 134

© 2006 Helen Frankenthaler/Universal Limited Art Editions: pages 133

© Lee Friedlander, courtesy Fraenkel Gallery, San Francisco: page 77

Photography by Blake Gardener: page iv

© Gilbert and George, Courtesy Jay Jopling/White Cube (London): pages iv, 156–57

Allen Ginsberg/Corbis: page 159

Digital photography by Jim Gipe, Pivot Media & Stephen Petegorsky Photography: pages xiii, 4 (fig. 1) Courtesy Williams College Archives and Special Collections, 5 (fig. 6) Courtesy Williams College Archives and Special Collections, 8 (fig. 21), 8–9 (fig. 29), 40, 41 (Dürer, Rembrandt), 43, 44, 53, 56, 57 (Barye, Delacroix), 60–61, 68–69, 70–71, 75, 76, 77, 80, 81, 84–85, 86, 89, 92–93, 97, 105, 106, 109, 110–11, 113 (Cambiaso), 114–15, 116, 124, 125, 126, 132, 133, 134, 135, 138, 140–41, 142, 146, 149, 153, 154, 159, 163, 166, 167 (Hine), 168, 175, 179, 182, 189 (Carrier-Belleuse)

Rube Goldberg is the ® and the © of Rube Goldberg Inc.: page 89

Matt Hamilton: page 11 (fig. 36)

© Ingeborg & Dr. Wolfgang Henze-Ketterer, Wichtrach/Bern: page 81

© 2006 Jenny Holzer/Artists Rights Society (ARS), New York: pages 164–65

© Nancy Reddin Kienholz, Courtesy of L.A. Louver Gallery: page 145

John M. Kuykendall Photography: page 9 (fig. 25)

Courtesy Gaston Lachaise Foundation: page 98

© 2006 The Jacob and Gwendolyn Lawrence Foundation, Seattle/Artists Rights Society (ARS), New York: pages 122–23, 126

LeClaire Custom Color: pages 9, 12–13, 73

Photograph © 1986 Robert Mapplethorpe: page 10 (fig. 31)

© 2006 Estate of John Marin/Artists Rights Society (ARS), New York: pages 82–83

Courtesy McKee Gallery: page 154

The works illustrated on pages 114 and 115 have been reproduced by permission of the Henry Moore Foundation.

© 2006 Robert Morris/Artists Rights Society (ARS), New York: page 151

(for Motherwell) Art © Dedalus Foundation, Inc./Licensed by VAGA, New York, NY: page 149

Courtesy of Matt Mullican and Tracy Williams, Ltd., New York: pages 169–71

Copyright © 2006 The Georgia O'Keeffe Foundation/Artists Rights Society (ARS), New York: pages 10 (fig. 30), 96 (Michael Agee), 84–85

Courtesy of Tony Oursler: page 176

© 2006 Estate of Pablo Picasso/Artists Rights Society (ARS), New York: page 75

Photo by David Reynolds: page 150

© Adrian Piper Research: page 163

© 2006 May Ray Trust/Artists Rights Society (ARS), NY/ADAGP, Paris: page 104

Courtesy of Faith Ringgold: pages 172–73

Art © Estate of Larry Rivers/Licensed by VAGA, New York, NY: page 144

Courtesy Tim Rollins and Kids of Survival and PPOW Gallery, New York: page 180

© Steve Rosenthal. All rights reserved: page 151

Courtesy of Cindy Sherman and Metro Pictures Gallery: page 168

Courtesy Brent Sikkema NYC: pages 186–87

Art © Estate of David Smith/Licensed by VAGA, New York, NY: pages 135, 136–37

© 1971 Aperture Foundation Inc., Paul Strand Archive: page 86

© 2006 Estate of Yves Tanguy/Artists Rights Society (ARS), New York: page 116

Courtesy The University of Arkansas Press 1995: page 19

Courtesy the James Van Der Zee Estate: page 97

© 2006 Andy Warhol Foundation for the Visual Arts/ARS, New York: pages iv, 132, 140–41, 142, 147, 158

Courtesy of Carrie Mae Weems and PPOW: pages 182–83

Photography by Nicholas Whitman: page 147

Williams College Archives and Special Collections: pages xiv–xv, 4 (figs. 2a, 2b), 4–5 (fig. 8), 5 (fig. 7), 6 (fig. 11), 6–7 (fig. 17), 7 (fig. 12), 8 (figs. 18, 19)

Courtesy Williamstown Art Conservation Center: page 34

Art © Estate of Grant Wood/Licensed by VAGA, New York, NY: pages 7, 107

List of Publications Cited

The following are published by the Williams College Museum of Art except where noted:

Labeltalk 1995

Labeltalk 1996

Labeltalk 1997

Labeltalk 2001

Labeltalk 2004

Bach, Suzanne, and William C. Siegmann, et al. *Assuming the Guise: African Masks Considered and Reconsidered.* 1991.

Edgerton, Samuel Y. *The Art of Mesoamerica, Before Columbus.* 1992.

Faison, S. Lane, Jr. *". . . and Gladly Teach."* 1990.

Grudin, Eva Ungar. *Stitching Memories: African-American Story Quilts.* 1989.

Kara Walker: Narratives of a Negress (brochure). 2003.

Kuo, Jason C. *Innovation within Tradition: The Painting of Huang Pin-Hung.* Hong Kong: Hanart Gallery in association with the Williams College Museum of Art, Williamstown, Massachusetts, 1989.

Mathews, Nancy Mowll, ed. *American Dreams: American Art to 1950 in the Williams College Museum of Art.* New York: Hudson Hills Press in association with the Williams College Museum of Art, 2001.

Noey, Christopher, and Janet Temos. *Art of India from the Williams College Museum of Art.* 1994.

Representing Slavery (brochure). 2003.